WOMEN AND HUMAN RIGHTS

WOMEN AND WORLD DEVELOPMENT SERIES

This series has been developed by the **UN-NGO Group on Women and Development** and makes available the most recent information, debate and action being taken on world development issues, and the impact on women. Each volume is fully illustrated and attractively presented. Each outlines its particular subject, as well as including an introduction to resources and guidance on how to use the books in workshops and seminars. The aim of each title is to bring women's concerns more directly and effectively into the development process, and to achieve an improvement in women's status in our rapidly changing world.

The Group was established in 1980 to organize the production and distribution of UN-NGO development education materials. It was the first time that United Nations agencies and non-governmental organizations had collaborated in this way, and the Group remains a unique example of co-operation between international and non-governmental institutions. Membership of the Group is open to all interested organizations.

SERIES TITLES – in order of scheduled publication

For full details, as well as order forms, please write to:
ZED BOOKS LTD, 57 CALEDONIAN ROAD, LONDON N1 9BU, U.K. and 165 First Avenue, Atlantic Highlands, New Jersey 07716, U.S.A.

WOMEN AND HUMAN RIGHTS

PREPARED BY KATARINA TOMAŠEVSKI

Zed Books Ltd · London & New York

Women and Human Rights was first published by Zed Books Ltd,
7 Cynthia Street, London N1 9JF, UK, and Room 400,
175 Fifth Avenue, New York, NY 10010, USA, in 1993.

Distributed in the USA exclusively by
St. Martin's Press, Inc., 175 Fifth Avenue,
New York, NY 10010, USA.

Second impression, 1995.
Third impression, 1999.

The views expressed in this publication do not necessarily reflect the
views of the United Nations.

Cover and book design by Lee Robinson.
Cover photo: Ruby Mera/UNICEF.
Typeset by Goodfellow & Egan, Cambridge.
Reprinted in Malaysia.

A catalogue record for this book is available from the British Library.

ISBN 1 85649 119 6 Hb
ISBN 1 85649 120 X Pb

CONTENTS

ACKNOWLEDGEMENTS

This book has been prepared by Dr Katarina Tomaševski, the Danish Centre for Human Rights, on behalf of the UN-NGO Group on Women and Development and made possible by contributions from:

- Baha'i International Community
- Danish International Development Agency (DANIDA)
- Finnish International Development Agency (FINNIDA)
- Norwegian Royal Ministry for Foreign Affairs
- Swedish International Development Agency (SIDA)
- United Nations Centre for Human Rights
- United Nations High Commission for Refugees (UNHCR)
- World Council of Churches

The content of this book has been approved by the UN-NGO Group on Women and Development. The following organizations have made a special contribution through their participation in the editorial panel formed for this publication:

- Article 19
- Baha'i International Community
- International Commission of Jurists
- International Council of Jewish Women
- International Council on Social Welfare
- International Council of Women
- International Federation of Red Cross and Red Crescent Societies
- International Federation of University Women
- International Women's Rights Action Watch
- Medical Women's International Association
- United Nations High Commission for Refugees (UNHCR)
- United Nations Centre for Human Rights
- United Nations Children's Fund (UNICEF)
- United Nations Division for the Advancement of Women (DAW)
- United Nations Educational, Scientific and Cultural Organization (UNESCO)
- United Nations Population Fund (UNFPA)
- Women's International League for Peace and Freedom
- World Federation of Methodist Women
- World Health Organization (WHO)
- World Union of Catholic Women's Organizations
- World University Service
- Zonta International

Overall co-ordination and management of the UN-NGO Group on Women and Development is provided by the United Nations Non-Governmental Liaison Service (NGLS), an inter-agency unit which fosters dialogue and co-operation between the United Nations system and the NGO community on development policy issues and North-South relations.

PREFACE

The editorial panel decided to invite Aung San Suu Kyi to write the preface for this book. All our efforts to communicate with her failed. We are thus reproducing here the speech delivered on her behalf by her son, Alexander Aris, on the occasion of the Nobel Prize Ceremony in her absentia in Oslo 10 December 1991.

Speech delivered on behalf of Aung San Suu Kyi, by her son Alexander Aris, on the occasion of the award to her *in absentia* of the Nobel Prize for Peace. Oslo, 10 December 1991

Your Majesties, Your Excellencies, Ladies and Gentlemen,

I stand before you here today to accept on behalf of my mother, Aung San Suu Kyi, this greatest of prizes, the Nobel Prize for Peace. Because circumstances do not permit my mother to be here in person, I will do my best to convey the sentiments I believe she would express.

Firstly, I know that she would begin by saying that she accepts the Nobel Prize for Peace not in her own name but in the name of all the people of Burma. She would say that this Prize belongs not to her but to all those men, women and children who, even as I speak, continue to sacrifice their well-being, their freedom and their lives in pursuit of a democratic Burma. Theirs is the prize and theirs will be the eventual victory in Burma's long struggle for peace, freedom and democracy.

Speaking as her son, however, I would add that I personally believe that by her own dedication and personal sacrifice she has come to be a worthy symbol through whom the plight of all the people of Burma may be recognized.

And no one must underestimate that plight. The plight of those in the countryside and towns, living in poverty and destitution, those in prison, battered and tortured; the plight of the young people, the hope of Burma, dying of malaria in the jungles to which they have fled; that of the Buddhist monks, beaten and dishonoured. Nor shall we forget the many senior and highly respected leaders besides my mother who are all incarcerated.

It is on their behalf that I thank you, from my heart, for this supreme honour. The Burmese people can today hold their heads a little higher in the knowledge that in this far distant land their suffering has been heard and heeded.

We must also remember that the lonely struggle taking place in a heavily guarded compound in Rangoon is part of the much larger struggle, worldwide, for the emancipation of the human spirit from political tyranny and psychological subjection. The Prize, I feel sure , is also intended to honour all those engaged in this struggle wherever they may be. It is not without reason that today's events in Oslo fall on the International Human Rights Day, celebrated throughout the world.

Mr Chairman, the whole international community has applauded the choice of your Committee. Just a few days ago, the United Nations passed a unanimous and historic resolution welcoming Secretary-General Javier Perez de Cuellar's statement on the significance of this award and endorsing his repeated appeals for my mother's early release from detention. Universal concern at the grave human rights situation in Burma was clearly expressed. Alone and isolated among the entire nations of the world a single dissenting voice was heard, from the military junta in Rangoon, too late and too weak.

This regime has, through almost 30 years of misrule, reduced the once prosperous 'Golden Land' of Burma to one of the world's most economically destitute nations. In their heart of hearts even those in power now in Rangoon must know that their eventual fate will be that of all totalitarian regimes which seek to impose their authority through fear, repression and hatred. When the present Burmese struggle for democracy erupted into the streets in 1988 it was the first of what became an international tidal wave of such movements throughout Eastern Europe, Asia and Africa. Today, in 1991, Burma stands conspicuous in its continued suffering at the hands of a repressive, intransigent junta, the State Law and Order Restoration Council. However, the example of those nations which have successfully achieved democracy holds out an important message to the Burmese people; that, in the last resort, through the sheer economic unworkability of totalitarianism this present regime will be swept away. And today, in the face of rising inflation, a mismanaged economy and near worthless currency, the Burmese government is undoubtedly reaping as it has sown.

However, it is my deepest hope that it will not be in the face of complete economic collapse that the regime will fall, but that the ruling junta may yet heed such appeals to basic humanity as that which the Nobel Committee has expressed in its award of this year's prize. I know that within the military government there are those to whom the present policies of fear and repression are abhorrent, violating as they do the most sacred principles of Burma's Buddhist heritage. This is no empty wishful thinking, but a conviction my mother reached in the course of her dealings with those in positions of authority, illustrated by the election victories of her party in constituencies comprised almost exclusively of military personnel and their families. It is my profoundest wish that these elements for moderation and reconciliation among those now in authority may make their sentiments felt in Burma's hour of deepest need.

I know that if she were free today my mother would in thanking you also ask you to pray that the oppressors and the oppressed should throw down their weapons and join together to build a nation founded on humanity in the spirit of peace.

Although my mother is often described as a political dissident who strives by peaceful means for democratic change, we should remember that her quest is basically spiritual. As she has said, 'The quintessential revolution is that of the spirit'; and she has written of the 'essential spiritual aims' of the struggle. The realization of this depends solely on human responsibility. At the root of that responsibility lies, and I quote, 'The concept of perfection, the urge to achieve it, the intelligence to find a path towards it, and the will to follow that path if not to the end, at least the distance needed to rise above individual limitation. ...' 'To live the full life,' she says, 'one must have the courage to bear the responsibility of the needs of others ... one must *want* to bear this responsibility.' And she links this firmly to her faith when she writes, '... Buddhism, the foundation of traditional Burmese culture, places the greatest value on man, who alone of all beings can achieve the supreme state of Buddhahood. Each man has in him the potential to realize the truth through his own will and endeavour and to help others to realize it.' Finally she says, 'The quest for democracy in Burma is the struggle of a people to live whole, meaningful lives as free and equal members of the world community. It is part of the unceasing human endeavour to prove that the spirit of man can transcend the flaws of his nature.'

This is the second time that my younger brother and I have accepted a great prize for my mother in Norway. Last year we travelled to Bergen to receive for her the Thorolf Rafto Prize for Human Rights, a wonderful prelude to this year's event. By now we have a very special feeling for the people of Norway. It is my hope that soon my mother will be able to share this feeling and to speak directly for herself instead of through me. Meanwhile this tremendous support for her and the people of Burma has served to bring together two peoples from opposite ends of the earth. I believe much will follow from the links now forged.

It only remains for me to thank you all from the bottom of my heart. Let us hope and pray that from today the wounds start to heal and that in the years to come the 1991 Nobel Prize for Peace will be seen as a historic step towards the achievement of true peace in Burma. The lessons of the past will not be forgotten, but it is our hope for the future that we celebrate today.

INTRODUCTION: WHY 'WOMEN AND HUMAN RIGHTS'?

IT IS A TRUISM that words are instruments rather than labels; the language we use reflects our image of reality. The terminology chosen here reflects this reality: women indeed do not enjoy the rights and freedoms to which they are entitled by the mere fact that they are human. Problems in attaining the full recognition and enjoyment of all human rights and fundamental freedoms for women are the main theme of this book.

Differences in the awareness of this problem can be seen in the language used in speaking about human rights, or specifically about the rights of female humans. In Canada the chosen term is 'droits de la personne', which represents a move from the traditional debate about 'la femme et les droits de l'homme', that is, 'women and the rights of men'. In Latin America the term 'derechos humanos', which encompasses both women and men, has been revised even further by those organizations that deal specifically with the human rights of women into 'derechos de las humanas', that is, 'rights of female humans'. This signifies a striving to discuss the continuing disregard of the human rights of women as the denial of the human in human rights.

The term 'women's rights' is not used here because it implies that women have some special or different rights as women. They do not. What are often portrayed as 'women's rights' are allowances that societies have made for motherhood, not for their womenhood. Not all women are mothers. More important, those who are are not mothers only – they are also work-ers, electors, medical doctors, political prisoners, trade union leaders, immigrants, soldiers, or refugees.

Throughout this book emphasis is placed on the implications of motherhood in the conventional approaches to women's rights. As long as women's role is confined to motherhood, their rights are reduced to those related to motherhood. For this reason the book pays far less attention to motherhood than many read-ers would expect. Rather, it argues that women do not have to earn societal recog-nition and protection of their human rights through motherhood. Women, as much as men, are entitled to full protec-tion of their rights and freedoms because they are human beings. Protection of motherhood is therefore addressed as only one component of the recognition and protection of equal rights for women, as a method whereby women are (or should be) compensated for performing a socially and economically useful function. The human rights of women as workers, pris-oners, or refugees should be (but more often are not) equal to those of male workers, prisoners, or refugees. The gen-der gap between the recognition and enjoyment of human rights and funda-mental freedoms is the main theme of this book.

In United Nations terminology, prob-lems concerning the human rights of women are often subsumed under the terms 'status of women' and 'advancement of women'. This book argues that the unequal status of women, constantly deplored as unsatisfactory, results from gender discrimination. Advancement of women is impossible unless and until their equal rights are fully protected. Again, ter-minology reflects our perception of prob-lems. By discussing the status of women in terms of the denial of equal rights we are moving the debate from an assessment of facts into the realm of remedies.

Human rights terminology embodies the demand that the unequal status of women be addressed as a violation of their rights, as a breach of the obligation of governments to guarantee equal rights to all.

The preparation of this book, in which numerous organizations and individuals took part, included discussions about the title; ultimately, the option of calling it 'Human Rights of Women' was rejected in favour of 'Women and Human Rights' mainly because we wanted to express and share our conclusion that the human rights of women have yet to be attained. This book is intended to make a contribution to this difficult uphill struggle, emphasizing that women have made a contribution to human rights that far exceeds the contribution that human rights have made to women. Two women, Daw Aung San Suu Kyi in 1991 and Rigoberta Menchú in 1992, have been awarded the Nobel Peace Prize for human rights work.

The incentive for this book was the convening of the World Conference on Human Rights. Many organizations, institutions and individuals felt that this provided a unique opportunity to place women on the human rights agenda. Indeed, the preparatory documents for this conference, in particular those submitted by non-governmental organizations (NGOs), reflect an increased global momentum. Their sheer number is impressive, their contents even more so. This development shows that women have become aware that the international human rights system has not – yet – paid sufficient attention to the female half of humanity, and also that an increasing number of women's and human rights organizations are determined to make the international human rights system work for women.

International human rights standards and procedures are perceived to be gender-neutral; this 'neutrality' often amounts in practice to a disregard of women, in

human rights as everywhere else. What women have learned from history is that their needs and interests – and their rights – are neither automatically recognized nor guaranteed unless they articulate them and fight for them. One specific purpose of this book is to describe the international human rights system so that women can use it more, and more effectively. Knowledge of existing human rights standards which should apply to women, but are more often than not unknown by the affected women themselves, is more than a tool: it is a weapon. Describing a particular act as a human rights violation gives it an importance that simply calling it unfair cannot give; it also opens the way for the affected women to seek redress and compensation, and helps to prevent further violations. The first step towards effective protection of women's human rights is knowledge of what these rights are, how they should be protected, and what redress is available to women whose rights are denied or violated. This book is therefore intended as an educational tool to assist women and their organizations to use existing human rights standards and procedures. Thus far women have rarely sought to remedy rights violations, often because they were unaware that they were entitled to have their rights protected, or did not know where to seek redress or even information concerning available remedies. Making such information accessible is a major task in the process of empowering women to assert and demand their rights and freedoms as human beings.

A recurrent theme of this book is its emphasis on the gaps between the women's agenda and the human rights agenda (ranging from standard-setting to policy, practice, and action) at all levels (from global to local) whereby human rights of women fall between the cracks. They are deleted from the human rights agenda because they pertain to women and from the women's agenda because human rights are seen to belong elsewhere. This book argues that a merger of the two is mutually reinforcing and should become a priority in the future work of both women's and human rights organizations.

Much as the decision to prepare this book was triggered by preparations for the World Conference on Human Rights, the need for it is clear from the paucity of the literature. The text itself is limited by the amount of information available, and its frequent theme is a plea to all concerned for more investigation of the real-life problems women experience in asserting and protecting their basic rights, and for the sharing of experiences on how to effect change. The little information that does exist is largely confined to academic publications that do not reach a wide audience. If it were possible to conduct a survey of the extent of knowledge of those rights that are universally recognized and therefore should be universally respected, the results would without doubt show that information about human rights is restricted to those who are able to exercise and enjoy them. The availability of human rights information is inversely correlated with the need for it: where needs are greatest, information is least. This has an obviously negative consequence: international human rights instruments are tools to be used by those whose rights they affirm and guarantee; the lack of knowledge about how these international instruments can be used prevents women from claiming their rights, and demanding redress for violations of them. The dearth of litigation – nationally and internationally – concerning violations of the human rights of women testifies to the fact that violations continue unreported and unchallenged. This contributes to their perpetuation. Silence, as we have learned too well, is the best friend of human rights violations.

In serving as a tool for action, this book is particularly intended to stimulate activism at the grassroots level. Its final part contains a set of suggestions for education, action and litigation, from the global to the individual level. The momentum of existing efforts to place equal rights for women on the global human rights agenda has begun to redress the traditional neglect of women. Many suggestions have already been made as to what to do and how, and some of these have been reproduced here in the hope that they will inspire other organizations and individuals to contribute to and strengthen the global process towards equal rights for all.

STRUCTURE AND CONTENTS ☐ This book describes the lack of attention to the human rights of women at all levels, from local to global, and encompassing all human rights and freedoms, from freedom from torture to political participation, from free and responsible parenthood to property rights. It outlines what has been done thus far to articulate and defend women's human rights, singles out illustrative examples of successes in attaining equal rights of women in different countries and areas, and indicates a range of issues where equal rights for women are still denied. Sometimes such rights are formally recognized but ignored in practice, but sometimes they are not even recognized, that is, women's human rights are openly and explicitly denied. The struggle for women's rights therefore necessitates a knowledge of what the problems are, because they vary a great deal, before one can venture into considering how best to address them.

The unfinished history of women's human rights is first summarized and then the pattern of problems today is outlined. Finally, the book describes the universal framework for the implementation of women's equal rights and the emerging women's human rights agenda.

The obvious starting point to discuss women's human rights is to outline their history. This is, however, virtually impossible. Women's rights are confined to the footnotes of history. Some illustrations are provided to demonstrate the dearth of information in this area but also, and more important, to pose a question: could it be true that history, or 'development' to use the vogue term, represents a retrogression rather than a development as far as women's equal rights are concerned? Available studies tend to agree that women did enjoy a broad spectrum of rights and freedoms early in history, but that subsequently these were diminished, restrained, and sometimes even abolished. It may well be true that the history of women's equal rights, once it is written, will prove that retrogression replaced progress through a large part of what we consider to be the continuous advance of civilization. The lesson we may have to learn from history is that neither a mere passage of time nor economic growth diminishes inequalities between the sexes. They may in fact be increased by some development models or even reinforced by legalizing women's unequal rights.

The concept of human rights was designed as a corrective to both political and economic development because, unless inequalities are specifically targeted, they tend to increase rather than diminish. Contemporary developments show that disregard of women results in increasing sex inequalities: because of their unequal status women bear a disproportionate share of the social burden, be it structural adjustment in the Third World or the transition of the Second World, the former Eastern Europe, to market economies.

Women's social status is still dominated by motherhood, and the role of women is often confined to child-bearing and child-rearing. As a consequence, equality is often confused with the protection of motherhood. It is increasingly accepted that special protection of motherhood, as an important social function, does not amount to reverse discrimination in favour of women. Nevertheless, such protective norms divert attention from the need to eradicate discrimination against women, not all of whom are mothers, and most of whom – as mothers – do not enjoy social support and protection. Controversies relating to women as objects of special protection (of motherhood, not womanhood), as opposed to women as subjects of human rights and fundamental freedoms, are still widespread.

The process of affirming human rights as inherent and inalienable properties of every human being constitutes part of modern history. The global recognition of human rights followed the Second World War: the history of human rights is short indeed. Women should enjoy all basic rights and fundamental freedoms but they do not. This book singles out just two illustrative examples that demonstrate that equal rights for women remain to be conquered: the rights of married women, and women's property rights.

Lesser rights for women relating to marriage and property originate in their treatment as dependants whose legal, economic and social status is derived from that of the 'head of the family'. Women's equality is thus doubly jeopardized: by their sex and by their marital and/or family status. In the economic sphere women's earnings are deemed supplementary to those of the 'breadwinner'. More important, much work performed by women is not recognized as an occupational activity. This point is highlighted in the section dealing with working women and women workers.

Women's opportunities to enjoy their rights and freedoms are often hindered by societal or religious norms that discriminate against women. The achievement of equal rights guarantees in the public sphere has been the first and the easier task of the women's rights movements. But governmental obligations towards women reach far beyond eliminating discrimination in the work of the public authorities: governments must take the lead in identifying and eliminating obstacles to the full realization of all women's rights and freedoms, whatever these may be. Social norms of conduct that treat women as sub- or half-human are powerful obstacles. Sometimes such norms are evidenced in the treatment of women as the property of their fathers and husbands; sometimes in the form of 'gender apartheid', namely the segregation of women and their prohibition from leaving their home and participating in any public activity; such a heritage is visible in the denial of the worth of women as women and their treatment as instruments for producing children.

Tackling such obstacles cannot be easy: most often, even women affected by them deem them to be 'natural' although they are, quite literally, man-made. The historical heritage of discrimination and inequalities has left us a monumental task. Opposition to the recognition of equal rights for women is decreasing but remains strong. Methods of addressing and eradicating obstacles to equal rights have to be adjusted to the national and local circumstances and accepted by all concerned. Advocates of equal rights for women are frequently in the paradoxical situation of lacking the support of the very women they aim to assist: the heritage of discrimination is internalized by women and thus perpetuated. The teaching and learning of equal rights for women becomes rejected as heretical or subversive. Education is therefore the key to both intergenerational transmission of gender discrimination and its gradual eradication.

Women cannot enjoy their rights and freedoms unless human rights are effectively protected. However, most violations of women's rights remain unchallenged. Action to expose and oppose violations victimizing women is a minuscule part of human rights action and litigation everywhere. The eradication of gender discrimination remains a challenge even within the international human rights system.

To be able to expose and oppose discrimination one needs to recognize it. The existing studies of discrimination against women reveal only partially its nature, scope, degree and, most important, its impact on women. Gender discrimination ranges from the explicit denial of equal rights to women, to women's inability to enjoy their formally recognized rights because they are prevented from doing so. Discrimination can be cloaked in law or exist in practice, it can be direct and indirect, it exists in the public and in the private sector. The typology of discrimination encompasses open, explicit discrimination which is still part of national law. One can still encounter many openly discriminatory rules in different countries in different areas. Moreover, apparently gender-neutral rules can have discriminatory effects on women. *De facto* inequalities, the unequal opportunities that women have, in practice, for exercising and enjoying their rights, and the lack of efforts to remedy the centuries of discriminatory heritage are evident worldwide and make the formal recognition of equal rights for women insufficient. It has long been recognized by human rights workers that equal treatment of persons in unequal situations perpetuates rather than challenges discrimination; hence, eradication of gender discrimination necessitates both a recognition of the discriminatory heritage and action to remedy its effects and to establish safeguards against its perpetuation.

Much has been achieved in conceptualizing human rights when these have been applied to women. First, women's rights have escaped the conventional, and erroneous, division of human rights into 'generations' (see pp. 56–7) and the accompanying ideological debates about trade-offs between civil and political, and economic, social and cultural rights. Women's rights have retained, and thereby strengthened, the conceptual universality of human rights. It was realized fairly early that global inequalities were an obstacle to the enjoyment of equal rights, that formal guarantees were insufficient and may in practice be meaningless. A strong link was therefore established between formal human rights guarantees and the factual possibilities for the exercise and enjoyment of equal rights by all women, particularly in developing countries. The parallel international action on women's rights and women-in-development is a good example for human rights work as a whole.

The important first step towards effective protection of women's rights is to recognize their violations. This is illustrated in this book by the examples of traditional practices detrimental to women, and violence against women. Their inclusion in the human rights agenda was hampered by views that the 'private' sphere should be exempted from human rights norms. In other words, what husbands, fathers, employers, colleagues and neighbours do to women, was deemed not to constitute a human rights issue. The worldwide movements that successfully argue that violence against women was a human rights issue are a good example of making human rights norms and procedure work for women.

International action on women's rights is dealt with towards the end of the book. It is true that global recognition of universal human rights owes its existence to the United Nations, and the book could easily have begun there, but a different sequence was followed in which substantive problems concerning women's rights were dealt with first. The reason is the gap between the international standards and policies and the actual problems women face. Whilst achievements in international standard-setting should not be underestimated, their real impact can be measured only through an examination of their application in the daily lives of women worldwide. A few case studies have been selected to illustrate how human rights apply – or should apply – to imprisoned women and refugees, categories particularly susceptible to violations.

The most important message of this book is that neither human rights in general, nor women's human rights in particular can be attained once and for all. Progress is slow and difficult and retrogression occurs easily. Progress necessitates changes at all levels, from individual to global. The global framework of universal human rights has provided legitimacy to all those working towards equal rights for women, and has given them tools by specifying the nature, meaning, content and implications of human rights for women. Many gaps within this framework still need to be closed, including those between global norms and local reality. Against the background of what has been accomplished thus far, the tasks ahead are by no means easy, but neither are they impossible.

Accomplishments in furthering equal rights for women, and particularly the recent strengthening of global demands to place women on the United Nations human rights agenda, promise that the history of women's rights will not remain unfinished. The final section of the book includes numerous examples of levels, areas and methods of work that have proved fruitful and can therefore provide guidance to others. Much attention is paid to forthcoming international events, because these may become signposts of change in the continuing history of women's human rights.

1 UNFINISHED HISTORY

We, women, do not know a lot about our own history and our own identity. We are unknown even to ourselves, and deprived of means for knowing ourselves. We tend to believe in myths about ourselves even when these conflict with our reality, we are hindered in seeing ourselves clearly. We are too busy looking at others and we remain in their shadow; we are told that the way these others see us is sufficient for our existence.[1]

THE HISTORY OF WOMEN'S HUMAN RIGHTS has not yet been written and remains largely unknown. This is partly a reflection of the traditional invisibility of women in history, but also a consequence of the novelty of human rights. It is worth recalling that human rights emerged as a term and a concept 200 years ago and became globally accepted 40 years ago. The human rights of women attained global attention only in the 1970s. This does not imply that earlier histories of women's movements and of their accomplishments in winning battles for women's rights should be dismissed because they did not use human rights terminology. It merely says that such histories are few and that many remain to be written.

EARLY DAYS ☐ The history of women's rights can in a brutal simplification be described as circular. A very early period of sex equality seems to have been followed by a long period of retrogression, then by efforts to regain some of the lost equality. Descriptions of the equal status of women in early history are sometimes

criticized as romanticizing, as going further and further back into history to identify examples of women's equality, and finding them a very, very long time ago. The following is an illustrative example from Africa:

Contrary to the more popularly held view, African women on a continent-wide scale enjoyed greater freedom and had both a legal and social equality which, among other things, enabled them to become effective heads of state and military strategists.

The recorded involvement of African women in state administration and military defence planning dates back about four thousand years, to the civilian rule in Egypt of Nebet during the Old Kingdom (c. 3100–2345 BC).

Indigenous Egyptian society was characterized by a strong matriarchy. As in many other parts of Africa, women played a central role in agriculture and their economic contribution was therefore greater than in nomadic hunting and pastoral societies. Some historians argue that women may, in fact, have 'discovered' agriculture in prehistoric times.

Monogamy was the prevalent form of marriage within the population. Royalty and court dignitaries practised polygamy in varying degrees, depending on wealth and status. Political and economic rights were transmitted through the women, who were seen as the more stable element within the family. No restriction barred Egyptian women from participating in the public affairs of society. Besides the opportunity to reign as monarchs in their own rights accorded to royal women, commoners were also able to excel based on merit.[2]

A common thread in the few documented histories of women's rights is their agreement on the downward trend in the societal recognition of gender equality, as an example from Asia shows:

Women did not always have an inferior status to men. In primitive communities men and women

1

tended to be viewed as equal since both had vital economic roles to play in supporting their families and communities. There are even instances of matrilineal and matriarchal societies in Malaysia, Java, the Philippines, and India.

Subjugation of women did not begin until the advent of the religions and became more intense as the centuries rolled on.

Hinduism, which dominates India today, regressed from a much more egalitarian status of women to an apex of subjugation around 700 AD when 'suttee' – the practice of burning widows on their husband's pyre – was considered a religious duty. In the Vedic period (1500 BC–500 AD) a great deal of freedom was attributed to religious causes. Maidens and bachelors were not admitted to heaven and the gods accepted no oblations from the unmarried. A wife was necessary and therefore esteemed for the performance of religious rituals. To prepare her for her role, she was initiated at the age of nine or ten and subsequently educated for six years. Marriages did not take place until the age of 16 or 17 when an educated and relatively mature young woman had much more say in the choice of her partner.

Women also had a role to play in agriculture and manufacturing as the people were frequently mobilized for war. However, as society became more settled, the economic need for women's labour diminished. Marriage was declared a substitute for religious initiation and consequently could take place at the age of nine or ten. Without education and with reduced religious and economic functions, women ceased to play a role in decision-making. Remarriage for women was banned around 500 AD because women were deemed married forever. Seclusion and veiling of women did not become the common practice until the invasion of Islam several centuries later.[3]

Descriptions of such a general downward trend in societal recognition of women's equality hides their efforts to challenge inequality. These are worth documenting even if they failed, because the lack of success signified the strength of resistance to equal rights for women. Women martyrs are rarely known, but in every society, in every generation, there were women who led the way. This example has been provided by Payam Akhavan:

Describing Fatimih Umm Salamih, who lived in Persia in the 19th century, Professor E.G. Browne claimed that 'the appearance of such a woman is, in any country and any age, a rare phenomenon, but in such a country as Persia it is a prodigy – nay, almost a miracle'.

She was born in 1817, and became known as Tahirih (The Pure One). She challenged the rules of the time, which relegated women to inferiority, and championed equality between men and women. She was murdered in 1852 and her body was thrown into a well which was then filled with stones. She was killed but not silenced; her last words were recorded: 'You can kill me as soon as you like, but you cannot stop the emancipation of women.'

All authors who try to describe the struggle for women's equal rights in history lament the shortage of documentation. The rare publications in this area are therefore precious. An excellent example is Kumari Jayawardena's study of movements for women's emancipation in Asia and the Middle East, previously confined, as she says, 'to the footnotes of history'. She brings to light the wealth of heritage of struggles by women – and men – to attain equal rights. Jayawardena describes thus efforts to attain the right to vote for women, and women's participation in labour movements:

Some of the early and unsuccessful attempts to obtain female suffrage were made by male reformers, for example in Iran (1911 and 1920) and the Philippines (1907), but the women themselves were also to lead the agitation as in China (1911), India (1917), Japan (1924) and Sri Lanka (1927). In some cases the agitation was peaceful, but in others it was less so. Women organized demonstrations and stormed the legislatures when these bodies failed to grant female suffrage; such militant agitation occurred in China in 1911 and 1924, and in Japan and Egypt in 1924.

The 1918 Rice Riots in Japan were triggered off when women port workers refused to load rice and were joined by other workers; this led to a long struggle and a political crisis. In China in 1922 many thousands of workers in 70 Shanghai silk factories went on strike, calling for increased wages and a ten-hour working day; this was the first important strike by Chinese women workers. In India and Sri Lanka, in the years after World War I, women workers were active participants in militant industrial agitation and strikes. To give only one example from the region, the most militant activists of the Ceylon Labour Union which led strikes in Sri Lanka in the 1920s were women factory workers in Colombo; they used to dress in red, were the most vociferous of the strikers and picketers, and formed a bodyguard for male trade union leaders during demonstrations. In Iran, Egypt and Turkey women were to join with men in the formation of left-wing political groups and trade unions, in spite of repression and adverse conditions for mobilizing the people.[4]

ENTER RIGHTS OF MAN □ Women's human rights are not automatically recognized in proclamations of the rights of men.

The French and American revolutions, with their emphasis on equality, liberty and fraternity, raised women's hopes for attaining rights of citizenship but these hopes were shattered by the conservative sex-role ideology of the male revolutionary leaders.[5]

Although it was – and still is – argued that the term 'men' subsumes women, a closer look at the rights of women reveals that this was seldom the case: the use of masculine nouns and pronouns more often than not signifies that the proclaimed rights are confined to the male sex. History provides ample evidence for this. There is probably no better example than the Declaration of the Rights of Man and Citizen of 1789, which in many ways established the foundations for the recognition and protection of human rights, at least those of men. As a response to the exclusion of women from this Declaration, in 1791 Olympe de Gauges published the Declaration of the Rights of Woman and Citizen,[6] but this document was never formally adopted or implemented and thus remains just a signpost of the awareness of the neglect of women in formulating human rights norms, and of the lack of political and public support to redress this neglect. Olympe de Gauges addressed her Declaration to Marie-Antoinette, and intended it to draw public attention to the male bias of the Declaration of the Rights of Man and Citizen, hailed then and now as the basis of human rights.

Both texts are given below, because their juxtaposition facilitates arguments in favour of the gender perspective in proclaiming basic human rights. True, human rights were and continue to be generic rather than gender-specific, but this does not preclude specific provisions aimed at guaranteeing women rights equal to those of men. A look at the two texts enables us to see that, regarding some rights, Olympe de Gauges considered it sufficient just to add 'and women' to reinforce the principle of rights being human rather than those of men only; she rewrote many provisions of the Declaration in order to present what necessitated equal rights for women. A reading of her text may leave an impression that she turned the traditional neglect of women into a specification of rights in order to benefit women at the expense of men; if so, this remains a rare example of such an effort. She broadened the notion of 'oppression', and the accepted legitimacy of resistance to oppression, to include the oppression of women by men. It took humanity almost 200 years to acknowledge that women are victimized by double oppression: that exercised by repressive political regimes, and that emanating from the society, neighbourhood, family, marriage, which denies women equal rights and opportunities.

The right to vote was confined at the time to male citizens. Women's protest actions, such as the refusal of Hubertine Auclert, the editor of the journal *La Citoyenne* (The Female Citizen), to pay taxes because she had no right to participate in decisions on taxation or the national budget,[7] did not change the denial to women of the right to political participation.

This exclusion of women from political participation was a consequence of the traditional confinement of women to the private sphere, leaving the public sphere to men. This view was reflected in a US Supreme Court decision of 1873:

The civil law, as well as nature herself, has always recognized a wide difference in the respective spheres and destinies of men and women. Man is, or should be, women's protector and defender. The constitution of the family organization, which is founded in divine ordinance, as well as in the nature of things, indicates the domestic sphere as that which belongs to the domain and function of womanhood.[8]

Olympe de Gauges demonstrated an imaginative use of human rights concepts to argue protection for women deprived of all rights, such as mothers of illegitimate children. Under freedom of expression she subsumed their right to challenge societal norms of silence and shame imposed on unmarried mothers, and their entitlement to demand responsible fatherhood.

CONQUERING THE RIGHT TO VOTE

☐ The admission of women into politics, and the recognition of their right to vote as the first prerequisite of their political participation, is a recent and still unfinished process. Its chronology is given in Table 1.1. The data show that in most countries, women have been granted the right to vote only in the last 30 years. It may come as a surprise to see the low position of some European countries in this Table (Switzerland granted women the right to vote only in 1971, and one of its cantons, Appenzell, in 1991 for communal and cantonal matters; Liechtenstein granted women the right to vote only in 1984). Kuwait remains an exception: women cannot vote. Countries which obtained their independence only late in the 20th century obviously could give women the right to vote only when men got it, namely after independence, and this they did fairly fast. In most countries, the first constitution drafted upon gaining independence recognized the right to vote for all adults.

The formal right to vote is, of course, the essential prerequisite for political participation, but much more is needed to make women's political participation effective. The United Nations publication *World's Women* reported that in 1977-88 no women held ministerial positions in 93 countries of the world, while their representation in national parliaments exceeded 20 per cent only in the former Eastern Europe and USSR.[9] This has deteriorated

PHOTO: LOUISE GUBB/UNICEF

Women voters in Furma, Ethiopia

in the meantime: 'From an average 33 per cent representation in pre-1989 state socialist parliaments, women now hold an average 10 per cent of parliamentary seats.'[10]

Data on women in political parties and trade unions remain scarce. These areas are documented – at best – by case studies. The gender issue in political participation is not yet on the agenda. Hence, quantitative analyses of women's political participation are hampered by the lack of data. Qualitative analyses, however, all confirm that women do not have equal access to political decision-making.

Much argumentation in the history of women's struggle to obtain the right to vote revolved around the inherently discriminatory practice of compelling women to pay taxes while preventing them from having a say in how their contribution was used. An illustrative example is the campaign of Kusunose Kita in Japan in 1872 against such discriminatory treatment. She

had inherited her husband's property and liability upon his death and became factually if not legally the head of household.

We women who are heads of households must respond to the demands of the government just as other ordinary heads of households, but because we are women, we do not enjoy equal rights. We have the right neither to vote for district council representatives nor to act as legal guarantors in matters of property ... My rights, compared to those of male heads of households, are totally ignored. Most reprehensible of all, the only equality I share with men who are heads of their households is the onerous duty of paying taxes.[11]

The struggle for equality continues. In the current political changes throughout Africa women are increasingly aware of the power of their votes:

As Kenya marches forward towards multi-party elections scheduled for not later than 23 February

Declaration of the Rights of Man and Citizen (1789)	Declaration of the Rights of Woman and Citizen (1791)*
1. Men are born and remain free and equal in rights; social distinction can be established only for the common benefit.	**1.** Women are born free and remain equal in rights to man; social distinctions can be established only for the common benefit.
2. The goal of every political association is the conservation of the natural and imprescriptible rights of man; these rights are liberty, security, and resistance to oppression.	**2.** The goal of every political association is the preservation of the irrevocable rights of woman and man; these rights are liberty, property, security, and especially resistance to oppression.
3. The source of all sovereignty is located in the nation; no body, no individual, can exercise authority which does not expressly emanate from it.	**3.** The principle of all sovereignty is located in the nation, which is none other than the union of women and men; no group, no individual, can exercise any authority which does not expressly emanate from it.
4. Liberty consists of being able to do anything that does not harm another person. Thus the exercise of the natural rights of each man has no limits except those which assure to the other members of society the enjoyment of these same rights; these limits can be determined only by law.	**4.** Liberty and justice consist of rendering to persons those things that belong to them; thus the exercise of woman's natural rights is limited only by the perpetual tyranny with which man oppresses her; these limits must be changed according to the laws of nature and reason.
5. The law prohibits all acts harmful to society. There can be no hindrance to what is not forbidden, and nobody can be forced to do what law does not order.	**5.** The laws of nature and reason prohibit all acts harmful to society; there can be no hindrance to what is not forbidden by these wise and divine laws, and nobody can be forced to do what the law does not command.
6. The law is the expression of the general will; all citizens must participate in its creation personally or through their representatives; law should be the same for all, whether it protects or punishes. All citizens being equal before the law are equally admissible to all public honours, positions, and employments, according to their capacity and with no distinctions other than those of their virtue and talent.	**6.** The law should be the expression of the general will; all female and male citizens must participate in its creation personally or through their representatives. It should be the same for all; female and male citizens, being equal before the law, should be equally admissible to all public honours, positions and employments, according to their capacity and with no distinctions other than those of their virtue and talent.
7. No man can be accused, arrested, or detained except in cases determined by the law, and according to the forms which it prescribes. Those who solicit, draw up, execute, or have executed arbitrary orders must be punished; but any citizen summoned or seized by virtue of the law must obey instantly; through resistance, the citizen renders himself culpable.	**7.** No woman is exempt: she can be accused, arrested, and detained in such cases as determined by law. Women, like men, must obey these rigorous laws.
8. The law should establish only punishments that are strictly and clearly necessary, and nobody can be punished except under a law established and promulgated prior to the offence and legally applied.	**8.** The law should establish only punishments that are strictly and obviously necessary. Nobody may be punished except under a law established and promulgated prior to the offence, and which is legally applicable to women.
9. Every man is presumed innocent until he has been found guilty; if it is judged indispensable to arrest him, all severity that is not necessary for making sure of his presence must be severely repressed by the law.	**9.** Since it is possible for a woman to be found guilty, then, in that event, the law must be enforced rigorously.

10. No one should be threatened for their opinions, even religious opinions, provided that their public demonstration does not disturb the public order established by the law.	**10.** No one should be threatened for their opinions, however divergent. Woman has the right to mount the scaffold; she should likewise have the right to speak in public, provided that her demonstrations do not disrupt public order as established by law.
11. Free communication of ideas and opinions is one of the most precious rights of man; every citizen can therefore freely speak, write and print; he is answerable for abuses of this liberty in cases determined by the law.	**11.** Free communication of ideas and opinions is one of the most precious rights of woman, since this liberty assures the legitimate paternity of fathers with regard to their children. Every female citizen can therefore freely say: 'I am the mother of a child that belongs to you,' without a barbaric prejudice forcing her to conceal the truth; she is also answerable for abuses of this liberty in cases determined by the law.
12. The guarantee of the rights of man and citizen necessitates a public utility; this guarantee should be established for the advantage of everyone, and not for the personal benefit of those entrusted with this utility.	**12.** The guarantee of the rights of woman and female citizen necessitates a public utility. This guarantee should be established for the advantage of everyone, not for the personal benefit of those entrusted with this utility.
13. For the maintenance of the public utility and for administrative expenses a tax is indispensable; it must be assessed for all citizens in proportion to their capacity to pay.	**13.** For the maintenance of the public utility and administrative expenses the contributions of women and men shall be equal; the woman shares in all forced labour and all painful tasks, therefore she should have the same share in the distribution of positions, tasks, assignments, honours and industry.
14. Citizens have the right to determine the need for public taxes, either by themselves or through their representatives, to consent to them freely, to investigate their use, and to determine their rate, basis, collection and duration.	**14.** Female and male citizens have the right to determine the need for public taxes, either by themselves or through their representatives. Female citizens can consent to this only if they are admitted to an equal share not only in wealth but also in public administration, and in their right to determine the proportion and extent of tax collection.
15. Society has the right to demand an accounting of their administration from every public agent.	**15.** The mass of women, allied for tax purposes to the mass of men, has the right to hold every public official accountable for their administration.
16. Any society in which the guarantee of rights is not assured, or the separation of powers not determined, has no constitution.	**16.** Any society in which the guarantee of rights is not assured, or the separation of powers not determined, has no constitution; the constitution is nullified if the majority of individuals who compose the nation have not co-operated in writing it.
17. The right of property is inviolable and sacred; nobody can be deprived of it except when public necessity certified by law clearly requires it, subject to just and prior compensation.	**17.** The right of property is inviolable and sacred to both sexes, jointly or separately; nobody can be deprived of it, since it is a true inheritance of nature, except when public necessity, certified by law, clearly requires it, subject to just and prior compensation.

* E. Kingdom (1990), 'Gendering rights' in A.-J. Arnaud and E. Kingdom (eds) *Women's Rights and the Rights of Men*, Enlightenment, Rights and Revolution Series, Aberdeen University Press, Farmers Hall, Aberdeen, pp. 104-107.

PHOTO: DAVID BARBOUR/UNICEF

Mostly men: many government delegations are still composed of men only

1993, for some, one of the most exciting developments in the democratization process is the seemingly unprecedented participation of women in the ongoing public political debate. Towards this goal, the first National Women's Convention took place in the Kenyatta International Conference Centre, Nairobi, on 22 February 1992. Here, women from all walks of life, including peasant farmers, social workers, petty traders, university lecturers, professional and business women, civil leaders, and political aspirants reiterated the centrality of women in all aspects of Kenya's development. Women's contribution in the agricultural, domestic, public, private and informal sectors was lauded amidst misgivings regarding what was perceived as a general trivialization of women's roles and images in society.

Ultimately it was concluded that women, who constitute more than half of Kenya's population, comprised a critical mass that had within it the power to determine the destiny of the country: the vote was the weapon that women could utilize to their advantage and for the general good of society. The vote was to be used wisely to elect candidates (female and male) who would be sensitive to the totality of women's realities and aspirations. The bottom line was the attainment of adequate representation of women at all key decision-making and policy-formulating bodies. This would ensure the passage and implementation of gender-sensitive legislation. This was deemed vital for a plethora of problems that plagued women.[12]

LESSONS FROM HISTORY: 'HE' DOES NOT INCLUDE 'HER' ☐ That women are not subsumed under 'men' in constitutions and laws we learned – or should have learned – from history. A notable case was the English Representation of the People Act of 1867, granting men the right to vote; the term 'man' was used throughout the text. On the basis of this

8

TABLE 1.1 CHRONOLOGY OF WOMEN'S RIGHT TO VOTE

1893 New Zealand
1901 Australia
1906 Finland
1913 Norway
1915 Denmark, Greenland, Iceland
1917 Canada, [USSR]
1918 Austria, Ireland, Poland, Sweden, United Kingdom
1919 Belgium, Germany, Luxembourg, Netherlands
1920 Czechoslovakia, USA
1923 Mongolia
1928 Ecuador
1931 Portugal, Spain, Sri Lanka
1932 Maldives, Thailand, Uruguay
1934 Brazil, Cuba, Turkey
1935 Burma
1936 Puerto Rico
1937 Pakistan, Philippines
1941 Panama
1942 Dominican Republic
1944 Bermuda, Bulgaria, France, Guadeloupe, Jamaica, Martinique
1945 Albania, Guatemala, Indonesia, Italy, Japan, Senegal, Solomon Islands
1946 Cameroon, Djibouti, Liberia, Romania, Trinidad and Tobago, Viet Nam, [Yugoslavia]
1947 Bangladesh, Bolivia, Malta, Venezuela
1948 Israel, Korea, Singapore, Surinam
1949 Chile, China, Costa Rica, Syria
1950 El Salvador, Haiti, India, Peru
1951 Antigua and Barbuda, Barbados, Dominica, Nepal
1952 Argentina, Bolivia, Côte d'Ivoire, Greece
1953 Bhutan, Mexico, Sudan
1954 Belize, Nigeria
1955 Ethiopia, Ghana, Honduras, Nicaragua

1956 Benin, Burkina Faso, Cambodia, Central African Republic, Chad, Comoros, Egypt, Gabon, Guinea, Laos, Mali, Mauritania, Mauritius, Niger, Somalia, Togo, Tunisia
1957 Colombia, Lebanon, Malaysia
1959 Madagascar, Tanzania
1960 Cyprus
1961 Burundi, Gambia, Rwanda, Sierra Leone
1962 Algeria, Bahamas, Monaco, Paraguay, Uganda
1963 Congo, Equatorial Guinea, Iran, Kenya, Libya, Morocco
1964 Afghanistan, Malawi, Zambia
1965 Botswana
1966 Guyana, Lesotho
1967 Grenada, St Christopher-Nevis, St Lucia, St Vincent and Grenadines, Yemen, Zaire
1968 Nauru, Swaziland
1971 Switzerland
1973 Jordan, San Marino
1975 Angola, Cape Verde, Papua New Guinea
1977 Guinea Bissau, Mozambique
1978 Zimbabwe
1980 Iraq, Vanuatu
1984 Liechtenstein
1989 Namibia

Note: This Table includes those countries for which information could be gathered and verified from the variety of existing sources, but does not encompass all countries.

TABLE 1.2 WORLD'S MINISTERS IN 1989: 4 PER CENT WOMEN

No women ministers

Afghanistan • Algeria • Angola • Antigua and Barbuda • Argentina • Bahamas • Bahrain • Belize • Bolivia • Botswana • Brunei Darussalam • Burma • Burundi • Cape Verde • Comoros • Congo • Costa Rica • Cyprus • [Czechoslavakia] • Djibouti • Dominican Republic • Ecuador • Ethiopia • France • Gabon • Grenada • Guinea • India • Iran • Iraq • Israel • Italy • Japan • Jordan • Kenya • Kuwait • Laos • Lebanon • Liechtenstein • Luxembourg • Malawi • Malaysia • Maldives • Mali • Malta • Marshall Islands • Mauretania • Micronesia • Mongolia • Morocco • Mozambique • Nauru • Niger • Nigeria • Oman • Panama • Papua New Guinea • Paraguay • Qatar • Rwanda • Samoa • Saudi Arabia • Sierra Leone • Singapore • Solomon Islands • Somalia • South Africa • St Lucia • St Vincent and Grenadines • Sudan • Switzerland • Tonga • Tunisia • Turkey • Tuvalu • United Arab Emirates • Vanuatu • Vietnam • Yemen • [Yugoslavia] • Zambia

Less than 10 per cent

Albania (4%) • Australia (9%) • Bangladesh (2%) • Barbados (6%) • Belgium (5%) • Benin (6%) • Brazil (8%) • Bulgaria (6%) • Cameroon (4%) • Central African Republic (6%) • Chad (4%) • Chile (4%) • China (7%) • Cote d'Ivoire (5%) • Cuba (3%) • El Salvador (6%) • Egypt (3%) • Equatorial Guinea (4%) • Fiji (9%) • Finland (17%) • Gambia (6%) • Ghana (3%) • Greece (4%) • Guinea Bissau (4%) • Haiti (7%) • Honduras (6%) • Hungary (5%) • Iceland (6%) • Indonesia (5%) • Jamaica (6%) • Kiribati (8%) • Lesotho (4%) Liberia (6%) • Libya (4%) • Madagascar (2%) • Mauritius (5%) • Mexico (7%) • Nepal (4%) • Netherlands (6%) • Nicaragua (6%) • Pakistan (7%) • Peru (5%) • Poland (4%) • Portugal (6%) • Sao Tome and Principe (8%) • Senegal (8%) • Seychelles (9%) • Spain (9%) • Sri Lanka (4%) • Surinam (6%) • Syria (3%) • Swaziland (7%) • Thailand (8%) • Togo (6%) • Uganda (3%) • United Kingdom (5%) • Uruguay (6%) • [USSR] (1%) • Zaire (3%) • Zimbabwe (9%)

More than 10 per cent

Austria (13%) • Bermuda (13%) • Burkina Faso (14%) • Canada (14%) • Colombia (21%) • Denmark (17%) • Dominica (11%) • Finland (7%) • Germany (10%) • Guatemala (11%) • Guyana (10%) • Ireland (10%) • New Zealand (15%) • Norway (33%) • Philippines (14%) • Romania (13%) • St Kitts and Nevis (10%) • Sweden (25%) • Tanzania (19%) • Trinidad and Tobago (19%) • USA (10%) • Venezuela (10%)

Source: *Women in government*. Statistical Extract from the DAW Database on Women in Decision-making, Division for the Advancement of Women, Vienna, March 1992.

law a woman, Mary Abbott, sought to have her name included in the electoral register, and her application was joined by 5,346 other women. A court case ensued and Mary Abbott lost. Despite the explicit provision of an earlier law that in all legislation 'words importing the masculine gender shall be deemed and taken to include females, unless the contrary as to gender and number is expressly provided', 'men' excluded 'women'. Evidence in support of this assertion proved that, historically, women had never been allowed to vote and their legal incapacity to do so was upheld.[13]

Human rights language aims to be gender-neutral, starting from the term 'human' which encompasses both men and women. In elaborating specific human rights, however, sexism prevails even today. Thus the 1989 Convention on the Rights of the Child reached its final stage of drafting using 'he' throughout the text, and were it not for the alert by UNICEF, UNESCO, ILO and FAO,[14] it might have been adopted as drafted. This is not hair-splitting: if the rights of women are not explicitly guaranteed they tend to remain unrecognized. In the case of the Convention on the Rights of the Child, the importance of eliminating discrimination against the girl child necessitates an emphasis on her rights. Proposals to include specific provisions relating to the discrimination against female children were, however, suggested too late, during the final stage of drafting of the Convention.[15]

The notion that problems have been solved in the industrialized countries is often erroneous. Thus the Committee of Ministers of the Council of Europe adopted a recommendation specifically on the elimination of sexism from language. The reasoning used by the Committee is sufficiently indicative of the long way still to go, even in that part of the world which calls itself 'developed':

[The Committee of Ministers] stressing the fundamental role of language in forming an individual's social identity, and the interaction which exists between language and social attitudes;

Convinced that the sexism characterizing current linguistic usage in most Council of Europe member states – whereby the masculine prevails over the feminine – is hindering the establishment of equality between women and men, since it obscures the existence of women as half of humanity, while denying the equality of women and men;

Noting also that the use of the masculine gender to denote people of both sexes is, in today's social context, a source of uncertainty about the people – men or women – involved.[16]

SEVENTY YEARS OF THE INTER-AMERICAN SYSTEM □ The protection of women's rights within the Organization of American States (OAS) predates that of the United Nations and thus provides evidence of early efforts towards equal rights for women. The obstacles to their success, before the universal recognition of human rights after the Second World War, were insurmountable.

The beginning goes back to 1923, when the Fifth International Conference of American States recommended 'the study of the means of abolishing the constitutional and legal incapacities of women for the purpose of securing, in due course and by means of the development of adequate capacities, the consequent responsibilites and the same civil and political rights for women that are today enjoyed by men'.[17] Ten years later it was acknowledged that no international measures concerning women's civil and political rights were feasible because of the resistance of national governments: 'The concession of [civil and political] rights belongs exclusively to the sovereign bodies of each State and an international conference ... cannot impose binding obligations on these matters

BY

HEWLETT & BRIGHT.

SALE OF

VALUABLE

SLAVES,

(On account of departure)

The Owner of the following named and valuable Slaves, being on the eve of departure for Europe, will cause the same to be offered for sale, at the NEW EXCHANGE, corner of St. Louis and Chartres streets, on *Saturday,* May 16, at Twelve o'Clock, *viz.*

1. SARAH, a mulatress, aged 45 years, a good cook and accustomed to house work in general, is an excellent and faithful nurse for sick persons, and in every respect a first rate character.

2. DENNIS, her son, a mulatto, aged 24 years, a first rate cook and steward for a vessel, having been in that capacity for many years on board one of the Mobile packets; is strictly honest, temperate, and a first rate subject.

3. CHOLE, a mulatress, aged 36 years, she is, without execption, one of the most competent servants in the country, a first rate washer and ironer, does up lace, a good cook, and for a bachelor who wishes a house-keeper she would be invaluable: she is also a good ladies' maid, having travelled to the North in that capacity.

4. FANNY, her daughter, a mulatress, aged 16 years, speaks French and English, is a superior hair-dresser, (pupil of Guilliac,) a good seamstress and ladies' maid, is smart, intelligent, and a first rate character.

5. DANDRIDGE, a mulatoo, aged 26 years, a first rate dining-room servant, a good painter and rough carpenter, and has but few equals for honesty and sobriety.

6. NANCY, his wife, aged about 24 years, a confidential house servant, good seamstress, mantuamaker and tailoress, a good cook, washer and ironer, etc.

7. MARY ANN, her child, a creole, aged 7 years, speaks French and English, is smart, active and intelligent.

8. FANNY or FRANCES, a mulatress, aged 22 years, is a first rate washer and ironer, good cook and house servant, and has an excellent character.

9. EMMA, an orphan, aged 10 or 11 years, speaks French and English, has been in the country 7 years, has been accustomed to waiting on table, sewing etc.; is intelligent and active.

10. FRANK, a mulatto, aged about 32 years speaks French and English, is a first rate hostler and coachman, understands perfectly well the management of horses, and is, in every respect, a first rate character, with the exception that he will occasionally drink, though not an habitual drunkard.

All the above named Slaves are acclimated and excellent subjects; they were purchased by their present vendor many years ago, and will, therefore, be severally warranted against all vices and maladies prescribed by law, save and except FRANK, who is fully guaranteed in every other respect but the one above mentioned.

TERMS:—One-half Cash, and the other half in notes at Six months, drawn and endorsed to the satisfaction of the Vendor, with special mortgage on the Slaves until final payment. The Acts of Sale to be passed before WILLIAM BOSWELL, *Notary Public*, at the expense of the Purchaser.

New-Orleans, May 13, 1835.

PRINTED BY BENJAMIN LEVY.

Advertising the sale of people: New Orleans, 1835

without curtailing the sovereign rights of the different states.[18]

Two years later a proposal was made to grant women full recognition of the rights and duties of citizenship in recognition of their role in promoting peace, namely of the manifest efficacy of the action of women in the social organization and the defense of peace because of the decisive influence which they exercise upon the moral upbringing of future generations.[19] In 1938 the situation of indigenous women was brought up, and the OAS was mandated to pay special attention to the problems of indigenous women.[20]

The activities of the OAS significantly changed after the Second World War, and in 1954 a series of resolutions on women was adopted, including one on economic, and another on political rights of women. The resolution on economic rights recommended, *inter alia*, the prohibition of wage differentials for equal work, because of sex or marital status, equal access of women to all kinds of apprenticeships and technical and vocational training, and the adoption of effective measures to protect industrial home work in order to prevent exploitation. The resolution on political rights recommended all governments to amend their laws for the purpose of granting full political rights to the women of their respective countries.[21]

SLAVERY OUTLAWED ☐ International treaties outlawed slavery long before human rights terminology came into usage. Moreover, trafficking in women was among the principal issues of the anti-slavery action from the very beginning. It is indicative of the slow and difficult path towards eradicating slavery that it was not abolished everywhere in the world. It persists in different forms, such as trafficking in people for the purpose of prostitution or organ transplantation, or debt bondage. The human rights body which deals with

slavery changed its name into Working Group on Contemporary Forms of Slavery to acknowledge the fact that slavery has not been abolished but modernized.

A particular form of contemporary slavery which affects women is forced prostitution. In dealing with the human rights aspects of prostitution there is still much confusion regarding the scope of protection that should apply – some argue that any prostitution violates human rights, others claim that prostitution can be a freely chosen profession. There is, however, full agreement that exploitation of prostitution is a human rights violation. A recent description of its impact on women says:

By reducing women to a commodity to be bought, sold, appropriated, exchanged or acquired, prostitution affected women as a group. It reinforced the societal equation of women to sex which reduced women to being less than human and contributed to sustaining women's second class status throughout the world.[22]

There is a set of universally applicable criteria against which national policies on prostitution can be evaluated. These include the Convention for the Suppression of the Traffic in Persons and of the Exploitation of the Prostitution of Others, which outlaws exploitation of prostitution and obliges governments to eliminate it. Article 6 of the Convention on the Elimination of All Forms of Discrimination against Women again prohibits exploitation of prostitution, and requires governments to undertake appropriate measures and report on them. There are special prohibitions on the exploitation of child prostitution and the protection of children against sexual abuse and trafficking which have been codified in the 1989 Convention on the Rights of the Child.

This international legal framework provides the basic principles and norms

SLAVERY: NOT ABOLISHED BUT MODERNIZED

During the eighteenth century the slave trade became the most flourishing branch of the fast-growing commerce of the new financial empires. The vast numbers of ships of all sizes and draughts crossing the Atlantic from West African ports and Arab slave-markets have never been counted, but the revenues of the insurance-brokers and investment bankers that serviced the slavers are written in the blood of thousands of victims ...

But the classical turning-point in the 'odious traffic', as Lord Mansfield was to call it, was reached on 22 June 1772, when that famous judge held that slavery had no standing in the law of England, so a writ of Habeas Corpus was good to release the slave Somersett from a ship then lying in the Thames. For a hundred years the abolition battle was waged, first on a national and soon on an international front – now an almost forgotten freedom struggle but by no means terminated yet.

Progress was infinitesimal. On 17 June 1788 a Bill passed the House of Commons by a vote of fifty-six to five, by which slavers were allowed to carry 'five men to every three tons in every ship' ... Parliamentary investigation of the trade followed.

Internationally, the initiative came from Britain. In 1806 Britain proposed to the United States a treaty ... under which the two nations 'agree to use their best endeavours to procure the co-operation of other Powers for the final and complete abolition of a trade so repugnant to the principles of justice and humanity', but the United States refused to sign it ... In 1814 Great Britain and the United States at last agreed 'to use their best endeavours' for the abolition of slave trade.

Until the League of Nations was founded at the end of the First World War, no sustained campaign of world-wide investigation and action had been feasible, for protection of human rights on so vast a scale required international political machinery to ensure it.

Under the leadership of Britain, a Slavery Convention was framed in 1926 and signed by over forty nations, including the United States, who committed themselves to the active tasks of abolition and emancipation. That was something, but it revealed that more was needed. Conventions do not execute themselves, and lagging signatories need to be kept up to their promises ... The Slavery Convention of 1926 expressed in twelve articles the maximum agreement obtainable at that time ... But it lacked clarity on many points and it neglected to provide machinery for supervising the application of the Convention.

A Protocol was concluded in 1953, by which the 1926 Convention was placed in the care of the United Nations. In September 1956 a new instrument was debated and approved under the title 'Supplementary Convention on the Abolition of Slavery, the Slave Trade and Institutions and Practices Similar to Slavery'. It went further than the 1926 Convention and covered abuses analogous to slavery, such as debt bondage, serfdom, the sale of women into marriage without their consent and the sham adoption of children to exploit their labour. Thus the United Nations is now in possession of two important instruments dealing with the problem of slavery. Ratification, however, has been rather slow, although there has been some progress towards that end in recent years.[23]

PHOTO: LAWYERS FOR HUMAN RIGHTS AND LEGAL AID (LHRLA)

Slavery still persists: trafficking in women, 1991

which states should apply. It has also established reporting systems which resulted in a wealth of authoritative information concerning laws, policies and practices of states regarding the multitude of contemporary forms of slavery. The United Nations human rights bodies continue to call for more effective measures towards abolition of all forms of slavery. In 1991, the Working Group on Contemporary Forms of Slavery elaborated a Programme of Action for Prevention of Traffic in Persons and the Exploitation of the Prostitution of Others, which has since been endorsed by the Sub-Commission and the Commission on Human Rights. This Programme is a vivid reminder of the fact that trafficking in people, mainly in women and children, has indeed been modernized:

It is noted with concern that the traffic in persons and the exploitation of the prostitution of others remain rife in various parts of the world. These phenomena are acquiring new forms and are being pursued on an industrial scale to a dangerous extent; hence the need for the development of a political and social will to combat them.

These ancient scourges are being transformed into sordid international businesses, making unprecedented use of advertising, modern techniques and the promotion of tourism for purposes of sexual exploitation. Above all these businesses exploit the poverty of the deprived countries; yet first and foremost they have their origin, and the greatest demand arises, in the developed countries.[24]

Strengthening the existing prohibitions on trafficking in people, and adopting additional ones, is indispensable, but insufficient, for its eradication. This was clearly recognized by the Working Group, and in the proposed Programme of Action it suggested in addition to legal measures and law enforcement three essential areas:

information and education; social measures (including development assistance); and rehabilitation and reintegration. The specific proposals of the Working Group include the following:

Special educational measures should be articulated and adopted on the basis of universally accepted ethical principles relating to human dignity, and directed both at the general public and at specific groups. Emphasis should be placed on the damaging effects these abuses have on the victims, on ways to assist victims, and on ways in which the abuses can be prevented, discovered and exposed.

For many countries, the application of local, national and regional programmes to benefit women and children who are victims of the traffic in persons requires substantial international assistance and calls for a greater commitment on the part of the international community, either through specific projects

or through development assistance.

Measures should be taken to ensure that the traffic in persons, particularly women and children, is not effected by means of bogus marriages, clandestine employment and immigration, domestic labour or false adoptions.

Legislative and other measures should be taken to prevent sex tourism and penalize those who organize it. Such measures should be adopted and implemented in both the countries from which the customers come (most often industrialized countries) and the countries to which they go (often developing countries). Using the enticement of sex with women and children to market tourism should be penalized on the same level as procurement.[25]

1. M. Lagarde (1990) 'Memoria feminista', *Otra Guatemala*, No. 12, August 1990, p. 17.
2. C. Qunta (1987) *Women in Southern Africa*, Skotaville Publishers, Johannesburg, pp. 23 and 29.
3. 'The cultural roots of Asian female subjugation', *Balai. Asian Journal*, No. 4, December 1987, p. 2.
4. K. Jayawardena (1986) *Feminism and Nationalism in the Third World*, Zed Books, London, pp. 19 and 23.
5. R.M. Kelly (1990) 'Women, the economy and the US constitution' in A.-J. Arnaoud and E. Kingdom (eds) *Women's Rights and the Rights of Man*, Enlightenment, Rights and Revolution Series, Aberdeen University Press, Farmers Hall, Aberdeen, p. 89.
6. O. de Gauges (1791) 'Declaration des droits de la femme et de la citoyenne' in B. Groulte (1986) *Oeuvres d'Olympe de Gauges*, Mercure de France, Paris.
7. H. Auclert (1982) *La Citoyenne. 1881/1891*, Syros, Paris.
8. *Bradwell v. Illinois* (1873) 83 US (16 Wall) 130.
9. United Nations (1991) *The World's Women 1970-1990. Trends and Statistics*, Social Statistics and Indicators, Series K, No. 8, New York, pp. 31-3.
10. B. Einhorn (1992) 'Concepts of women's rights' in V.M. Moghadam (ed.) *Privatization and Democratization in Central and Eastern Europe and the Soviet Union: The Gender Dimension*, WIDER, Helsinki, January 1992, p. 63.
11. S.L. Sievers (1983) *Flowers in Salt. The Beginnings of Feminist Consciousness in Modern Japan*, Stanford University Press, p. 29.
12. T. Kanongo (1992) 'Perceiving women in Kenya's history', *Africa World Review*, May-October, 1992, p. 16.
13. T.D. Fergus (1988) 'Women and the parliamentary franchise in Great Britain' in S. McLean and N. Burrows (eds) *The Legal Relevance of Gender. Some*

Aspects of Sex-Based Discrimination, Humanities Press International, Atlantic Highlands, pp. 88-9.
14. 'Gender-neutral language', in: technical review of the text of the Draft Convention on the Rights of the Child, UN Doc. E/CN.4/1989/WG.1/CRP.1 of 15 October 1988, p. 5.
15. Ibid., pp. 7-8.
16. Council of Europe – Recommendation No. R (90) 4 of the Committee of Ministers to Member States on the Elimination of Sexism from Language of 21 February 1990, preamble.
17. Fifth International Conference of American States (1923) *Resolutions*, Santiago, Chile, 1923, pp. 6-7.
18. Seventh International Conference of American States (1933) *Final Act*, Montevideo, 3-26 December 1933, Florensa, 1934, pp. 42-3.
19. *Final Act of the Inter-American Conference for the Maintenance of Peace*, Buenos Aires, 1-23 December 1936, pp. 12-13.
20. Eighth International Conference of American States (1938) *Final Act*, Lima, Torres Aquirre, pp. 29-30.
21. Tenth Inter-American Conference (1954) *Final Act*, Caracas, 1-28 March 1954, Pan American Union, Washington DC, pp. 67-9.
22. 'Seminar on Action against Traffic in Women and Forced Prostitution: Note by the Secretary-General', UN Doc. E/CN.4/Sub.2/AC.2/1992/8 of 16 April 1992, para. 54 (g).
23. J. A. Joyce (1978) *The New Politics of Human Rights*, Macmillan Press, London, pp. 12-18.
24. Report of the Working Group on Contemporary Forms of Slavery on its sixteenth session, UN Doc. E/CN.4/Sub.2/1991/41 of 19 August 1991, p. 36, paras. 1 and 3.
25. Ibid., pp. 37-40, paras. 13, 18, 27 and 30.

2 FROM THE PROTECTION OF MOTHERHOOD TO EQUAL RIGHTS

Whilst not denying that reproductive freedom has significance for both sexes, it remains crucial that any policy designed to expand or contract reproductive choice honestly confronts the fundamental point that the primary bearers of interests in human reproduction remain women, who carry the social, physical, psychological and practical burdens of childbearing and -rearing.[1]

THROUGHOUT THIS BOOK emphasis is placed on the need to refrain from the conventional, but still widespread, reduction of the human rights of women to motherhood. For this reason, the book pays far less attention to motherhood than many readers would have expected. Human rights require that women do not have to earn societal recognition and protection through motherhood, that women are, as much as men, entitled to full protection of their rights and freedoms because they are human beings.

Nevertheless, the issue of motherhood and its implications for equal rights of women cannot and should not be avoided. The biological fact remains that women bear children and men do not. Societal and legal protection aims to compensate for this biological difference and accords protection to women regarding pregnancy and child-bearing. This protection derives from the recognition that child-bearing has a high societal value. Protection of motherhood is compensation to those women who perform a socially valued function, it is not granted them merely because they are women.

FAMILY PLANNING ☐ If equal rights for women remain controversial, issues relating to family planning represent a continuing and worldwide subject of disputation. There really is no single controversy but many, and these vary in time and place. At one end of the spectrum are recent controversies relating to women's access to medically assisted procreation which enables them to have children without having intercourse with a male partner. At the other, victims of rape are denied access to abortion and forced to bear children resulting from rape. While abortion is fully legalized and made free of charge in some countries, it is strictly prohibited in others. Such prohibitions are usually justified on the grounds of protection of the life of the unborn child, and treat abortion as homicide. Some countries recognize that human rights ought to guide family planning, while others pursue population control policies that deny the very notion of human rights. Enforced abortion may be one of the methods used in population control.

It is important to emphasize that human rights norms relating to family planning address both parents rather than only the prospective mother. Reducing the discussion of family planning to women may indeed contribute to the tolerance of irresponsible fatherhood, which is quite common worldwide. However, the exercise of human rights in family planning is necessarily focused on women because they bear children, and obstacles to their access to information and services jeopardize not only their rights, but their health and their lives.

The human rights principles in family planning have been summarized by the

PHOTO: SEAN SPRAGUE/UNICEF

Family planning clinic in Mali

United Nations Population Fund (UNFPA) as follows:

The principle that reproductive choice is a basic human right is widely accepted.

The 1968 Teheran International Conference on Human Rights stated it in terms of a basic right. 'Parents have a basic human right to determine freely and responsibly the number and spacing of their children.'

Since then, the basic right to making decisions about child-bearing has been elaborated and reaffirmed by a number of international documents and instruments. These include World Population Plan of Action of 1974 and the recommendations of the International Conference on Population held in Mexico in 1984 and the Amsterdam Declaration of 1989.

These international declarations, resolutions and instruments expressed a political commitment to ensuring reproductive choice regarding the number and spacing of children, and to have access to the means to do so has become an enforceable right with the ratification of the Convention on the Elimination of All Forms of Discrimination against Women. Article 16(e) of the Convention recognizes the right of women, on an equal basis with men, to decide on child-bearing and to have access to the information and means to exercise this right. Several other clauses mandate the provision of family planning information, counselling and services.

At the national level, political commitment to the right to decide on child-bearing is usually implied by policy support to family planning although the objectives of family planning policies and programmes are mostly expressed in terms of health and demographic goals to be achieved. In some countries,

18

**constitutional provisions and laws
guarantee the right of access to family
planning services although political
commitment is still widely varied among
and within countries.²**

The denial of or respect for women's
human rights in this area has significant
implications for their health. The evidence
that denial of access to family planning
and to reproductive health services takes a
heavy toll on women's health and lives
was summarized in an earlier book in this
series, *Women and Health.*³ Such evidence
is used for action. On 8 May 1992 the
International Planned Parenthood Federation (IPPF) instituted 'Flowers for
Mothers': 500,000 flowers, one for each
of the women who die every year from
pregnancy-related complications.⁴

A dividing line between the developed
and developing world with regard to access
to family planning and reproductive health
services does not follow the usual criteria
of Gross National Product (GNP) or level
of industrialization. Recent court cases in
the USA testify to continued resistance to
allowing women access to abortion; abortion has indeed become one of the most
divisive political issues, not only in the
USA. In Canada, restrictions upon
women's access to abortion were lifted in
1988 by a Supreme Court decision; the
Court said: 'Forcing a woman, by threat
of criminal sanction, to carry a foetus to
term unless she meets certain criteria
unrelated to her own priorities and aspirations, is a profound interference with a
woman's body and thus an infringement
of security of the person.'⁵ The new
Brazilian Constitution of 1988 declared
family planning to be a constitutional
right.

Women's right to access to information
about family planning in Ireland was
upheld by the Court of Justice of the
European Community (EC) in October
1991. The Court held that abortion constitutes a service, hence it could be freely
advertised throughout the EC. The
Commission on Human Rights of the
Council of Europe had articulated its
views on the primacy of women's rights
regarding abortion in 1980. It stated that
the 'right to life' of a foetus could not be
construed so as to jeopardize the mother,
and added: 'This would mean that the
"unborn life" of the foetus would be
regarded as being of a higher value than
the life of the pregnant woman.'⁶

In Eastern Europe, recent political and
economic changes may have jeopardized
women's access to family planning and
reproductive health services. Abortion has
become a much debated issue during the
reunification of Germany; in Poland proposed legislation prompted much opposition from women's and human rights
organizations; at the end of 1991 a workshop on women's health and reproductive
rights, held in Prague, concluded that 'as
new laws are drawn up, it is vital that
women's groups become involved in political activism to ensure that their rights are
maintained at national and international
levels.'⁷

There are many different obstacles to
women's access to family planning. One
of these, the requirement of husband's
authorization, is a direct consequence of
unequal rights for women. In quite a few
countries the law empowers the husband
to veto his wife's access to family planning. An example from Ethiopia demonstrates how effective the removal of this
veto can be: in 1982 the husband's authorization was no longer required for women
attending family planning clinics and the
attendance at clinics increased by 26 per
cent immediately.⁸

EQUAL RIGHTS AND MOTHERHOOD

☐ Human rights norms do not treat
people as if they were all equal, because

Controversial Chinese family planning

they are not. These norms demand that people be recognized as having equal rights. Thus disabled persons have been accorded a specific set of rights to compensate for their disability and prevent it from being a handicap. Similarly, pregnant women and mothers with small children have been accorded special protection, not because they are women, but because child-bearing and child-rearing necessitate social and economic support. The main aim of human rights is to accord everyone equal opportunities for free and full development, hence the methods of eliminating discrimination include redressing factual inequalities that might curtail the enjoyment of human rights.

The progress from protection of motherhood to equal rights for women is best described by taking international labour standards as an example. International legal protection for women workers actually predates human rights. The first norms were adopted in 1919, virtually as soon as the International Labour Office (ILO) was established. Not surprisingly, these protective norms dealt primarily with the protection of motherhood. Women were thus protected from night work, from particularly strenuous manual labour, from working in mines. For many decades such norms were deemed essential for the protection of rights of women workers; virtually all of them treated women as mothers or prospective mothers. It took the ILO 60 years to recognize formally that male workers can be fathers, in its 1981 Convention and Recommendation on Workers with Family Responsibilities. This change of terminology evidenced the belated recognition that both men and women may be parents and exercise parental duties.

ILO standard-setting for the protection of women workers is illustrative of the evolving notion of gender equality. At the very beginning of its establishment, the

ILO adopted its first convention on maternity protection, which granted women workers in industrial and commercial undertakings maternity leave, employment security and an entitlement to breast-feed their children during working hours. The focus on maternity protection marked the first decades of international protection. Equal access to employment, and equal treatment in employment, emerged as priority concerns in the 1950s. Thereafter, at first implicitly, and later explicitly, it was recognized that a woman had the right to support herself, equal to that recognized much earlier for men. It took 20 more years to tackle the sharing of support of one's family between the two sexes; previously it had been taken for granted that men were obliged – but also entitled – to be considered 'breadwinners'. Moreover, during the 1970s the content of equal rights for women workers changed. The ILO explicitly recognized that identical treatment of men and women perpetuates inequality; the terminology and provisions of subsequent instruments changed to include equal opportunities for women, not only equal treatment.

TOWARDS RESPONSIBLE FATHERHOOD ☐ If child-bearing is biologically determined, child-rearing is not. The sharing of parental duties is far from being accepted worldwide, let alone practised. Women raise and educate their children, and their attitude towards their daughters is a significant factor determining what their daughters will teach their own daughters. Whatever human rights documents say or demand remains irrelevant to their lives if this fact is not known, internalized and practised.

The change ought to be introduced and supported, sometimes even enforced, 'top-down'; this is what human rights are all about. Governments have to take a firm stand against gender discrimination and provide leadership towards its eradication. Their commitment was evidenced, for example, by the initiative of the South Asian Association for Regional Co-operation (SAARC) to declare 1990 the Year of the Girl Child. This initiative aimed to address the inter-generational transmission of gender discrimination at the family level:

It is the male child who usually gets the lion's share of available resources: of food and maternal attention, of health care and education. And, as the male progresses from infancy to adulthood, those advantages multiply in terms of access to paid employment and decision-making roles. This deeply entrenched preference for males in many societies encourages neglect and exploitation of the girl child and ultimately lowers the status of women. Stereotyped and robbed of her self-esteem, the girl child very often faces a life of servitude and eventually becomes a role model for her own children.[9]

An Expert Group Meeting on Population and Women, held in Botswana in June 1992, formulated a series of recommendations addressing, *inter alia*, the promotion of responsible fatherhood:

Governments and non-governmental organizations should promote responsible parenthood. Children are entitled to the material and emotional support of both fathers and mothers, who should provide for all their children of both sexes on an equitable basis. Governments should adopt specific measures to facilitate the realization of these rights.

Governments should strengthen efforts to promote and encourage, through information, education and communication, as well as through employment legislation and institutional support, the active involvement of men in all areas of family responsibility, including family planning, child-rearing and housework, so that family responsibilities can be fully shared by both partners.

Family planning programmes, in their efforts to reach both women and men, should be consonant with the cultural setting, sensitive to local constraints on women, and should provide all aspects of quality care and services, including counselling, reliable information on contraceptive methods, informed consent and access to a wide range of contraceptives.

Government and non-governmental organizations should develop culturally sensitive health education to increase the awareness of health rights of all members of the family. Efforts should also be made to achieve equal rights of access to appropriate preventive and curative health care regardless of age, gender or family position. Issues such as rape, incest, child abuse, domestic violence and exploitation based on age and gender require special attention. Programmes are required to promote acceptance among men and women of equal rights in sexual relationships.[10]

WHERE DO WOMEN GO FOR HELP IN MAINTAINING CHILDREN?

'Now you cannot rely on the extended family any more. If you are faced with a problem where your husband gives you trouble, the only place to go to today is the courts. If you try to go to your extended family members they will reject you because they will say "We did not see you come into our homestead being made into a wife, so we cannot go into your problems. Go and solve them yourself."'

Thus a group of market women in a slum at the outskirts of Manzini (Swaziland) express their grievances. Women engaged in the daily struggle of maintaining their children and providing for their welfare cannot get much help from the idealized vision of the Swazi society where children were maintained by all members of the extended family. The main problem is described clearly by a group of seamstresses:

'It is this money problem. Everybody has to work, and maintenance now is not only food, it includes maybe medical expenses or taking the child to school. So if you educate another person's child it becomes more expensive for you.'

With the extended family not any more – and the state not yet – able to provide support in child maintenance, women have little choice. A young woman working as a cleaner in Manzini thus did not hesitate to seek help at a legal aid office, although this ran contrary to the customary norms of not challenging the husband and settling private matters within the family.

'I know about the law on maintenance, that the father is supposed to maintain his children. I heard it on the radio when they talked about the rights of children, and I have also heard it from different people. I didn't know what to do, but some people advised me to instruct a lawyer. But I did not have money to do that. So I came to this office to get assistance to get maintenance and I do not feel any problems with that.'

A nurse described the seriousness of the situation:

'I think maintenance is a big problem. I am working at one of clinics around Manzini and usually more than half of the children I see every day have maintenance problems. You find that the mother is working for the kid and the father is not there. Or the father is but he doesn't support the kids. Most malnutrition is because of that.'[11]

1. S. McLean (1989) 'Women, rights and reproduction' in S. McLean (ed.) *Legal Issues in Human Reproduction*, Gower, Aldershot, p. 215.

2. Statement by UNFPA at the Third Session of the Preparatory Committee for the World Conference on Human Rights, Geneva, 14-18 September 1992.

3. Patricia Smyke (1991) *Women and Health*, Zed Books, London.

4. 'Mothers remembered in flower ceremony', *Open File*, A News Digest of the International Planned Parenthood Federation, London, June 1992, pp. 1-2.

5. R.J. Cook and B.M. Dickens (1988) 'International developments in abortion laws: 1977-88', *American Journal of Public Health*, Vol. 78, No. 10, October 1988, p. 1309.

6. European Commission on Human Rights, Decision in the case of X v. the United Kingdom of 13 May 1980, Application 8416/79, D.R. 19, p. 244.

7. 'Women's reproductive rights in Eastern Europe', *Open File* January 1992, p. 1.

8. Family Guidance Association of Ethiopia, *1982 Annual Report*, Addis Ababa, 1982 mimeograph.

9. 'Girls and boys on equal terms', *Convention on the Rights of the Child Information Kit,* Background note No. 6, UN Centre for Human Rights and UNICEF, 1991.

10. Recommendations of the UN Expert Group Meeting on Population and Women, Gaborone, Botswana, 22-26 June 1992.

11. K. Poulsen and M. Jensen (1992) *Legal Aid and Education in Ghana and Swaziland, A Comparative Analysis with a Human Rights Perspective*, Danchurchaid, Copenhagen, January, pp. 43-4.

3 EDUCATION FOR EMPOWERMENT

This process of empowering entails much more than awareness of alternatives, women's rights and the nature of their requirements. It involves the breakdown of powerful sex stereotyping, which prevents women from demanding their rights from men in positions of authority.[1]

HUMAN RIGHTS ARE INCREASINGLY DEFINED by one word only: empowerment. For women, the process of empowerment entails breaking away from the cycle of learned and taught submission to discrimination, carried on from one generation of women to the next. The issue of education in the human rights context thus goes beyond inequalities in access to formal education for women; it necessitates addressing the orientation, contents and impact of education on women. In both cases human rights argumentation regularly runs counter to the current situation, which is itself based on centuries of discrimination against women.

Most controversies concerning the equal rights of women relate to the private rather than the public sphere. In particular they involve challenges to the right of international and national human rights bodies to question the heritage of discriminatory practices and attitudes. Requirements for the elimination of gender discrimination are often at variance with religious norms and cultural practices, thus with societal norms. Many of these requirements interfere in family life and sometimes lack the support of the very women they aim to benefit.

There exist few surveys of public attitudes concerning equal rights for women. Those that do exist cannot be taken as representative of the global or indeed any national situation; the results illustrate obstacles to equal rights for women. In UNESCO's public opinion surveys relating to human rights and family planning, carried out in 1978–81 in Ecuador, Egypt, Mauritius and the Philippines, knowledge of and support for human rights varied a great deal. In Ecuador, for example, 62 per cent of the respondents knew nothing about human rights. In the other three countries, the respondents did know about human rights, particularly those in the private sphere, relating to family, work and property. Their attitudes were summarized as follows:

Those rights that are formulated in a way which stresses women's independence from, and equality with, men within the family, are least well known and find least favour with both men and women.

The idea that 'every wife has the right to work outside her home without her husband's permission' was universally unpalatable. In Egypt and Mauritius it met with less support than any other of the women's rights; in fact, more than three-quarters of those interviewed disagreed with the proposition.

In Egypt, apart from the shared problematic area of the rights of married women, there was widespread disagreement with the right of the woman 'to equal inheritance with the man': 52 per cent of those interviewed rejected this.

In Ecuador, where few (4 per cent) disagreed that women should have the right to be elected to government posts, over a quarter (28 per cent) said that

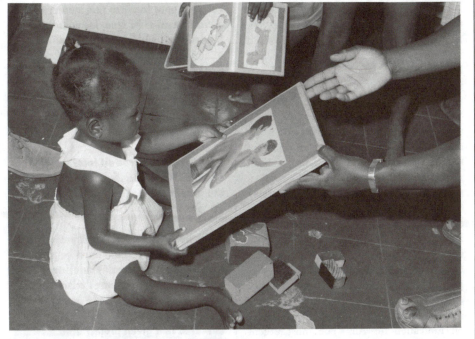

PHOTO: VICKERS/UNICEF

Education starts early: a UNICEF day-care centre in Jamaica

married women should not work outside the house, and a third (34 per cent) did not support women's rights to equal pay for equal work.

It might be assumed that women would know more about their rights, and be more favourably disposed to them, than men. However, there is no clear-cut relationship of this sort.

On the question of wives working outside the home without husbands' permission, men were actually somewhat less likely to oppose this (63 per cent disagreed) than working women, 66 per cent of whom disapproved; an overwhelming 80 per cent of housewives, on the other hand, rejected the idea. Similarly, on the issue of equal inheritance, men were rather more in agreement than was either group of women [working women and housewives].[2]

Following these findings, Margaret Gallagher, the author of the final study based on these surveys, suggested how the attitudes jeopardizing progress of equal rights for women should be tackled:

Attention needs to be paid not only – or even primarily – to the introduction of human rights and their implications into formal educational curricula, but particularly to ways of reaching those whose formal education stops at an age before such concepts as 'rights', 'responsibilites', 'equality', and so on can have any real meaning to them. Non-formal programmes, aimed at a basic redefinition of the status of married women, at recognition of domestic labour as economic activity, at a re-evaluation of the parental and domestic responsibilities of men, would improve the attitudinal environment which currently militates against the practice of equal rights within the family.[3]

ACCESS TO EDUCATION ☐ The history of women's education began with heated controversies about women's right to education, and this battle has been won. Women, today, enjoy a formally and explicitly recognized right to education, but few specific and effective guarantees have been put in place to ensure that women's access to education is secured. Voluminous evidence of different sex ratios throughout the world, and throughout the educational systems, testifies to the fact that equal access to education has been achieved in few countries: 'To date, progress in female enrolments has largely been a by-product of educational expansion, rather than a result of specific efforts aimed at getting girls into school by making schools more accessible.'[4] The necessity to redress this neglect of the fact that formally recognized equal rights do not change unequal access to education was acknowledged in the World Declaration on Education for All: 'The most urgent priority is to ensure access to, and improve the quality of, education for girls and women, and to remove every obstacle that hampers their active participation.'[5]

Numerous measures are necessary to make equal access to education for girls effective. UNICEF has provided guidance by suggesting, *inter alia*, the following:

Recruiting and training teachers locally and providing schools within the village are factors which repeatedly characterize successful programmes. When the teachers come from the same village, they have the knowledge and appreciation of the local lifestyle and customs, and the support and advice of parents and the community. Avoiding interference with the demands of rural life is most important. The reality for many families is that their children need to help with household and farming chores as a matter of survival. When cultural practices place the bulk of this burden on girls, it is critical that educational activities do not clash with these responsibilities. Far too many girls have remained out of school for this reason.

For very poor families this means that education must be free, including no hidden costs such as uniforms, shoes or examination fees. Costs of girls' schooling also need to be lowered by providing scholarships and day-care facilities for siblings and by adjusting school timings to fit schedules of rural children.

Special efforts to recruit local females and train them locally not only improve the enrolment levels of girls, but also provide important role models for them.

While designing educational projects and programmes, attention must be paid to target girls as the main beneficiary of programmes. A conscious decision at all levels needs to be made to have the maximum number of girls enrolled and educated in a given project area.[6]

EDUCATION AGAINST DISCRIMINATION □ Women were formally excluded from access to education throughout a large part of history and even when granted admission to educational institutions this did not entail a recognition of their right to education nor equality between sexes. Education for women was argued along functionalist lines, it was intended to reinforce their role as wives and mothers and thereby constitute a social benefit. Benjamin Rush argued early in the 19th century that education for women was necessary because they are future mothers of (male) citizens, while Frances (Fanny) Wright saw women's education as beneficial for the institution of marriage.[7]

Protests against education which perpetuated women's oppression have been voiced throughout history. A good example is the 'Proclamation of the Wives and Daughters of Tiensin', issued in December 1924 by the Chinese women's

Adult literacy programme in Zimbabwe

movement. This Proclamation required not only that access to education be equal for boys and girls, but also that the orientation of education be changed:

Let [the women's] legal, financial and educational situation be equal to that of men. They must have dignity and equal rights. From the lowest to the highest grades of elementary school, let boys and girls receive the same instruction and let the special classes 'for girls' be eliminated. Let all careers be open to girls, let them choose ... Let the old educational system which produced 'good wives and tender mothers' be abolished and one created which turns girls into real human beings.[8]

Evidence of the perpetuation of intergenerational transmission of discrimination is provided by a UNICEF study of the contemporary situation of female children in Nepal:

It is necessary to understand that girls are socialized from the very beginning to accept their situation and the ideology of male supremacy which makes them prey to a whole range of discriminatory practices. This means that not only are girls and women socially and ideologically unequipped to retaliate against (or even question) the implicit and explicit injustices to which they are subjected, but that, in the absence of alternative models of role and conduct, they actually espouse and propagate the dominant social and cultural values that militate against their gender group. For this reason, women would need powerful social, cultural and economic cues to develop a sense of self-worth and transmit this sentiment to the succeeding generation. Educating women to treat themselves and their daughters better should accompany attempts to create a 'critical consciousness' in women (and men) about their situation.[9]

The Lesser Child: The Girl in India, a study prepared for the Government of India on the occasion of the Year of the Girl Child, describes the challenge:

If laws could guarantee their own enforcement there would never be any injustice. On paper the rights of the girl are unequivocally protected, enshrined in the Constitution and the various laws of the land.

We have never been guilty of the lack of good intentions towards our daughters. But what we do stand indicted for is assuming that they can be a substitute for the relentless effort that alone can transform intention into practice.[10]

Numerous obstacles impede the transformation of intentions into practice. The economic arguments against educating girls reinforce the traditional neglect of their education: 'Education costs include direct expenses such as tuition and school supplies, opportunity costs of lost work by daughters at home or in the marketplace, and cultural costs of going against society's norms of female behaviour. Because of cultural and labour market restrictions on women's work in many poor countries, the private benefits to the family that pays for a daughter's education are often not large enough to offset the costs.'[11]

Faced with those compounded obstacles, it is hardly surprising that girls are discriminated against in education as in other crucial areas. And this is where human rights action of governments comes into the picture: because increased investment in educating girls does not happen spontaneously, governments must make it happen to prevent the perpetuation of *de facto* discrimination against girls. This is the most useful aspect of human rights as a tool for action: they constitute an obligation on governments. It is a truism that governments perform their obligations best when their conduct is scrutinized and breaches of their obligations reported, litigated and remedied. Too little such pressure has been focused

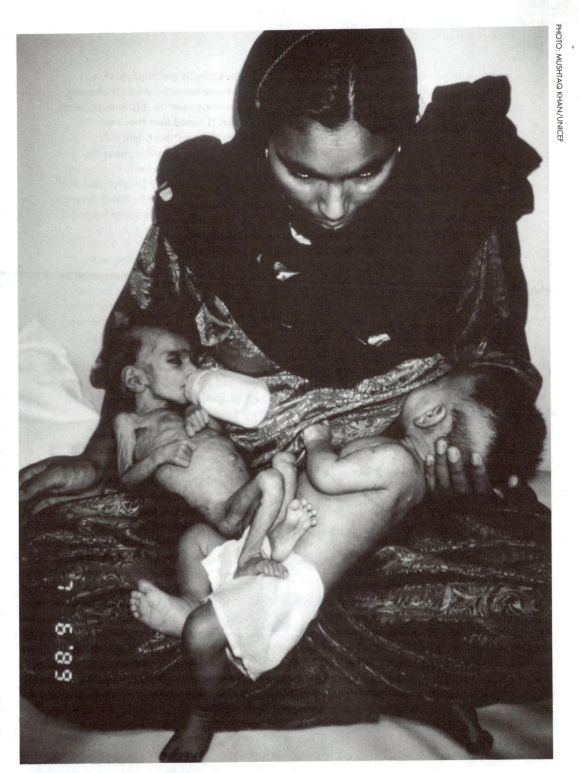

Education against discrimination: baby girl is dying, baby boy is breast fed

on their investment in the right of girls to equal education. When the issue is addressed, solutions are not easy, but far from impossible to find. It was thus found that an effective inducement to parents to send their daughters to school is to compensate them for the loss of the girls' work at home.

Dr Bouthaina Shaaban has vividly described what an uphill struggle gender equality represents, even for those women who have had the advantage of formal education:

During the course of her research for Both Right and Left Handed, Dr Shabaan discovered that although women have become professionals and politicians and have excelled in many fields, at home they are still considered the weaker sex, and are frequently expected to act as servants. 'In fact, the more successful the woman is in her profession, the greater is the pressure exerted on her at home to prove that she is still a "woman" with connotations

of "weak, docile and feminine", she notes. However, sadder still is the way many women react to this unreasonable pressure. 'I found that these women, who, for the most part, had rich experiences and valuable thoughts, were fettered by their own fears of seeming odd or ridiculous, or of jeopardizing their chances of a happy family life if they did not behave according to inherited social traditions.'

There is a widespread feeling in the [Middle Eastern] region – propagated by male 'hypocrites' – 'that just because women go out to work, to school or to university, they are now fully liberated and independent. The aim of these hypocrites is to make women feel grateful for the slight progress they have made and to stop them from going beyond this. Yet the real battle has only just begun,' warns Dr Shaaban.[12]

1. *World Survey of the Role of Women in Development* (1986) Salkes, No. E.8.IV.3, United Nations, New York.
2. M. Gallagher (1985) *Becoming Aware: Human Rights and the Family*, Paris, UNESCO, pp. 20–30.
3. Ibid., p. 85.
4. *Educating Girls: Strategies to Increase Access, Persistence and Achievement* (1991) ABEL Research Study, USAID, Washington DC, December, p. 14.
5. The World Declaration on Education for All, Jomtien, Thailand, 1990, Article 3(3).
6. UNICEF (1992) *Educating Girls and Women. A Moral Imperative*, New York, pp. 29–33.
7. F. Wright (1972) *Life, Letters and Lectures 1834–1844*,

Arno Press, New York.
8. J. Chesneaux et al. (1977) *China from the 1911 Revolution to Liberation*, The Harvester Press, Sussex, pp. 179–80.
9. D. Grover (1991) *Hamra Chelibetiharu. An Analysis of the Situation of Girl Children in Nepal*, UNICEF, Kathmandu, p. 6.
10. *The Lesser Child: The Girl in India* (1990) Delhi, p. 19.
11. E.M. King (1990) *Educating Girls and Women: Investing in Development*, The World Bank, Washington, DC, p. 2.
12. 'The new Arab woman: fact or feminist fantasy?' *The Middle East*, February 1989, p. 7.

4 CHALLENGING UNEQUAL RIGHTS

Achieving the same status for married and unmarried women is a goal separate from that of securing equal developmental opportunities for women and men.[1]

IT MAY SEEM PECULIAR that the law often punishes women for marrying, by decreasing the rights they may exercise once married, but this is part of historical heritage worldwide.

A CLOSER LOOK AT MARRIAGE ☐ In 1765, Blackstone, one of the 'fathers' of English law, said: 'By marriage, the husband and wife are one person in law: that is, the very being or legal existence of the woman is suspended during marriage or at least is incorporated and consolidated into that of the husband.'[2] Two hundred years later this view is still being upheld. Indeed, the struggle to increase the scope of married women's rights to equal those of unmarried women has been and remains a part of the global striving towards equal rights for women.

Human rights norms postulate the right of everyone to marry and to found a family but the essential requirement is that free consent be given for marriage, but this cannot apply to children. Indeed, knowledge about the widespread practice of child marriages prompted the adoption of the 1962 Convention on Consent to Marriage, Minimum Age for Marriage and Registration of Marriages.[3] This Convention has been ratified by only 35 countries.

The small number of countries bound by this Convention testifies to the fact that marriages of girl children are widespread.

This obviates the requirement of consent because, clearly, a child cannot give informed and free consent to marriage, but in any case this is, in practice, nullified by the fact that a girl child's consent is not sought. In African countries, most of which recognize the dual system of statutory and customary marriages, there is an infinite variety of practices. The age of the bride can be seven or eight and indeed a girl can be promised to her future husband even before she is born:

Early marriage is another serious problem which girls face as opposed to boys: girls are given away for marriage at the ages between 11 and 13 and start producing children at an early age. Birth to women between the ages of 11 and 13 who are not fully mature can permanently injure their health, and the maternal mortality rate is three times greater than that of the 20–24 year age group.[4]

Marriage is often arranged by the couple's families. In fact under many customary laws a woman must obtain her family's consent to marry, regardless of her age. The bride price undermines the status of the woman before and after marriage. A woman cannot divorce unless her family repays the bride price to her husband's family.

Even if the woman is not a minor when she marries, she often does not have an equal opportunity to exercise her rights. In many parts of the world the institution of marriage includes various forms of polygamy. A description of a recent debate in Malaysia illustrates the current situation:

The issue of polygamy continues to divide the sexes in Malaysia, with most women united in denouncing polygamy and men's reactions ranging from criticism to active support of the practice. Although Islam does not advocate polygamy, provisions in the Koran which allow a man to take up to four wives in specific and exceptional circumstances are treated

marriage bride price

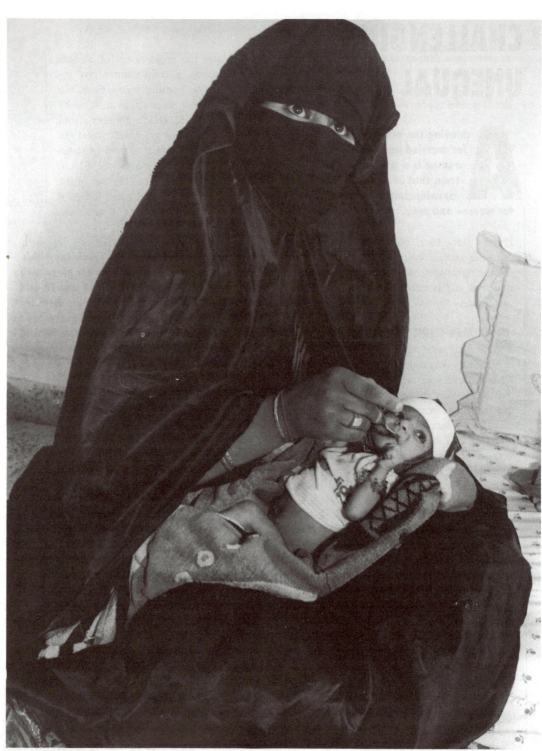

Hidden from public sight: a young mother with her baby

by some men as a blanket licence to take extra wives.

The latest call for facilitating polygamy came from Perlis State's Islamic Religious Department Director, Mohamed Saad Mehmad, who at the seminar on 4 August [1991] urged women to allow their husbands to take second, third and fourth wives as a way of preventing extramarital affairs and alleviating the problem of unmarried women.[5]

Unequal rights in marriage have become a frequent topic of inquiry on the agenda of international human rights treaty bodies. Not only the Committee on the Elimination of All Forms of Discrimination Against Women (CEDAW), but other human rights bodies, are faced with different national approaches to marriage which are reflected in governmental reports. These reports often point out explicit gender discrimination. In its report under the International Covenant on Civil and Political Rights (ICCPR), Guinea stated that statutory requirements for marriage included 'the payment of a dowry of GF 500', and added: 'Polygamy is permitted under Guinean law but is subject to the requirement of consent by the female spouse or spouses.'[6]

Married women are still required to have their husbands' permission to seek family planning advice or to enter employment; they are not considered independent – or equal – in migration or issues of citizenship. The concept of the 'head of the family' in land ownership and land reform, or in loans and credits, jeopardizes the status of women in many countries. International norms guaranteeing married women equality of rights with unmarried women, let alone with men, still leave much to be desired.

The Convention on the Nationality of Married Women is a good example of the global level of commitment to equal rights for married women. Although it was adopted in 1957,[7] this Convention has thus far been ratified by 57 states only, well below one-third of the countries in the world. It is true that the aims of this Convention have been largely incorporated in the Women's Convention and the Convention on the Rights of the Child, but the sad fact remains that the number and composition of the parties to this Convention testify to the low level of commitment to the elimination of child marriages. It is striking that none of the superpowers (China, France, United Kingdom, USA, the former USSR) are among the parties to this Convention.

Because of the persistence of open discrimination against married women in the area of citizenship it is not surprising that quite a number (of the existing few) international cases successfully challenged it. The Inter-American Court on Human Rights, in its Advisory Opinion, which had been sought by Costa Rica regarding amendments to its Constitution, declared that 'the right accorded to women to acquire the nationality of their husbands was an outgrowth of conjugal inequality' and that legal solutions 'which favour only one of the spouses ... constitute discrimination'.[8] Similarly, in the case of Aumeeruddy Cziffra, the Human Rights Committee declared that the legislation of Mauritius, which precluded women from transmitting their citizenship to their children, constituted gender discrimination.[9] Such cases are brought by women, nationally and internationally, with increasing frequency and success. (See Chapters 9 and 10.)

In many countries such discrimination is not challenged. In Gabon, for example, a woman must renounce her citizenship when marrying a foreigner (no similar requirement exists for Gabonese men marrying foreigners) and if she is subse-

Access to justice against wife abuse: this Bolivian cartoon tells it simply and clearly

quently divorced, she cannot regain her original Gabonese citizenship.[10]

Married women tend to be discriminated against as women and as married women, the latter by the assumption that they are financially dependent on their husbands. Few countries have changed their law in order to eliminate sex prejudice, in so far as a married woman must prove that she is a breadwinner before she may claim entitlements stemming from the fact that she is the breadwinner. Married women are sometimes openly discriminated against in social security matters.

Traditional family patterns have left their mark as regards the entitlements a working wife can claim in her own right. The financial dependency which used to be the common lot of women is reflected in provisions which are now outdated, and in any case discriminatory. Any rights a married woman may have acquired through her own employment are denied her because of the protection she can obtain as a dependent person; in the most favourable of circumstances her rights may be recognized provided she meets certain conditions which are never required of men.[11]

PROPERTY ☐ Access to productive resources for women is a prerequisite for their participation in development. Seeking to ensure their access may raise such issues as title to land, and credit and banking facilities, as well as the provision of information and advice about new technology and technical training. In projects not dealing directly with women, it may be important to avoid any aggravation of their situation in this respect.[12]

The origin of problems concerning women's property rights is the treatment of women as the property of their fathers, husbands, even sons. Women's rights have been developing in a similar way to

TABLE 4.1 STATES PARTIES TO THE CONVENTION ON CONSENT TO MARRIAGE, MINIMUM AGE FOR MARRIAGE AND REGISTRATION OF MARRIAGES

● Antigua and Barbuda	● Mali
● Argentina	● Mexico
● Austria	● Mongolia
● Barbados	● Netherlands
● Benin	● New Zealand
● Brazil	● Niger
● Burkina Faso	● Norway
● Cuba	● Philippines
● [Czechoslovakia]	● Poland
● Denmark	● Samoa
● Dominican Republic	● Spain
● Fiji	● Sweden
● Finland	● Trinidad and Tobago
● Germany	● Tunisia
● Guatemala	● Venezuela
● Guinea	● Yemen
● Hungary	● [Yugoslavia]
● Iceland	

human rights: in human rights the most important challenge was to change the view according to which people were the property of their state; in women's rights much change has been attained in abolishing the ownership of women by their fathers, husbands and sons, but the challenge remains, particularly in the area of property rights:

When dealing with property and the legal position of women in African culture we must ask the puzzling question whether women (and children) are able to own property, or whether women (and children) are themselves considered to be property (owned by men). Where bride-wealth persists as a sign of the transfer of rights over the labour and reproductive capacity of women, does this imply that women are to some extent considered as property?[13]

Access to land and land tenure is one of the crucial issues both in development and in human rights, but a systematic exami-

TABLE 4.2 STATES PARTIES TO THE CONVENTION ON THE NATIONALITY OF MARRIED WOMEN

- Albania
- Antigua and Barbuda
- Argentina
- Australia
- Austria
- Bahamas
- Barbados
- Belarus
- Brazil
- Bulgaria
- Canada
- Cuba
- Cyprus
- [Czechoslovakia]
- Denmark
- Dominican Republic
- Ecuador
- Fiji
- Finland
- Germany
- Ghana
- Guatemala
- Hungary
- Iceland
- Ireland
- Israel
- Jamaica
- Lesotho
- Libya
- Luxembourg
- Malawi
- Malaysia
- Mali
- Malta
- Mauritius
- Mexico
- Netherlands
- New Zealand
- Nicaragua
- Norway
- Poland
- Romania
- Russia
- St. Lucia
- Sierra Leone
- Singapore
- Sri Lanka
- Swaziland
- Sweden
- Tanzania
- Trinidad and Tobago
- Tunisia
- Uganda
- Ukraine
- Venezuela
- [Yugoslavia]
- Zambia

however, land rights are not addressed.

Moreover, there appears to be a move within the United Nations human rights bodies towards protecting existing property rights as human rights. Recent international policy documents call for additional efforts in standard-setting and demand the protection of private property rights within human rights.[16] This is a significant departure from the previous view that human rights necessitate a reconsideration of property rights. A decade ago Erica-Irene Daes in her study of limitations upon human rights made a distinction between individual, that is, legal rights, which include property rights, and human rights, and stated: 'In cases where purely property rights are involved, the resulting conflict between such rights and the "general welfare" could well be resolved in the community's interest.'[17] This controversy is likely to have wide-ranging implications in the very definition of what human rights in development are and/or should be.

The approach which protects private property results in treating land as a commodity to be bought and sold rather than as an essential resource to which access is necessary for those whose livelihood depends on it. The latter, although it constitutes a key human rights requirement, remains a distant goal.

In his 1990 report, the United Nations Special Rapporteur on Economic, Social and Cultural Rights reviewed the existing human rights provisions relating to land rights and pointed out that these give states powers to mould land tenure and restrict land ownership, but such powers are seldom used. Therefore he asked: 'Can or should the human rights organs of the United Nations either encourage or persuade States to make more effective use of their existing legal powers to guarantee a more equitable distribution of land in the social interest?'[18]

nation of pertinent human rights considerations is yet to be undertaken. Land rights are sometimes encompassed in the study of development interventions,[14] but the lack of suggestions as to how to reconcile the existing property rights with demands for access to land impedes the application of a human rights approach. Many international pronouncements have been made concerning access to land and land reform;[15] these, however, represent recommendations rather than binding instruments. In the binding human rights instruments,

Women's access to land, and their land

rights, crucial for rural development, are poorly documented in all statistics. Accurate data on land tenure are scarce. Moreover, they are never gender-specific. It is known from qualitative analyses that women are denied land ownership in many countries, but the extent of their access to land is unknown.[19]

The awareness of gender discrimination in property rights has been demonstrated in numerous calls upon international and national bodies to remedy this. Thus the Nairobi Forward-looking Strategies included a recommendation to remedy this discriminatory approach:

The assumptions that underlie a large part of the relevant legislation, regulations and household surveys that confine the role of supporter and head of household to men hinder women's access to credit, loans and material and non-material resources. Changes are needed in these areas to secure for women equal access to resources. There is a need to eliminate terms such as 'head of household' and introduce others that are comprehensive enough to reflect women's role appropriately in legal documents and household surveys to guarantee the rights of these women.[20]

Much earlier, following the initiative of the Commission on the Status of Women, the Economic and Social Council (ECOSOC) found that statutory matrimonial conditions in many countries were incompatible with the principle of equal rights for women,[21] and later demanded that the existing inequality of inheritance rights be remedied by granting women equal rank in the order of succession and equal shares in the same degree of relationship.[22] These demands remain unmet. What the male orientation in agricultural policies may amount to in practice has been described by one African woman affected by it:

This one they call farmer; send in teachers to teach him to farm (while I'm out growing the food); lend him money for tractors and tillers (while I'm out growing the food); promise him fortunes if he'd only raise cotton (while I'm out growing the food).[23]

Women are doubly jeopardized in property rights: as women, and, again, as married women. As women they often cannot inherit property from their parents or husbands. The legal consequence of marriage has been, throughout history, that women lose much of their (previously unenviable) legal capacity. This remains the situation in many countries. In Rwanda, for example, a married woman cannot enter into contracts, buy or sell property, including land, or even open a bank account without the authorization of her husband.[24] A precedent-setting case before the Human Rights Committee led to its finding that Peruvian legislation, which allows only the husband to represent the matrimonial property before the courts, was discriminatory; it asked the government to remedy such discrimination.[25]

A combination of customary and contemporary law severely restricts property rights of women in Africa:

Under customary law the status of the woman is usually that of a minor whereby she is always under the control of a male: either her father, brother or husband. This means that in terms of real property, where this is communal or clan property, a woman has no capacity to exercise ownership rights over it.

Under the customary law all the property acquired by the spouses, except personal goods, belong to the husband who is entitled to retain all of it at the dissolution of the marriage. At divorce under customary law the wife is often entitled only to her personal goods and no more than a handful of kitchen utensils.

In most African countries (Nigeria, Ghana, Burundi,

Women are involved worldwide in assisting other women: an encounter in Chad

Zaire, for example) by law the husband controls his wife's property, in particular, property acquired by her after marriage, and she cannot enter into contracts that would jeopardize the husband's rights in such property. In practice, she cannot enter into a loan or purchase agreement without her husband's consent.[26]

A UNESCO survey of rural women's land ownership in different periods of African history found that the 'modernization' of legal systems or of agricultural policies often eliminated the previous common usage of land, and led to the exclusion of women from land ownership: 'With independence, the new states retained that imported land ownership legislation while also making use of the pseudo-traditional types of tenure which dropped the idea of community usufruct (which was fair to women) and made men the sole owners.'[27]

WOMEN IN THE HUMAN RIGHTS MOVEMENT □ Daw Aung San Suu Kyi was awarded the Nobel Peace Prize in 1991 for her contribution to human rights. The following year, Rigoberta Menchú received the Nobel Peace Prize for her work on indigenous rights. This recognition of women's contribution to human rights exceeds our knowledge of how much women have contributed worldwide. Much as it is occasionally remembered that women always worked – and continue working – for the rights of all, men and women alike, they remain largely unknown.

The history of the Universal Declaration of Human Rights was linked to Eleanor Roosevelt and many commentators claimed that without her persistence the Declaration would not have been drafted or adopted. Outside the United Nations, women's human rights work is best documented in Latin America. Indeed, the Mothers of the Playa de Mayo have

become known internationally. Their work remains a unique example of the mobilization of women within the human rights movement:

It is ironic that in violating human rights repressive states may sow seeds of new forms of resistance. Groups of relatives of the disappeared of Latin America who confront their governments as mothers seeking their missing children and as wives seeking their missing husbands are an important example of such resistance.

The experiences of these groups reveal the ironic circumstances created by the repressive state. On the one hand, the state valorized motherhood and the family; on the other hand, it simultaneously undertook systematic repression through the use of forced disappearance. As a result, the repressive state has found itself confronting new forms of resistance based precisely on motherhood and the family. Using the language of sacrifice and the traditional values associated with motherhood as both political protection and political tools, these women have been willing to take public action during the worst years of repression ...

While these 'motherist' groups are only part of the larger human rights movement in Latin America, they reveal how protest is shaped by particular types of repression ... Through dramatic acts of civil disobedience – launching street demonstrations with flowers, candles and photos of their missing relatives, staging hunger strikes, chaining themselves to government buildings, blocking traffic – the women in these movements counter the cults of 'everyday death' with celebrations of everyday life. By presenting writs of habeas corpus to the supreme courts in their respective countries (often without the help of lawyers, who fear for their lives), while at the same time remaining sceptical of the legal process, these women demonstrate both the potential and limitations of law within their societies. Perhaps what is most striking about these groups is that they are led primarily by women who would never in their lives before have considered demonstrating

Madres de Playa de Mayo, wearing white scarves, have become a symbol of resistance to repression in Latin America

Women protesting political imprisonment in South Korea

in the street against the government on any issue whatsoever. As in past resistance movements, these women use the image of the weak and powerless female to their advantage as a protective means for mobilization, resistance and survival. As in the bread riots of the past centuries, these women represent the defiant transformation of the powerless victim into the political actor.[28]

In January 1992 an Amnesty International urgent action document reported that Professor Wangari Mathaai, the founder of the Green Belt Movement in Kenya and a prominent environmental expert, had been arrested the previous day.[29] She and eleven other members of the Forum for the Restoration of Democracy were charged with 'publishing a false rumour which is likely to cause fear and alarm to the public'; they were released on bail awaiting trial. Wangari Mathaai continued

her activities for protecting human rights of others and joined the Mothers' Hunger Strike in Nairobi, demanding the release of political prisoners. She and three other women hunger-strikers were beaten unconscious by the riot police on 3 March 1992 and taken to hospital by their supporters. She is still awaiting her trial. Her work has been described as follows:

And it is in Kenya, incidentally, where a woman, Wangari Mathaai, Africa's leading environmentalist, is responsible for a programme that has attracted worldwide attention. Under Mathaai's leadership the Green Belt Movement has enlisted 50,000 women and school children to plant more than 10 million trees.[30]

In 1988 the small Pacific island of Belau (Palau), administered as a USA trust territory, entered world news with reports of its efforts to remain nuclear-free. But global attention was really attracted by the fact that the battle was led and won by women.

The referendum of 1979, by a 92 per cent majority, had approved the constitution of Belau, which prohibited the placing of any nuclear material or installations on the island. Subsequent to this referendum the US government proposed to Belau a 'compact of free association', which would have granted the USA the option of using the island as a military base and introducing nuclear weapons. Approval of this 'compact', however, necessitated amending the anti-nuclear constitution. The Congress of Belau adopted a constitutional amendment whereby the two-thirds majority required to amend the anti-nuclear constitution was changed to a simple majority; the constitution was adjusted accordingly and the 'compact' ratified. In August 1987 the Belauan women started a

legal case challenging this change. Threats and harassment failed to deter them and in March 1988 they won their case: the court declared the changes to be unconstitutional and reaffirmed that Belau should remain nuclear-free. During a visit to Washington to testify at the US Senate hearings against the 'compact', Gabriella Ngirmang, one of the women leaders, explained the background to the women's activism:

In Belau women play an important role in issues of policy, as I suspect is the case in Washington as well. Women traditionally own and divide land. We control the clan money. We traditionally select our chiefs; women place and remove them; having observed their upbringing closely, we are able to decide which men have talent to represent our interests.[31]

1. R.J. Cook (1990) 'Reservations to the Convention on the Elimination of All Forms of Discrimination against Women', *Virginia Journal of International Law*, Vol. 30, No. 3, Spring 1990, p. 670.
2. W. Blackstone (1765) *Commentaries on the Laws of England*, Vol. 1, Oxford, p. 15, III.
3. The Convention on Consent to Marriage, Minimum Age for Marriage and Registration of Marriages was adopted on 10 December 1962 and entered into force on 9 December 1964. *United Nations Treaty Series*, Vol. 521, p. 231.
4. 'Study on traditional practices affecting the health of women and children. Final report by the Special Rapporteur, Mrs Halima Embarek Warzazi', UN Doc. E/CN.4/Sub.2/1991/6 of 5 July 1991, para. 30.
5. 'Malaysia: states differ on approach to polygamy', *Far Eastern Economic Review*, 22 August 1991, p. 18.
6. 'Initial report of Guinea', UN Doc. CCPR/C/6Add.11 of 25 November 1987, p. 26.
7. The Convention on the Nationality of Married Women was adopted on 20 February 1957 and entered into force on 11 August 1958. *United Nations Treaty Series*, Vol. 309, p. 65.
8. Amendments to the naturalization provisions of the Constitution of Costa Rica, 1984, Advisory Opinion of the Inter-American Court on Human Rights of 19 January 1984, Series A, Judgments and Opinions, No. 4, paras. 64 and 68.
9. Human Rights Committee, Communication No. R.9/35.
10. 'Implementation in Africa of the Convention on the Elimination of All Forms of Discrimination against Women', UN Doc. E/ACA/CM.13/27 (1987) para. 33.
11. A. M. Brocas (1990) *Women and Social Security. Progress towards Equality of Treatment*, International

Labour Office, Geneva, p. 30.
12. OECD/DAC (1984), 'Guiding principles to aid agencies for supporting the role of women in development, adopted on 29 November 1983', in *Development Cooperation. 1984 Review*, OECD, Paris, November 1984, p. 180.
13. J.S. Gay (1990) 'Who needs this workshop? Who will benefit from it?' in J. Stewart and A. Armstrong (eds) *The Legal Situation of Women in Southern Africa*, Women and Law in Southern Africa, Vol. II, University of Zimbabwe Publications, Harare, p. 228.
14. Cf. M.R. Brown and W.C. Thiesenhusen (1983), 'Access to land and water', *Land Reform, Land Settlement and Cooperatives*, FAO, Rome, No. 1/2, pp. 1–14; and G. Feder and R. Noronha (1987), 'Land rights systems and agricultural development in sub-Saharan Africa', *The World Bank Research Observer*, Vol. 2, No. 2, July 1987, pp. 143–69.
15. Cf. K. Tomaševski (ed.) (1987) *The Right to Food. Guide through Applicable International Law*, Martinus Nijhoff Publishers.
16. United Nations Commission on Human Rights, 'Respect for the right of everyone to own property alone as well as in association with others', Resolution 1991/19 of 1 March 1991.
17. E.-I. Daes, Special Rapporteur *The Individual's Duties to the Community and the Limitations of Human Rights and Freedoms under Article 29 of the Universal Declaration of Human Rights*, United Nations, New York, E.82.XIV.1, paras. 264–7 and 1021.
18. 'Realization of economic, social and cultural rights'. Progress report prepared by Mr Danilo Turk, Special Rapporteur, UN Doc. E/CN.4/Sub.2/1990/19 of 6 July 1990, para. 137 (d).
19. Cf. J. Masrevery (1975) *Agrarian Law and Judicial*

Systems, FAO, Rome; M.R. Brown and W.C. Thiesenhusen, 'Access to land and water', *Land Reform: Land Settlement and Cooperatives*, No. 1/2, 1983.

20. 'Nairobi Forward-looking Strategies for the Advancement of Women', UN Doc. A/CONF.116/28 of 15 September 1985, para. 295.

21. United Nations Economic and Social Council, Resolution 547 I (XVIII) of 12 July 1954.

22. United Nations Economic and Social Council, Resolution 884 D (XXXIV) of 16 July 1962.

23. US Congress Office of Technology Assessment, *Africa Tomorrow: Issues in Technology, Agriculture and US Foreign Aid*, Washington, DC, December 1985, p. 71.

24. 'Implementation in Africa of the Convention on the Elimination of All Forms of Discrimination against Women', UN Doc. E/ECA/CM.13/27 (1987), para. 51.

25. Human Rights Committee, Communication No. 202/1986.

26. 'Comparative study of national laws on the rights and status of women in Africa', UN Doc. ECA/ATCRW/3.5(ii)(b)/89/3 (1989) p. 9.

27. Submission by UNESCO, in 'Respect for the right of everyone to own property alone as well as in association with others and its contribution to the economic and social development of Member States. Report of the Secretary-General', UN Doc. A/45/523 of 22 October 1990, pp. 43–4.

28. J.G. Schirmer (1988) '"Those who die for life cannot be called dead": women and human rights protest in Latin America', *Human Rights Yearbook*, Harvard Law School, Cambridge, Massachusetts, Vol. 1, 1988, pp. 41–3.

29. Amnesty International (1992) 'Legal concern: Professor Wangari Mathaai (f), Chairman, Green Belt Movement', Doc. AFR 32/01/92 of 14 January 1992.

30. J. Ellis (1991) 'Spreading the word', *Zontian*, September/ October/November 1991, p. 15.

31. 'Belau Court Decision: the Supreme Court has found in favour of the women's legal challenge!' *Pacific News Bulletin*, Vol. 3, No. 2, April/May 1988, p. 3.

5 THE KEY: NON-DISCRIMINATION

Inevitably, as one layer of the discrimination phenomenon is peeled away, other layers appear.[1] Gender discrimination is so firmly imbedded in the history of humanity that it is often not perceived as discrimination. Because women have always been burdened with unpaid household work and absent from public life this is deemed to be a natural state of affairs – this is the way it has always been. To challenge such practices and the deeply rooted attitudes on which these are based is a tremendous task indeed.

THE CHALLENGE TO INEQUALITY is inherent in the very notion of human rights. The main postulate is that all human beings have equal rights, which are properties inherent to human beings. Sex was included in the universally prohibited grounds for discrimination by the United Nations Charter, and all further human rights instruments reinforced and further extended this prohibition. The most important change was attained by the Women's Convention which demands not only that women should be accorded rights equal to those of men, namely that there should be no *de jure* discrimination, but that they should be able to enjoy all these formally accorded rights. This requires that other-than-legal obstacles be identified and eliminated. Eliminating *de facto* discrimination is much more complex and difficult than enacting laws which recognize equal rights for all.

What is discrimination? An employer who hires the best qualified candidate is not discriminating. However, if an employer refuses to hire a female candidate because she is female although equally as qualified as her male colleagues, he is probably discriminating on grounds of sex. The prohibition of discrimination does not imply that no differentiation should be made between people, but that such differentiation should be on the basis of objective and reasonable criteria, not on the grounds of sex, race, ethnic origin, or colour.

Not every differentiation constitutes discrimination. Because human beings are not equal, to treat them with this recognition in mind is legitimate. In differentiating, three modes are relevant: firstly, distinctions are in fact made; secondly, they are based on the specific grounds or criteria out of which international human rights law prohibits some while allowing others, and, thirdly, the outcome of the process of differentiating may result in the nullification or impairment of equal rights, in which case it is considered discriminatory. The Human Rights Committee laid down the distinction between differentiation and discrimination as follows: 'Not every differentiation of treatment will constitute discrimination, if the criteria for such differentiation are reasonable and objective and if the aim is to achieve a purpose which is legitimate under the Covenant.'[2]

To provide guidance on how this should apply it is necessary to define the key terms 'reasonable', 'objective' and 'legitimate'. For the first, it seems accepted that reasonable is the opposite of arbitrary. The basic characteristic of discrimination is the irrelevance of the criterion used to discriminate, while those discriminating are attributing negative connotations to irrelevant criteria, such as sex, race, colour, or ethnic origin.

International human rights law specifies prohibited grounds of discrimination (race, colour, sex, language, religion, political or other opinion, ethnic or national origin) and these have been extended further, to cover social origin, property or economic position, birth, age, disability, sexual orientation, state of health, medical history, marital or family status. Further, this law lists types of discrimination and areas where discrimination is prohibited.

For the public authorities, non-discrimination entails a whole range of obligations which reach far beyond a legal prohibition on discrimination. The Human Rights Committee declared that equal and effective protection against discrimination is an autonomous right. This view emanates from Article 26 of the International Covenant on Civil and Political Rights (ICCPR) which states that all individuals are equal before the law and equally entitled to protection by the law against any discrimination. The Human Rights Committee also extended protection against discrimination to include all human rights, civil, political, economic, social and cultural. In a series of cases the Committee applied prohibition of discrimination to unemployment benefits, social security, and immigration law, thus broadening access to remedy beyond civil and political rights. Thereby a broad range of social rights and social policies has been brought into the realm of litigation if discrimination is at issue. This is an important improvement because economic and social rights were until recently considered to be unenforceable by court action. Non-discrimination should thus apply in all areas regulated by public authorities.

The Human Rights Committee asks questions on gender discrimination of every government which reports on its implementation of the ICCPR. This reflects the fact that gender discrimination exists worldwide, and also indicates the importance of addressing it as one of the crucial human rights issues.

Non-discrimination entails corrective and compensatory policies in favour of those categories that are vulnerable to dis-

crimination and those that have been subjected to it. The Committee found that governments have an obligation to undertake 'affirmative action designed to ensure the positive enjoyment of rights'. Such affirmative action may consist of laws, policies, measures or actions needed to remedy discrimination in fact; that is, to redress *de facto* inequalities. When aimed at redressing inequalities, in order to enable people to enjoy and exercise their rights on an equal footing, differential treatment is necessary and therefore 'action needed to correct discrimination in fact is a case of legitimate differentiation'.[3]

The chronology of international prohibitions of gender discrimination shows how much improved is our knowledge of what constitutes discrimination. In the beginning it was considered sufficient to state simply and clearly that discrimination on the basis of sex was prohibited. The more women used this prohibition to challenge gender discrimination the broader it became, because many practices which originally had not been recognized as discriminatory were proved to discriminate against women. Definitions of discrimination thus became increasingly detailed. A comparison of the wording of the Universal Declaration and the Women's Convention demonstrates this well:

**Universal Declaration of Human Rights (1948):
'Everyone is entitled to all the rights and freedoms ... without distinction of any kind, such as race, colour, sex, ...'**

Women's Convention (1979): 'the term "discrimination against women" shall mean any distinction, exclusion or restriction made on the basis of sex which has the effect or purpose of impairing or nullifying the recognition, enjoyment or exercise by women, irrespective of their marital status, on a basis of equality of men and women, of human rights and fundamental freedoms in the political, economic, social, cultural, civil or any other field.'

TABLE 5.1 CHRONOLOGY OF MAIN HUMAN RIGHTS INSTRUMENTS

1945 United Nations Charter

1948 Universal Declaration of Human Rights

American Declaration of the Rights and Duties of Man

Convention on the Prevention and Punishment of Genocide

1949 Convention on the Suppression of Traffic in Persons

1950 European Convention for the Protection of Human Rights and Fundamental Freedoms

1951 Convention on the Status of Refugees

1952 Convention on the Political Rights of Women

1953 Protocol amending the 1926 Slavery Convention

1956 Supplementary Convention on the Abolition of Slavery

1957 Convention on the Nationality of Married Women

Abolition of Forced Labour Convention

1958 Discrimination (Employment and Occupation) Convention

1960 Convention against Discrimination (in Education)

1961 European Social Charter

1962 Convention on Consent to Marriage, Minimum Age for Marriage and Registration of Marriages

1965 Recommendation on Consent to Marriage, Minimum Age for Marriage and Registration of Marriages

International Convention on the Elimination of All Forms of Racial Discrimination

1966 International Covenant on Economic, Social and Cultural Rights

International Covenant on Civil and Political Rights

Protocol relating to the Status of Refugees

1967 Declaration on the Elimination of Discrimination against Women

1968 Proclamation of Teheran

1969 American Convention on Human Rights

Declaration on Social Progress and Development

1971 Declaration on the Rights of Mentally Retarded Persons

1973 International Convention on the Suppression and Punishment of Apartheid

1974 Universal Declaration on the Eradication of Hunger and Malnutrition

Declaration on the Protection of Women and Children in Emergency and Armed Conflict

1975 Declaration on the Rights of Disabled Persons

Declaration on the Protection of All Persons from Being Subjected to Torture and Other Cruel, Inhuman or Degrading Treatment or Punishment

1978 Declaration on Race and Racial Prejudice

1979 Convention on the Elimination of All Forms of Discrimination against Women

1981 African Charter of Human and Peoples' Rights

Declaration on the Elimination of All Forms of Intolerance and of Discrimination Based on Religion or Belief

1984 Convention against Torture and Inhuman or Degrading Treatment or Punishment

1989 Convention on the Rights of the Child

1991 International Convention for the Protection of Human Rights of All Migrant Workers and Their Families

International action has moved beyond detailed enumerations and descriptions of prohibited discrimination to reviewing the outcome of specific laws, policies or practices, whereby these can be challenged if their impact is discriminatory. Moreover, it is increasingly argued that the most effective way to combat discrimination is to switch the burden of proof – all those differentiating would be subject to the burden of proving that such differentiation is necessary and legitimate, thus consistent with the prohibition of discrimination.

OUTLAWING GENDER DISCRIMINATION ☐ Non-discrimination requires

governments to undertake direct action to ensure the observance of non-discrimination by all public authorities and in all the public services, that is, in all the areas which are under direct control of the national authority. Indirect action involves taking measures to ensure the acceptance and implementation of non-discrimination in areas where the national authority does not exercise direct control.

One may assume – wrongly – that, as a result of 40 years of international activities towards the prohibition of discrimination, all countries have prohibited gender discrimination, at least in principle. This is not the case. While no worldwide study has been carried out to show in how many and in which countries discrimination against women is not prohibited, some information is available from a variety of scattered documents. Thus an analysis of national constitutions reveals that some omitted to include sex among prohibited grounds of discrimination: Egypt, Uganda, Zambia and Zimbabwe, for example.[4] A recent analysis of the situation in Uganda emphasized the following:

The 1967 Constitution of the Republic of Uganda does not outlaw discrimination on the grounds of sex. The Constitution

TABLE 5.2 HUMAN RIGHTS GUARANTEED IN MAIN INTERNATIONAL TREATIES

- Right to self-determination
- Non-discrimination
- Prohibition of apartheid
- Right to effective remedy for violations
- Prohibition of retroactivity for criminal offences
- Prohibition of imprisonment for contractual obligations
- Right to procedural guarantees in criminal trials
- Right to life
- Right to physical and moral integrity
- Prohibition of torture and of cruel, inhuman or degrading treatment or punishment
- Prohibition of slavery, of forced labour and of trafficking in persons
- Right to recognition of legal personality
- Right to liberty and security
- Prohibition of arbitrary arrest, detention and exile
- Right to freedom of movement and residence
- Right to seek asylum
- Right to privacy
- Right to freedom of thought, conscience and religion
- Right to freedom of expression
- Right to freedom of peaceful assembly
- Right to freedom of association
- Right to marry and to found a family
- Right to protection of motherhood and childhood
- Right to a nationality
- Right to work
- Right to food
- Right to social security
- Right to enjoy the highest standard of physical and mental health
- Right to education
- Right to participation in cultural life

permits discriminatory adoption, marriage, divorce, burial, division of property upon death, as regulated by personal law and customary laws. In these areas women's oppression and subordination is most pronounced. The Constitution, by permitting discriminatory family and customary laws and by not expressly outlawing sex discrimination perpetuates legal inequality and women's subordination.[5]

PHOTO: S. ERRINGTON/UNHCR

Women's work is often backbreaking

A different problem was described by the representatives of Thailand during the presentation of its initial report to CEDAW:

The definition of the word 'discrimination' was still unclear in Thai law, as Thailand had no sex discrimination act to provide such a definition, although if it involved a violation of rights, the civil and political codes could be used to protect basic rights. Development of such a law was on the agenda for the future.[6]

The international human rights system permits complaints for violations of civil and political, but not economic and social rights. In 1987 the Human Rights Committee created a precedent by changing this rule in two cases. Not surprisingly, both related to unequal rights of married women. The two women, Mrs Broeks and Mrs Zwaan de Vries, both from the Netherlands, complained to the Committee against the then discriminatory provisions

of Dutch law, which excluded married women from an entitlement to unemployment benefits.

The Committee was faced with a significant dilemma: it had to decide to what extent the prohibition of discrimination under the International Covenant on Civil and Political Rights (ICCPR) extended to economic, social and cultural rights. The Covenant stipulates, in its Article 26, that everybody is entitled – without any discrimination – to the equal protection of the law, including equal and effective protection against discrimination. This decision entailed considering whether the grounds of discrimination (sex, marital status) and areas of discrimination (social security, specifically unemployment benefits), covered by different international treaties which have different monitoring bodies, could be subsumed under the protection against discrimination guaranteed by the ICCPR. The Committee decided not only that it could, but that such protection should be granted.

The two cases were similar. Both women claimed unemployment benefits, which they would have obtained had they been unmarried or had they been married men, but found themselves rejected because they were married women. The Dutch law of the time stipulated that unemployment 'benefits could not be claimed by those married women who were neither breadwinners nor permanently separated from their husbands'. The government further explained that the law had reflected 'the prevailing views in society in general concerning the roles of men and women within marriage and society', whereby the employed married men were always considered "breadwinners" while married women were not.[7] The Committee decided that this was discriminatory: 'a married woman, in order to receive the [unemployment] benefits, has to prove that she was a "breadwinner" – a condition that did not apply to married men. Thus a differentiation which appears on one level to be one of status is in fact one of sex, placing married women at a disadvantage as compared with married men.'[8]

The Netherlands changed its legislation in 1985 and deleted this discriminatory provision. For many other countries, however, such a change remains an unattained goal. Individual complaints of similar types of discrimination from all countries that ratified the Optional Protocol can be submitted to the Human Rights Committee, but unfortunately this has not led to a broader utilization of this procedure.

E LIMINATING DISCRIMINATION: WOMEN AT WORK □ Many changes

have been enacted in many countries when laws were proved to discriminate against women. One example is the unification of retirement age; previously non-discrimination was deemed to necessitate that the retirement age for women be lower than that for men:

Discrimination between men and women with regard to retirement age has drawn sharp criticism in several countries.

In the United States plans to fix a lower pensionable age for women than for men have been condemned as discriminatory ... In the United Kingdom the Equal Opportunities Commission in 1978 proposed a compromise solution. Instead of 60 for women and 65 for men, pensionable age would be set at 63 for all: this suggestion has provoked a lively nation-wide debate.

In March 1975 the Tokyo High Court found the arrangement whereby men retired at the age of 55 and women at 50 unacceptable: it was unjustified, discriminatory towards women, and for this reason was contrary both to the law of the land and to good practice.

In Italy the Court of Cassation in December 1981 declared any clause in a work contract which obliged women to retire earlier than men, thereby hampering the progress of their careers and making it more difficult for them to obtain various benefits, to be illegal and incompatible with the country's Constitution.[9]

Protective norms which apparently favoured women workers have recently been challenged because their effects may be discriminatory. This is hardly a recent phenomenon, although awareness of the necessity to eradicate discrimination today results in abolishing such norms. This was not the case at the beginning of international protection of women workers.

An illustrative example is the 1919 Advisory Opinion of the Permanent Court of International Justice (PCIJ) concerning the interpretation of the 1919 ILO Convention on the Night Work of Women. This Convention protected women from night work, but it also prohibited them

According to statistics, she is not working

from working at night and thus from increasing their earnings.

The case was brought up by the United Kingdom, which sought an authoritative interpretation of this prohibition as it affected women engineers. The specific question that the PCIJ had to answer was whether the 1919 Convention precluded British women engineers, that is, women who were holding, or striving to obtain, managerial positions in electrical companies, from such work because it required night work. It was unclear whether this Convention prohibited all women in industrial enterprises from night work, or applied only to women involved in manual labour.

The Court decided, by six votes to five, that prohibition of night work applied to all women, including those in managerial positions.[10] In the subsequent revisions of this Convention, first in 1934 and then in 1948, women in managerial positions were

exempted and flexibility in interpretation was written into the text of the Convention to prevent provisions aimed at benefiting women from actually harming them.

The majority of women in the world work, but a minority are recognized as 'workers' with the corollary rights of safe working environment, equal wages, paid vacation, and sick leave. The majority of working women are not paid for their work because they are not recognized as workers: The main shortcoming of all global economic statistics from women's point of view is, without doubt, the invisibility of the unpaid labour in households and the informal and agricultural sectors, a major part of which, in all countries, is performed by women.[11] This vast gap between working women and women workers hinders recognition of the basic rights of women as workers: only a small minority of working women are formally employed. Consequently, most are invisible, unprotected, underpaid or unpaid, and more often than not exploited. The Development Assistance Committee (DAC) of the OECD recently called for the creation of a legal framework that would guarantee equal rights for women, and especially for the removal of 'legal restrictions on the full economic and political participation of women'.[12]

Efforts to document the nature and scope of women's work have not yet brought about the formal recognition of women's work. This is not a question of formalities but of the recognition of basic rights; the right to work is included among fundamental human rights. To be recognized as a 'worker' it is not enough to work – the law everywhere insists on a contractual relationship between the employer and the employee. Most women do not have contracts with their husbands or fathers; most women producing food have no contracts whatsoever, neither protecting their labour nor giving them a title to its product. Thus, in so far as economic statistics and labour legislation are concerned, they do not work. In the worst case scenario, such women are considered a burden on society.

The protection of women workers is one of the most thoroughly regulated areas of international human rights protection. The number of specific international standards, their detailed provisions and effective supervision make this area a notable success of the international community. Its impact on women's lives – much as in other areas – necessitates further and stronger national measures to apply protection to women in need of it:

Just as women face untold miseries and injustices at the hands of their families, they are not any better off at their places of work. It's usually worse. Mostly, women are threatened and pressurized not to join trade unions. If they insist,

they're told it'll be at the risk of their honour and self-respect. Note that this is a threat, violent in intent, enough to intimidate most women who are already defenceless.[13]

Despite these odds some women have joined unions. For example, a group of women took up the case of various violations in a garment factory in Karachi. They met the Chief Minister who ordered the Labour Department to look into the matter. The employers were forced to make some amends. But a heavy price was exacted – the services of the women who had raised the issue were terminated. Our survey team met these women, and their cases in the Labour Court are still pending. They have formed a union and an intense battle is going on. The management not only unleashed systematic harassment and intimidation, they also resorted to a vilification campaign against these women through character assassination.[14]

A good example of the need to recognize gender discrimination is child labour, where the genderless category of child workers may often hide the double discrimination affecting female child workers:

It may be wondered why working girls call for separate study. Should not research focus just on children who work, whichever sex they belong to? Is the concentration on girls not a case of looking for sex discrimination where it does not exist? And since the children who work in factories, mines and other hazardous occupations are mostly boys, is it not invidious to focus attention on working girls when the brunt of exploitation is visibly borne by male children?

To sum up, we can say that there are significant differences between the situation of the working girl and that of the working boy in the household, in agriculture and in unorganized industry. These differences manifest themselves in a variety of ways: the sex typing of work, the value imputed to such work and its influence on the attitudes of parents and access to education. As a result of certain cultural restraints, the female child in the

TABLE 5.3 INTERNATIONAL PROTECTION OF WOMEN WORKERS 1919–91

1919 Maternity Protection Convention
Night Work (Women) Convention
Anthrax Prevention
Recommendation
Lead Poisoning (Women and
Children) Recommendation
Labour Inspection (Health Services)
Recommendation

1921 Maternity Protection (Agriculture)
Recommendation
Night Work of Women
(Agriculture) Recommendation
Living-in Conditions (Agriculture)
Recommendation

1922 Migration Statistics
Recommendation

1923 Labour Inspection Recommendation

1926 Migration (Protection of Females at
Sea) Recommendation

1927 Sickness Insurance (Industry)
Convention
Sickness Insurance
Recommendation

1928 Minimum Wage-Fixing Machinery
Recommendation

1930 Forced Labour (Regulation)
Recommendation

1933 Old-Age Insurance (Industry)
Convention
Old-Age Insurance (Agriculture)
Convention
Invalidity Insurance (Industry)
Convention
Invalidity Insurance (Agriculture)
Convention
Survivors' Insurance (Industry)
Convention
Survivors' Insurance (Agriculture)
Convention
Invalidity, Old-Age and Survivors'
Insurance Recommendation

1934 Night Work (Women) Convention
(Revised)

1935 Underground Work (Women)
Convention
Unemployment (Young Persons)
Recommendation

1936 Sickness Insurance (Sea) Convention
Seamen's Welfare in Ports
Recommendation

1937 Public Works (National Planning)
Recommendation

1938 Convention Concerning Statistics of
Wages and Hours of Work

1939 Vocational Training
Recommendation
Migration for Employment (Co-
operation between States)
Recommendation

1944 Income Security Recommendation
Medical Care Recommendation
Social Policy in Dependent
Territories Recommendation
Employment (Transition from War
to Peace) Recommendation

1945 Social Policy in Dependent
Territories (Supplementary
Provisions) Recommendation

1946 Night Work of Young Persons
(Non-Industrial Occupations)
Recommendation

1947 Labour Inspection Convention
Social Policy (Non-Metropolitan
Territories) Convention
Labour Standards (Non-
Metropolitan Territories)
Convention
Labour Inspection Recommendation

1948 Night Work (Women) Convention
(Revised)
Employment Service
Recommendation

1949 Migration for Employment
Convention (Revised)
Migration for Employment
Recommendation (Revised)

1950 Vocational Training (Adults)
Recommendation

1951 Equal Remuneration Convention
Equal Remuneration
Recommendation
Minimum Wage-Fixing Machinery
(Agriculture) Recommendation

1952 Social Security (Minimum

Standards) Convention

Maternity Protection Convention
(Revised)

Maternity Protection
Recommendation

1953 Protection of Workers' Health
Recommendation

1956 Vocational Training (Agriculture)
Recommendation

Welfare Facilities Recommendation

1958 Plantations Convention

Discrimination (Employment and
Occupation) Convention

Plantations Recommendation

Discrimination (Employment and
Occupation) Recommendation

1959 Occupational Health Services
Recommendation

1960 Consultation (Industrial and
National Levels) Recommendation

Radiation Protection
Recommendation

1961 Workers' Housing Recommendation

1962 Social Policy (Basic Aims and
Standards) Convention

Reduction of Hours of Work
Recommendation

Vocational Training
Recommendation

1963 Termination of Employment
Recommendation

1964 Employment Policy Convention

Employment Policy Recommendation

Hygiene (Commerce and Offices)
Recommendation

1965 Minimum Age (Underground
Work) Convention

Employment (Women with Family
Responsibilities) Recommendation

1967 Maximum Weight Convention

Invalidity, Old-Age and Survivors'
Benefits Convention

Maximum Weight
Recommendation

Invalidity, Old-Age and Survivors'
Benefits Recommendation

1969 Labour Inspection (Agriculture)

Convention

1970 Accommodation of Crews
(Supplementary Provisions)
Convention

Special Youth Schemes
Recommendation

1971 Benzene Convention

Benzene Recommendation

1974 Paid Educational Leave Convention

Paid Educational Leave
Recommendation

1975 Rural Workers' Organizations
Recommendation

Human Resources Development
Recommendation

1977 Nursing Personnel Recommendation

1980 Older Workers Recommendation

1981 Workers with Family
Responsibilities Convention

Workers with Family
Responsibilities Recommendation

Termination of Employment
Convention

1983 Vocational Rehabilitation and
Employment (Disabled Persons)
Convention

Vocational Rehabilitation and
Employment (Disabled Persons)
Recommendation

1985 Labour Statistics Recommendation

1987 Seafarers' Welfare Convention

Seafarers' Welfare Recommendation

1988 Safety and Health in Construction
Convention

Employment Promotion and
Protection against Unemployment
Convention

Safety and Health in Construction
Recommendation

1989 Indigenous and Tribal Peoples
Convention

1990 Night Work Convention

Protocol of 1990 to the Night Work
(Women) Convention (Revised),
1948

Chemicals Recommendation

Night Work Recommendation

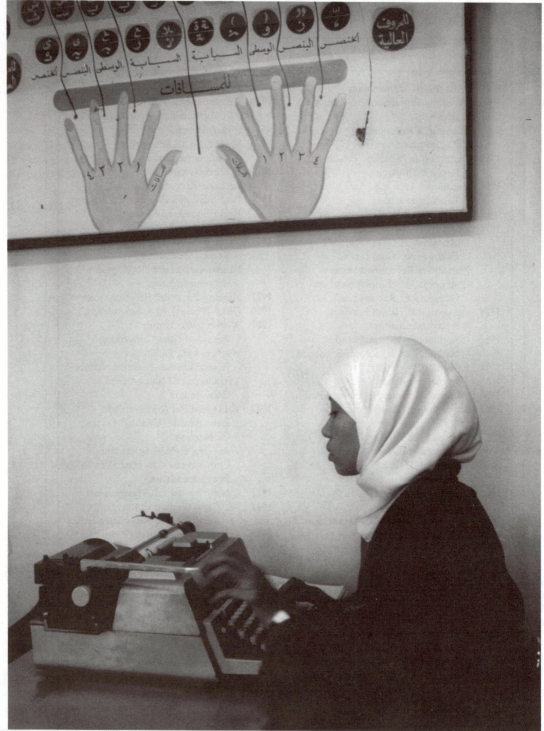

Vocational training for Palestinian women in Gaza

unorganized industry is spared the health hazards that the male child faces in mines, workshops or factories; the same stereotypes keep her home helping her mother. When she is out of public sight, she is out of mind. Devalued as a child, denied equal access to education and often devoid of skills, she carries into her womanhood all the accumulated burdens of her past. The challenge facing programmes, policy and law is to offer the working girls the opportunity to grow, to change and to be free.[15]

Women workers in industrialized countries are deemed to enjoy broader labour protection than those in developing countries. Nevertheless, it should not be assumed that all problems have been solved and that further action is unnecessary. Just one example from the United Kingdom demonstrates that gender discrimination persists virtually everywhere:

Women continue to bear the brunt of poverty under a social security system biased towards men, according to a report published yesterday by the Equal Opportunities Commission.

The study found that only a minority of women earned enough to enjoy full economic independence because the rise in women's paid work had been largely concentrated in part-time, low-paid jobs.

Women found that many such jobs – chosen to fit in with the demands of their families – offered fewer hours than they needed and less employment protection. Black women are likely to have been particularly harshly affected.

The study[16] found that women faced financial disincentives to obtaining paid work and that their interrupted working lives and lower earnings put them at a disadvantage in relation to men in the social security system.[17]

1. S. McLean and N. Burrows (eds) (1988) *The Legal Relevance of Gender. Some Aspects of Sex-Based Discrimination*, Humanities Press International, Atlantic Highlands, New Jersey, p. 15.
2. UN Doc. CCPR/C/21/Rev.1/Add.1, para. 12.
3. Human Rights Committee – General Comment 4 (13), UN Doc. CCPR/C/21/Rev.1 of 19 May 1989.
4. 'Comparative study of national laws on the rights and status of women in Africa', UN Doc. ECA/ATRCW/3.5(ii)(b)/89/3 (1989), pp. 3-4.
5. F.L. Egunyu-Asemo (1990) 'Women and the law in Uganda', Kampala, mimeograph, p. 2.
6. *Report of the Committee on the Elimination of All Forms of Discrimination against Women, Ninth Session*, UN Doc. A/45/38 (1990), para. 239.
7. F.H. Zwaan de Vries *v.* The Netherlands, Communication No. 182/1984, Decision of 9 April 1987, UN Doc. CCPR/C/29/D/182/1984 of 16 April 1984, para. 8.2.
8. Ibid., para. 14.
9. A. M. Brocas et al. (1990) *Women and Social Security. Progress towards Equality of Treatment*, International Labour Office, Geneva, pp. 46–7.
10. Advisory Opinion on the Interpretation of the Convention of 1919 Concerning Employment of Women During the Night (1932), Permanent Court of International Justice, The Hague, Series A/B, No.50, p. 382.
11. H. Pietila and J. Vickers, (1990) *Making Women Matter. The Role of the United Nations*, Zed Books, London, p. 10.
12. *Development Co-operation, 1991 Report*, OECD, Paris, 1991, p. 56.
13. N. Ahmed (1991) 'Trade unions', *SUBHA*, a newsletter on women and development, Karachi, Vol. 5, Summer 1991, p. 6.
14. K. Ali (1991) 'It's *our* right too', in Ibid., pp. 10–11.
15. N. Burra (1989) 'Out of sight, out of mind: working girls in India', *International Labour Review*, Vol. 128, No.5, pp. 651 and 660.
16. R. Lister (1992) *Women's Economic Dependency and Social Security*, Equal Opportunities Commission, Manchester.
17. J. Jones and B. Clement, 'Social security system biased against women', *The Independent*, London, 1 May 1992, p. 6.

6 REDRESSING INEQUALITIES

Economic aid does not bring independence. Adult literacy and education in legal rights is a must in any scheme to help women who are being oppressed.[1]

IT IS SELF-EVIDENT that action against discrimination requires knowledge of the pattern of discrimination. Nevertheless, it is not always accepted that the much-lamented unequal status of women represents the result of discrimination. More often it is attributed to 'objective' factors, usually to the differences existing in the level of development.

The United Nations Development Programme (UNDP) Human Development Report included a human development index (HDI), and further elaborated a gender-sensitive one. For women it reflects, in a single figure, combined quantitative estimates of: life expectancy; adult literacy; average years of schooling; employment; and wage rates for those employed. This precedent-setting measure of the impact of the heritage of gender discrimination has, not surprisingly, revealed that the ranking of countries differs a great deal once gender-neutral categories are replaced by gender-sensitive data. Thus the gender-neutral HDI categorized the highest ranking countries as Canada, Japan and Norway, but when gender-sensitive HDI was applied the highest ranking countries were Sweden, Finland and Norway.

This effort has also revealed the dearth of gender-specific statistics: data are available for 33 countries only. Gender discrimination has to be exposed before it can be effectively opposed. As long as women remain hidden in genderless statis-tics, gender discrimination remains undocumented. This hinders efforts to provide evidence: the proverbial rule that what cannot be quantified does not exist inhibits development policies aimed at redressing women's disadvantages.

The implications of introducing human rights into development are far-reaching. Once human rights are accepted as human, that is, universal, human rights obligations reach far beyond national borders. Wide disparities in the opportunities to enjoy human rights thereby become one of the principal challenges in human rights, and the principal challenge in development. Equal access to education, health care, housing, income-generation or employment, or social assistance, has not been accepted as an individual entitlement in many countries, let alone at the global level.

Earlier decades divided human rights into three generations, relegating economic and social rights to the second generation,

TABLE 6.1 FEMALE HDI AS PERCENTAGE OF MALE HDI

- Sweden 96.16
- Finland 94.47
- Norway 93.48
- France 92.72
- Denmark 92.20
- Australia 90.48
- [Czechoslovakia] 90.25
- New Zealand 89.95
- Paraguay 88.82
- Belgium 86.57
- Austria 86.47
- USA 86.26
- Netherlands 86.26
- United Kingdom 85.09
- Italy 83.82
- Portugal 83.36

- Germany 83.32
- Switzerland 80.92
- Sri Lanka 79.59
- Philippines 78.67
- Japan 77.56
- Greece 76.10
- Ireland 74.89
- Luxembourg 74.88
- Burma 74.07
- Cyprus 72.32
- Hong Kong 71.10
- Singapore 70.87
- Costa Rica 70.61
- Swaziland 68.74
- Korea 65.53
- Kenya 58.60

SOURCE: UNITED NATIONS DEVELOPMENT PROGRAMME – *HUMAN DEVELOPMENT REPORT 1992*, OXFORD UNIVERSITY PRESS, P. 21.

and development and solidarity to the third and last. The focus of human rights activism is 'first generation rights', particularly abuses of physical force against people. Governmental obligations emanating from individual entitlements to the necessities for survival are poorly defined, nationally and internationally, and abuses of power in this area are not yet conceptualized as human rights violations. A brief resolution on human rights based on solidarity was adopted by the General Assembly in 1989, stating that 'the severe suffering of innumerable human beings through the world ... calls for the strengthening of a common sense of human solidarity'.[2]

Although there are no intergovernmental policies based on solidarity, a shared sense of human solidarity is visible in the multitude of private, citizens', and non-governmental activities which range from fund-raising for development projects to challenging official policies and practices in the North, as these largely determine development options in the South. This human sense of solidarity has resulted in numerous international actions for the benefit of those deprived of opportunities for survival and development. Although human rights are seldom explicitly mentioned, the human rights rationale permeates many consciousness-raising campaigns:

As the nature of the misery is forcefully presented to the general public, the possibility of politically ignoring the question becomes, to that extent, unviable ... More exposure has led to more awareness, and that seems to have led to more concern and to a sense of obligation which many people have felt they had to act on.[3]

The notion of sustainable development emerged with the awareness that self-destructive development can only be short-lived. This awareness had been generated and was reinforced by evidence that non-renewable environmental resources must be protected. People were treated as perpetrators of environmental damage rather than beneficiaries (or objects) of environmental protection, and protection of the people themselves lagged far behind protection of the environment. Individual human beings were, moreover, subsumed under renewable resources. People are still often referred to as 'human capital'[4] or – at best – as human resources. The idea that destruction of a single human being jeopardizes humanity as a species has been advocated by human rights, following its main postulate that all individuals have equal rights, hence, jeopardy of rights of any single individual challenges the *human* in human rights.

The most important obstacle for the effective application of human rights to development is the lack of means of redress for those harmed by development interventions. Because human rights activism always emerges in response to what is perceived as violations of human rights, the lack of remedies precludes it from being effective. Access to remedy for human rights violations is still – and likely to remain – exclusively individualistic: remedies can be sought by the individuals whose individual rights have been (allegedly) violated. This is obviously insufficient to challenge structural and policy problems in development.

WOMEN-IN-DEVELOPMENT ☐ Development assistance to women entails recognition and protection of their rights. The reason is, simply, that gender inequality is an obstacle to the improvement of the position of women. Human rights standards have been developed for the purpose of eliminating this obstacle, hence their application can complement and strengthen the women-in-development policies within international development co-operation.

The Women-in-Development (WID) approach differs from the human rights approach. The former addresses women as a disadvantaged group and elaborates special projects for them. The notion that women constitute a group and the effectiveness of women's projects have been subjected to criticism, and their appropriateness questioned. Human rights aim to secure equal rights for all human beings and outlaw all discrimination, including that based on sex. This entails compensatory measures to redress the impact of the prevailing gender discrimination. Thereby the human rights approach and WID come close, and sometimes overlap. Nevertheless, they follow different paths.

Reviews of development co-operation carried out to determine its impact on women have revealed that aid was as likely to harm as to help women; they confirm that the neglect of discrimination reinforces it. The assumption that there is no gender distinction in the access to aid was proved to be wrong. Effects of aid are different for women and men recipients, not because of their sex, but as a consequence of institutionalized gender discrimination. A negative impact of aid on women was identified in many cases, and explicit policies on women were adopted, notably by the OECD in 1984.[5]

Efforts to redress the damage caused by genderless aid policies were hampered by the absence of gender distinctions in the data used in conventional development research and planning. Thus women's participation in the labour force was underreported, women's work ignored, women's ownership of land or access to agricultural loans unknown, wage differentials by sex impossible to document. Genderless categories such as 'peasants', 'the rural poor' or 'the landless' prevailed. Only after gathering gender-specific data have inequalities become visible and gender discrimination documented. The 1989 World Survey on the Role of Women in Development noted 'a dramatic increase of research on economic variables taking the factor of sex into account'.[6]

Evaluations of development projects identified those types which are particularly harmful for women, such as those which increase, rather than diminish their workload, modernization programmes which displace women workers without providing them with an alternative source of income, or rural works programmes consisting of hard manual labour for destitute women with half the remuneration given to men. For example:

One area where women have regularly been harmed rather than helped is the modernization of agriculture. The negative impact on women's access to land has been identified in the case of the least developed countries, for example: 'Their [the women's] situation has been made worse by the modernization process whereby the disappearance of communal land tenure has caused them to be dispossessed of their land and men have been recognized as the new owners.'[7]

The other area where development projects have undermined women's status is the introduction of labour-eliminating technology. This can be illustrated by an example from Bangladesh. The rural electrification programme in Bangladesh, financed through international development co-operation, introduced rice-processing mills. These mills displaced women workers: one rice-processing mill eliminated the full-time work of sixty-four women. This labour-displacing effect was not even taken into account when the aid intervention was planned. The

**work of women had been invisible from
the official information consulted, and
their elimination from rice-processing as
well.**[8]

WID policies prompted analyses of the
absence of women in development co-
operation agencies. It transpired that the
gender bias in development co-operation
was *inter alia* a reflection of the gender
composition of the staff. No gender-
specific data exist in the area of execution
of development projects. Development
personnel are referred to in gender neutral
terms, and their composition confirms that
the use of gender neutral categories reflects
a dominantly male personnel. Development experts are assumed to be male,
which they usually are. While no systematic data have been collected, it is estimated
that only five or ten per cent of development experts are women.[9] The introduction
of women's concerns into development
co-operation brought about demands for
change in the gender composition of
development agencies.

The search for causes of harm to
women identified institutionalized discrimination against them in virtually every
aspect of development: political, economic, social, cultural, and – last but not least
– legal. Gender inequalities are often
reflected in, and strengthened by, discriminatory laws. These legalize the denial of
equal rights to women. Law is not an area
of primary concern in development, nor
are rights of women incorporated in
guidelines concerning women in development aid. The exception is the OECD
Guiding Principles which require donors
to secure the commitment of recipient
countries to the rights of women. In particular, they require recognition of the
right of women 'to participate in the process of development, and to benefit from
its fruits'.

Participation in development includes

taking part in decision-making, not only in
carrying out development projects. The
recognition of women's rights therefore
encompasses all aspects and all levels of
development. Moreover, it spans the full
range of the rights of women – civil and
political, economic and social.

The framework for the recognition and
promotion of women's rights has been
established by the Convention on the
Elimination of All Forms of Discrimination against Women (the Women's
Convention). This can easily be applied in
international development co-operation
because it lays down universal standards
concerning the rights of women which
also constitute international obligations for
governments. Because the Convention
regulates the full scope of women's rights,
its standards can be applied throughout
development co-operation.

Before similarities between women's
rights and WID guidelines are discussed,
an important difference should be mentioned. The OECD Guiding Principles
address the core issue of gender discrimination only implicitly; surprisingly, a document adopted with the ultimate purpose of
redressing discrimination fails to mention
it. The Women's Convention devotes
most of its substantive provisions to gender discrimination. The Convention's provisions and the women-in-development
guidelines both include an important, and
also controversial, principle – that of
reverse discrimination:

**Women's Convention: 'Adoption ... of temporary
special measures aimed at accelerating de facto
equality between men and women ... shall in no
way entail as a consequence the maintenance of
unequal or separate standards.'**

**OECD/DAC Guidelines: 'At least initially, it may be
necessary to co-operate with recipient governments
to identify special categories of projects explicitly
designed with women as the principal beneficiaries;**

it is essential, however, that at the same time, project design should ensure that women are involved as fully as possible in all development projects.'

Access of women to productive resources, especially to land, has also been similarly dealt with. The longest and the most detailed provision of the Women's Convention lays down the rights of rural women. This area has been dealt with by the OECD in a less systematic and detailed manner (see box right).

The impact of development on women depends on two interrelated factors: on the project's impact on women's role in the local community, and on family obligations of women which determine their actual and possible participation in the project. Projects designed as if women had no constraints for participating in, and benefiting from development, regularly fail to achieve desired results. Women's participation is neither equal nor identical to that of men; in the case of households headed by women, this has been described in the following manner:

Although the term suggests that women can head households in the same way men do, for rural women this is seldom the case. A woman does not assume all of her husband's rights just because he is out of the picture. She cannot dispose of property ... and she may not have the authority to adopt new technology. But she assumes many of his obligations, including his work tasks and the financial support of the family. Moreover, there remains her own work; unlike a male household head, she has no wife.[10]

The human rights approach demands equality in the enjoyment of all rights and freedoms. The existing inequalities thus need to be evaluated against the prohibition of discrimination and governmental obligation to eradicate it.

OECD/DAC GUIDELINES
Access to productive resources for women is a prerequisite for their participation in development. Seeking to ensure their access may raise such issues as title of land and credit and banking facilities, as well as the provision of information and advice about new technology and technical training.

WOMEN'S CONVENTION:
States Parties shall take into account the particular problems faced by rural women and the significant roles which rural women play in the economic survival of their families, including their work in the non-monetized sectors of the economy, and shall take all appropriate measures to ensure the application of the provisions of the present Convention to women in rural areas.

States Parties shall take all appropriate measures to eliminate discrimination against women in rural areas in order to ensure, on the basis of equality of men and women, that they participate in and benefit from rural development and, in particular, shall ensure to such women the right:

(a) To participate in the elaboration and implementation of development planning at all levels;

(b) To have access to adequate health care facilities, including information, counselling and services in family planning;

(c) To benefit directly from social security programmes;

(d) To obtain all types of training and education, formal and non-formal, including that relating to functional literacy, as well as, *inter alia*, the benefit of all community and extension services, in order to increase their technical proficiency;

(e) To organize self-help groups in order to obtain equal access to economic opportunities through employment or self-employment;

(f) To participate in all community activities;

(g) To have access to agricultural credit and loans, marketing facilities, appropriate technology and equal treatment in land and agrarian reform as well as in land resettlement schemes;

(h) To enjoy adequate living conditions, particularly in relation to housing, sanitation, electricity and water supply, transport and communications.

REMEDYING CONSEQUENCES: WOMEN'S PROJECTS □

The initial steps undertaken within development to improve women's position consisted of 'women's projects', designed to benefit women only, thus applying a target-group approach. This approach has had a two-fold justification: 1) it meant the implementation of the newly adopted WID policies; and 2) it fitted the established development priorities: women have regularly been identified as among the poorest of the poor.

While the human rights approach aims to eradicate gender discrimination, women's projects are based on defining women as a group. Thus the Norwegian Strategy for Assistance to Women says that 'women as a group have common interests independent of the culture, religion, class position and political conditions they live under'.[11] However, differences in the economic and social status of women, added to their divergent age and family obligations, undermine such a group identity. This is one of the main reasons for the failure of

many women's projects. Translated into human rights terminology, such projects attempted to reinforce sex distinctions rather than trying to diminish their negative consequences. The assumption that women are a group has been criticized within development circles. Winifred Weekes-Vagliani concluded that it was adopted for the administrative convenience of donors. Her critique emphasized that such an approach constituted a form of reductionism, confining women to their traditional role rather than recognizing the multiplicity of their roles:[12]

'Women's projects' were by and large confined to the traditionally conceived female domain of family planning, health care, child welfare, nutrition, and expanded into home economics, crafts, and other means of enabling women to earn some supplementary income. Separate projects for women have been justified only as the first step in those developing countries where the improvement of women's status faced obstacles enforced by religious and social norms. The Swedish International Develop-

---

WHY IS IT BETTER TO LEND TO WOMEN THAN TO MEN?

Banks do not want to lend money to women. If a woman wants to borrow from a bank, the manager will ask her to bring her husband along, so that he can discuss the business.

I had wanted to make sure that at least 50 per cent of the borrowers were women. This was not easy as women were not willing to borrow. They believed they would not be able to handle the money. Their husbands were not enthusiastic about their getting loans either.

When 50 per cent was finally achieved, we noticed significant results.

Money going through women in a household brought more benefits to the household than money entering the household through men. With a woman, when she brings in more income, the immediate beneficiaries of the income are the children. They get top priority from their mother. The woman's second priority is her household – to improve living conditions, a few more utensils, a stronger roof maybe. But a man has a different set of priorities which do not give the family a top position. Why then should we approach a household through men?[13]

Muhammad Yunus, Director of
Grameen Bank

ment Agency's (SIDA) evaluation of a women's project in Ethiopia thus concluded that 'separation is sometimes necessary under patriarchal structures, for women to gain experience and confidence, enabling them to integrate with men on more equal terms'.[14]

Such separation became institutionalized in quite a few developing countries. Women's institutions and ministries have been set up to co-ordinate the women's component of development. One reason for the widespread criticism of this approach is the low priority for WID, both in funding and in the limited role for women which such separation implicitly promoted. The critics object to the sidelining of women to gender-segregated activities, which reinforces obstacles to their equal participation in development.

TACKLING CAUSES: WOMEN'S EQUAL RIGHTS ☐ The main target of the criticism of 'women's projects' has been problem avoidance: they addressed the consequences of gender discrimination instead of tackling discrimination itself. Challenging gender discrimination is not easy; it often necessitates criticism of a government's policy and practice. Moreover, gender discrimination is frequently institutionalized, and enforced by religious, social and cultural norms. Problem avoidance has also sometimes been noted in the work of non-governmental organizations (NGOs). They have been eager to display 'sensitivity to local cultures and ability to work successfully at the community level. They do not want to be accused of cultural imperialism by tampering with sex roles, roles that are enforced by family and community and thus are most resistant to change.'[15]

Development aid donors show reluctance to tackle the human rights policies of developing countries' governments. This reluctance is understandable but not

---

LEGAL LITERACY FOR RURAL WOMEN – UGANDA

- It has been estimated that 50 per cent of Ugandans above the age of 15 are illiterate and of these 60 per cent are women. Enjoyment of human rights among women who have no access to the contents of the law is therefore minimal.
- Attempts have been made to redress this problem, for example, by running radio programmes. This is indeed well-intentioned and would have had impact were it not for certain inherent problems.
- Women in Uganda are not only illiterate, they are also very poor and cannot afford to buy radios. They have a workload which denies them nearly any moment to sit down and listen to the radio. The nature of the work of a rural woman is such that she is away in the fields most of the day or, if she is at home, carrying out yet another labour intensive activity. The problem therefore still remains: how to disseminate the substance of the law to overwhelmingly big numbers of an illiterate rural population.
- It is common knowledge that Africans love folklore and story telling. Customs and norms are passed on by word of mouth from generation to generation. Among the Iteso, for example, it is the role of women, especially the old, to tell stories to young children. This is usually done in the evenings after ... a hard day's work. It might be useful to explore these avenues and to find a specific method to make known the substance of the law to the traditional teachers – the women.[16]

---

justifiable: international human rights standards, which include the eradication of gender discrimination, are binding upon all governments. Not addressing breaches of human rights obligations undermines the binding force of human rights and contributes to their violation. Moreover, non-recognition of the rights of women undermines development itself. Projects which aim to improve the status of women need to secure women's rights to make these improvements sustainable; this has been recognized in evaluations of development projects. A review of Danish International Development Agency (DANIDA) supported women's projects thus noted: 'Women do not own means of production like land, livestock and capital. This situation has not been recognized, nor appreciably improved, by the DANIDA projects.'[17] A similar critique of the reluctance to tackle the issue of women's rights was included in the evaluation of Norwegian development aid to Kenya:

The situation of women could be improved considerably through legislation. Gender inequality in Kenya is partly founded in differences between legal rights for women and men. Donors could undoubtedly have a role to play in this context by raising the issue of women's legal position in their discussions with the Kenyan authorities.[18]

A BRIEF REVIEW OF LEGAL EMPOWER-MENT PROGRAMMES IN LATIN AMERICA

CLADEM (Comite Latinoamericano para la defense de los Derechos de la Mujer), the Latin American Committee for the Defence of Women's Rights published, in February 1991, an overview of legal information, education and training programmes for and by women in Argentina, Costa Rica, Ecuador, Mexico and Peru.

These programmes combine legal literacy and critical studies, the latter based on the assessment of conventional legal literacy courses which fail to move beyond lecturing on legal norms and procedures to the population which is perceived in terms of passive recipients to whom one ought to extend the knowledge of the law. The purpose of such programmes is defined as follows:

Legal empowerment has to include the critique of the contents of laws, of the knowledge of legal and institutional mechanisms, and of their origin, and to broaden to the necessity of formulating

LEGAL LITERACY FOR RURAL WOMEN –
SRI LANKA
- The Lawyers for Human Rights and Development (LHRD) Women's Desk conducted several educational workshops on law and human rights for the benefit of women workers and women in general.
- On July 26, 1992, a legal literacy workshop for FTZ (Free Trade Zone) women workers was conducted at Amandoluwa Temple. 22 women participated in this workshop. Women expressed fear that they might lose their jobs if the employers came to know of their participation in this type of literacy campaign.
- On May 22, 1992, Women's Desk held a workshop at Biyagama. Due to fear in the minds of workers, only about 10 women participated in this workshop. Due to poor attendance it was converted into a legal aid clinic. The women came out with many problems they were facing. Women's Desk members explained to the workers their legal rights and how to seek relief in respect of their problems.[19]

proposals for reform of discriminatory laws with the aim of establishing, clearly, that the objective is not only to attain formal legal equality, namely, the recognition of the same legal status for women as men have, but to work towards real equality.

Legal literacy is thus defined as an instrument of empowerment going far beyond the use of laws and procedures as they are: the idea is not to familiarize women with the labyrinths and meanderings of the legal system so that they would get trapped within them, but to enable women who are active in social and community organizations to develop a critical platform regarding the legal system and facilitate their action for change regarding governmental institutions, political parties, and trade unions.

The legal empowerment programmes start from the assessment that problems which affect women are neither natural, nor individual, nor isolated but gender-based, and the knowledge of women's human rights contributes to self-esteem and the sense of worth of each woman. The critique of the existing law is necessary because these do not respond to injustices with which women are faced, not being gender-specific. Group sessions facilitate the awareness of problems being gender-specific:

Starting from the very knowledge of the women's problems as they tell them themselves, we move on to elaborate the contents of law regarding family violence, family rights, labour rights, and agrarian law, taking as the point of reference the specific cases related by the women. This way we manage to demystify the law and to make it accessible to these women in a simple legal language comprehensible to all, while not departing from the rigorous legal analysis. Such analysis facilitates group integration and the sharing of awareness of the gender-specific problems which women face.[20]

RIGHT TO HEALTH? □ In May 1992 the World Health Assembly (WHA) called for the implementation of international policies aimed at improving women's health. It acknowledged that many previous resolutions have called for action, but recognized with dismay 'the lack of adequate sex-specific data; and the fact that there is insufficient knowledge of the specific consequences of diseases for women'.[21] WHA meets annually and consists of representatives of all members of the World Health Organization (WHO), specifically ministers or ministries of health. The mandate of WHA is international health policy. The link between health and human rights may not be obvious; hence it is useful to recall that this same WHA made this link explicit in 1985 specifically concerning women. The WHA recorded its concern at the slow progress in the improvement of women's health and also in the safeguarding of women's rights, and noted 'the close relationship between equal rights for men and women and the participation of women in health activities and in the promotion of health for all, particularly as decision-makers'.[22] This parallel between the slow progress in women's health and in their enjoyment of equal rights may reflect their correlation. Much evidence of this slow progress in women's health is available, including *Women and Health*[23] (in this series), and this will not be dealt with here; rather links between health and women's human rights will be highlighted.

Guaranteed access to health care services for all people remains an issue of disagreement. At the time of drafting the text of Article 12 of the International Covenant on Economic, Social and Cultural Rights (ICESCR), WHO was reluctant to acquiesce to the proposed obligation for the state to guarantee access to medical care, since it was committed not to 'attempt to force States to adopt any particular method of [providing] medical care'.[24] It has therefore never advocated the provision of health services on the basis of individual entitlement. The human rights approach insists on the centrality of guaranteed access to health care. Article 12 of the ICESCR thus obliges governments to create conditions which would assure to all medical service and medical attention in the event of sickness'.

It should not be forgotten that there is no such thing as free health care service: if services are free for the user, someone else has to cover the cost. The existing models of providing health care are diverse. It is widely acknowledged that the national government has the responsibility for the health of the population, but how far this responsibility should reach has not been clarified.

Women encounter numerous obstacles in their access to health care. If this is not guaranteed as a human right, neither women – nor men nor children – can enjoy it. However, women are additionally jeopardized in access to health care because of their unequal rights. The WHA has urged governments to introduce laws and regulations to provide access to free medical services for pregnant women, particularly in cases of high-risk pregnancy, at delivery, and during the child's first year when immunization is crucial for its survival.[25] Alice Armstrong described the jeopardy of women's access to health care as follows:

Many hospitals and clinics in Swaziland require a woman to prove that she has her husband's (or guardian's) permission before she can receive medical treatment. In most cases, this requires that a permission form be signed by the husband. That this practice may cause hardship to the woman is self-evident. She may be separated from her husband, either by agreement, by desertion, or by necessity. Her husband may refuse his permission unreasonably. She may have travelled many miles only to arrive at a clinic and find that she must return home to get a permission form signed. Finally that an adult woman is required to get 'permission' before attending to the medical needs of her own body is a violation of her self-respect and liberty.

Why is it that the practice of requiring spousal permission is so prevalent in Swaziland? And why are most abortions performed not legally, by medical practitioners, but illegally and dangerously?

The practice that exists among health workers in Swaziland of requiring spousal permission probably stems from two sources. The first is a desire to uphold Swazi tradition. Many health workers feel that by requiring a woman to provide her husband's permission they are supporting the traditions and customs which are so important to the

Swazi nation as a whole. They may also feel that they have a legal duty to uphold these traditions ... Secondly, a health worker may fear that s/he may be criminally liable for giving treatment to a woman without permission, which is usually termed 'consent'. This confusion probably arises from the fact that a doctor may be found criminally liable for assault if s/he operates on a patient without that patient's consent.[26]

The Committee on Economic, Social and Cultural Rights has not yet addressed the implications of the right to health in Article 12, but the Human Rights Committee did make an effort to define the state's role in protecting human life, concluding that the state was obliged to undertake measures 'to eliminate epidemics and malnutrition'.[27] It thus reinforced the traditional responsibility of public health authorities regarding epidemics, but refrained from defining the obligation of the governments in eliminating malnutrition. Little has been achieved in international law-making, largely because in international law food is considered a commodity rather than an individual entitlement. Individual entitlements aimed at preventing and reducing malnutrition have been proposed by United Nations human rights bodies,[28] and WHO has recently defined malnutrition as 'preventable noncommunicable disease'.[29] Even so, the recognition of legal entitlements is still lacking.

WOMEN AND AIDS ☐ The interplay between human rights and health can be described by taking AIDS as an example. AIDS has shown, more clearly than any other current global problem, the importance of including equal rights for women in health policies.

During the AIDS epidemic there have been instances where preference was given to women as part of screening-out possible male homosexuals in employment.

AIDS is still perceived as a male disease: a woman with AIDS in Poland

Male homosexuals were declared a 'high-risk group' early in the pandemic. We have thus had rare examples of reverse gender discrimination in the context of AIDS. In the United Kingdom, for example, the Equal Opportunities Commission issued in 1987 a report on discriminatory recruitment practices of Dan Air, which justified their refusal to employ male stewards on the grounds that they were more likely to be HIV-infected than were female stewards. As the Commission found no evidence that 'the employment of male cabin staff on aircraft would cause the disease to be transmitted to other staff or passengers', Dan Air was ordered to modify its employment policy.[30]

Such instances have not changed the main trend in responding to AIDS, characterized by the neglect of women. Much as in other areas, there is a paucity of data to show how much of an impact HIV/AIDS has had on women, even to document the spread of HIV infections in women. Globally, women constitute between one-third and one-half of those HIV-infected and with AIDS, while in some regions women are infected in larger numbers than men. Analyses of the orientation of research on women and HIV/AIDS showed that HIV transmission from rather than to women was the focus.

The 1986 International AIDS Conference, when women and HIV/AIDS were first placed on the agenda, documented the neglect of women in AIDS prevention. This was further substantiated at the International Conference on the Implications of AIDS for Mothers and Children, with two principal conclusions: (1) in most countries, AIDS prevention programmes for women do not exist; and (2) where programmes for women do exist, they are often designed exclusively to reach female sex workers.[31] This discriminatory attitude, in which HIV transmission from women has been given prominence

at the expense of HIV transmission to women, hides the fact that women's risk of infection through intercourse is at least double, and maybe four times greater than, the risk for men.[32] While definite quantifications are not available, the conclusions of all investigations confirm women's higher susceptibility to sexually acquired HIV infection.

Women have often been targeted by AIDS prevention measures in order to prevent infection of their future children. HIV screening of pregnant women has been applied in many countries and, in quite a few, compulsory HIV screening of all pregnant women has been introduced by law, or made part of the national AIDS prevention and control programme. Surveys revealed a variety of attitudes among pregnant women: women attending an ante-natal clinic in Brazzaville said that they would not mind an HIV test but the test result would not influence their decision on child-bearing; in Berlin the introduction of HIV screening resulted in fewer women attending the clinic; in London 1,500 pregnant women were asked whether they would take an HIV test and 1,491 said they would not.[33] Therefore, a conclusion has been reached that pregnant women do not provide a mandate for routine HIV testing.[34]

One study of the needs of HIV-positive women carried out in Kigali (Rwanda) revealed that inability to bear another child was among the main concerns of these women.[35] Moreover, the pressure against child-bearing by HIV-infected women extended to 'uncompromising condemnations of decisions by HIV-infected women to conceive or bear children'.[36] Despite the full concordance of research results on the point that knowledge of seropositivity does not have an important influence on pregnancy decisions, and complaints about the pressure against child-bearing exercised upon HIV-infected women, interventions are often based on the assumption that HIV-positive women will avoid pregnancy.

In 1990 CEDAW adopted a recommendation on the avoidance of discrimination against women in responding to AIDS. The incentive was found in the need to reach beyond the impact of the epidemic on women, and also to consider the impact of the responses to epidemic. CEDAW recommended:

(a) That States Parties intensify efforts in disseminating information to increase public awareness of the risk of HIV infection and AIDS, especially in women and children, and of its effects on them;

(b) That programmes to combat AIDS should give special attention to the rights and needs of women and children, and to the factors relating to the reproductive role of women and their subordinate position in some societies which make them especially vulnerable

to HIV infection;

(c) That States Parties ensure the active participation of women in primary health care and take measures to enhance their role as care providers, health workers and educators in the prevention of infection with HIV;

(d) That all States Parties include in their reports under Article 12 of the Convention information on the effects of AIDS on the situation of women and on the action taken to cater to the needs of those women who are infected and to prevent specific discrimination against women in response to AIDS.

The impact of this recommendation depends, as with any other human rights instrument, on the monitoring of national practices to identify instances where women are discriminated against, and on effective measures to remedy such discrimination.

1. F. Raj (1989) *Women in India: Their Legal Rights*, International Women's Rights Action Watch Seminar, Vienna, 20–22 February 1989, p. 13.
2. United Nations, 'Human rights based on solidarity', General Assembly resolution 44/148 of 15 December 1989, preamble.
3. A. Sen (1986) 'Famine and fraternity', *London Review of Books* 12 (3 July 1986), p. 6.
4. *The World Bank Annual Report 1990*, Washington DC, p. 59.
5. 'Guiding principles to aid agencies for supporting the role of women in development' in *Development Co-operation. 1984 Review*, Paris, OECD, 1984, Annex II, p. 179.
6. United Nations '1989 world survey on the role of women in development', Centre for Social Development and Humanitarian Affairs, UN Doc. ST/CSDHA/6, New York, 1989, p. 7.
7. *The Least Developed Countries, 1986 Report*, New York, UNCTAD, 1987, para. 179.
8. K. Tomaševski (1988) *Foreign Aid and Human Rights: Case Studies of Bangladesh and Kenya*, The Danish Centre for Human Rights, Copenhagen, p. 63.
9. Cf. T. Bleie, 'From demands to institutionalization – from institutionalization to practice?' in K. Rupesinghe (ed.) (1987) *Development Assistance in the Year 2000*, Institute for Social Research, Oslo, pp. 236–66.
10. S. Reynolds Whyte et al. (1987) *Women in DANIDA-supported Development Projects: An Evaluation*,

DANIDA, Copenhagen, January, p. 40.
11. *The Norwegian Strategy for Assistance to Women*, NORAD, Oslo, 1985, p. 5.
12. Cf. W. Weekes-Vagliani (1985) *The Integration of Women in Development Projects*, OECD Development Centre, Paris, pp. 14–42.
13. M. Yunus (1992) 'Credit: a human right', *We. Weekend Magazine*, The International News, Karachi, May 7–14 1992, p. 11.
14. M. Albinh et al. (1982) *Integrating Women as a Means of Rural Development: A Case Study of the Swedish CADU Project 1967–74 (Ethiopia)*, SIDA, Stockholm, September 1982, p. 73.
15. S. W. Yudelman (1987) 'The integration of women into development projects: observations on the NGO experience in general and in Latin America in particular', *World Development*, 15, Supplement, p. 181.
16. A. Akwi Ogojo (1991) 'Superstitions undermine RCs', *ARISE*, October–December 1991, pp. 16–17
17. S. Reynolds Whyte et al. (1987) *Women in DANIDA-supported Development Projects: An Evaluation*, Copenhagen, DANIDA, January 1987, p. 3.
18. *Kenya: Case Study and Norwegian Aid Review*, Bergen, CHR Michelsen Institute, 1987, p. 61.
19. 'Legal literacy for women', *Kantha* (newsletter of the Women's Desk of the Lawyers for Human Rights and Development), No. 2, 1991, Colombo, Sri Lanka.
20. R. Vaspuez (1991) *Capacitacion legal a mujeres*, CLA-DEM, Lima.

21. World Health Assembly, 'Women, health and development', resolution WHA 45.25 of 17 June 1992, preamble.

22. Ibid., WHA38.27 of 17 May 1985, preamble.

23. Patricia Smyke (1991) *Women and Health*, London, Zed Books.

24. WHO Official Records, No. 4, February 1947, p. 9.

25. World Health Assembly, 'WHO long-term programme for maternal and child health', resolution WHA32.42 of 25 May 1979, para. 2.

26. A. Armstrong, 'Traditionalism and access to health care: law relevant to women's health in Swaziland', in: A. Armstrong and W. Ncube *Women and Law in Southern Africa* (1987) Zimbabwe Publishing House, Harare, pp. 222 and 232.

27. Human Rights Committee, General Comment 6 [16], Article 6, UN Doc. CCPR/C/21/Rev.1 of 19 May 1989, para. 5.

28. A. Eide, *Right to Adequate Food as a Human Right*, United Nations Publication, Sales No. E.89.XIV.2, Centre for Human Rights, Geneva, 1989.

29. World Health Organization, 'Global estimates for health situation assessment and projections, 1990', Doc. WHO/HST/90.2, mimeograph, Geneva, 1990, p. 36.

30. *The Independent* (London), 3 February 1987.

31. K. Carovano et al., 'Women are more than mothers: developing effective AIDS prevention strategies for women and children', Abstract 1.3, International Conference on the Implications of AIDS for Mothers and Children, Paris, 1989.

32. J. Mantell et al., 'Women and AIDS prevention', *Journal of Primary Prevention*, Vol. 9, Nos. 1–2, Fall/Winter 1988, p. 20.

33. J. Mariasy and M. Radlett, 'Women face new dilemmas', *AIDS Watch*, International Planned Parenthood Federation, No. 5, 1989, pp. 2–3.

34. L. Sherr et al., 'The psychological cost of HIV screening in ante-natal clinics', Abstract D.16, International Conference on the Implications of AIDS for Mothers and Children, Paris, 1989.

35. P. Keogg, 'An evaluation of the social service needs of HIV-positive women enrolled in a cohort study in Kigali, Rwanda', Project San Francisco, 1988, mimeograph.

36. K. Nolan, 'Ethical issues in caring for pregnant women and newborns at risk for HIV infection', Hastings Center, February 1989, mimeograph, p. 18.

MONA MAHMUDNEZHAD

Mona was the youngest of the ten Baha'i women executed in Shiraz, Iran, on 18 June 1983. She was seventeen. Her outstanding courage in the face of imprisonment, torture and execution has touched the hearts of people around the world. These women were all arrested and executed because of their belief in the Baha'i faith. In the final effort to make them sign the prepared documents of recantation, the women were hanged one at a time, so the others had to watch. It is said that Mona asked to be the last to be hanged, so that she could pray for the strength of each one of them.

Mona was a beautiful young girl, skilled in arts and poetry. At the time of her arrest, she was teaching Baha'i children who had been expelled from school because of their religion. She had been arrested along with her father; her mother was subsequently arrested as well. It is remarkable that Mona spent her nine months of imprisonment comforting and cheering up other prisoners, most of whom were older than her.

Before her execution, she had told her mother: 'When they put the rope around my neck I will say a prayer. It will be a prayer for the happiness and success of humanity.'

Source: The Baha'i International Community

7 PROTECTING THE MOST VULNERABLE

For millions of persons, every day lived is either a day escaped from death, torture, violence, deprivation of liberty, degradation, or other forms of gross violations of human rights.[1]

ONE AIM OF HUMAN RIGHTS is to prevent abuses of power; obviously power can be abused by those who have it against the powerless. Human rights are a tool to empower those who are not in a position to assert and protect their rights.

Human rights activism emerged in response to abuses targeting people deprived of their liberty. The perception of human rights as limited to the protection of prisoners is still widespread. Indeed, when asked about the substance of human rights most people would state that this involves protection against torture, ill-treatment, summary executions, arbitrary arrest and disappearances. The most widely known human rights NGO, Amnesty International, is regularly taken to represent what human rights are all about; in fact its mandate is limited to prisoners of conscience and safeguards against ill-treatment and the death penalty.

The necessity to protect people who are themselves unable to protect their rights hardly needs explaining. What needs to be explained is that the gender-neutral term 'people' includes women who are exposed to double jeopardy: as members of a vulnerable category and as women; hence their need for protection differs from that of men. This is explored below, taking up three typical (gender-neutral) human rights themes: prisoners, refugees, and the disabled.

IMPRISONED WOMEN □ The human rights of prisoners are more frequently violated than are those of persons at liberty, and human rights litigation evolved first and foremost to protect persons deprived of their liberty. For example, applications to the European Commission of Human Rights alleging violations of prisoners' rights constituted 56 per cent of all applications in 1968, decreasing to 12 per cent in 1989.[2] Most complaints relate to ill-treatment and its harmful effects. Those specifically addressing women are virtually non-existent.

Human rights standards have been broadened from the protection of prisoners from ill-treatment, to safeguards against damage to health created by conditions of imprisonment (and treatment), and to guarantees for the prisoner's retention of the basic human rights. Except for the general prohibition of discrimination, and specific mention of motherhood, these standards remain gender-neutral. This neglect of women has been explained as follows: 'The world of prisons has been created by men for men and although it would be quite simple to introduce a sound penal policy for women's prisons, it has not been done in practice.'[3]

At the beginning of the international litigation for the protection of human rights of prisoners, in the 1960s, the concept of inherent limitations of human rights was accepted by international human rights bodies. In the 1970s and 1980s this concept of 'inherent limitations' was gradually abolished and a different approach to prisoners' human rights started gaining acceptance, namely, that because prisoners are in the custody of the state, they acquire a specific set of rights. Thus, this recognition of special rights of prisoners was derived from their dependent status: '[the

PHOTO: PETER WILLIAMS/WCC

Radio studio at the women's prison in Barcelona

prisoner] acquires new rights against the State which imprisons him.'[4] This view, however, is not universally accepted; a contrary view holds that prisoners have forfeited their rights by the commission of an offence. In addition, because prisoners are deprived of the exercise of many rights and freedoms by virtue of their imprisonment, the status of their remaining rights often appears unclear.

Deprivation of liberty is widely used as punishment for crime. Because it is serious punishment itself, human rights standards challenge the imposition of additional hardship upon prisoners. This can be explained simply: people are sent to prison *as* a punishment, not *for* punishment. The 1990 Basic Principles for the Treatment of Prisoners have affirmed that human rights apply to prisoners 'except for those limitations that are demonstrably necessitated by the fact of incarceration'.[5] Prisoners are, however, an easy target for

coercive or restrictive measures, because their options for resisting and denouncing them, and for securing remedies, are limited. The existing international standards have therefore affirmed the following three distinct but interrelated principles: (1) Deprivation of liberty does not entail the loss of human rights; all persons deprived of their liberty retain their basic rights, except for those that are necessarily and legitimately limited by imprisonment. (2) The state is responsible for all persons in its custody and is obliged to provide them with adequate living conditions and ensure their humane treatment. (3) The fundamental human rights principle of non-discrimination requires that neither prisoners as a category nor individual inmates be discriminated against, on the grounds of sex or any other grounds.

The basic principles of protecting human rights of prisoners are codified in the ICCPR. Interpreting it, the Human

Rights Committee stressed that 'the humane treatment and respect for the dignity of all persons deprived of their liberty is a basic standard of universal application which cannot depend entirely on material resources', and added that 'ultimate responsibility for the observance of this principle rests with the State as regards all institutions where persons are lawfully held against their will (prisons, hospitals, detention camps, correctional institutions).'[6]

It may seem strange that the few specific norms to protect the rights of imprisoned women have not been enacted internationally. This issue was not included in the Women's Convention and thus remains scattered in the range of international instruments (listed in Table 7.1) which only reiterate the prohibition of discrimination on various grounds, including sex. The only specific resolution in regard to imprisoned women was adopted by the Economic and Social Council, in 1986, on physical violence against detained women, and it called upon 'all Member States that have not yet done so to take appropriate measures urgently, as necessary, to eradicate acts of physical violence against detained women.'[7]

This omission is usually explained by the fact that women constitute a small minority of the prison population; nevertheless, their small numbers cannot diminish their basic human rights. Moreover, women seem to be the fastest-growing category of the prison population not only in Europe but worldwide.[8] A recent Council of Europe survey of comparative prison demography noted 'an increase in the proportion of women in practically all prison populations' in the period 1983–88. The highest rates of growth were identified in Spain (373 per cent), Portugal (232 per cent) and the Netherlands (110 per cent).[9]

Information on women in prison is scarce, while projects looking into women's problems, aside from the recent attention on sexual abuse and the traditional focus on motherhood, are virtually non-existent. Problems faced by imprisoned women thus remain largely unknown. More research needs to be carried out to determine whether these are similar, comparable or different from problems that men experience and thus whether women need kinds of protection different from those designed for men. The first, and thus far only, United Nations survey of the treatment of women in criminal justice systems revealed that although awareness of problems existed to some extent, solutions were reported from only a tiny minority of countries:

About 50 per cent of the countries reported that female offenders presented administrators of their criminal justice systems with particular or unique difficulties, caused by the treatment and handling of females in custody. The unique problems or difficulties typically cited were issues of pregnancy or child care, lack of protection from victimization, the need for quarters separate from those used for males, and the need for trained female criminal justice personnel.

As regards essential treatment conditions, however, only 16 per cent [of countries] reported the availability of separate quarters for the female offender, 10 per cent reported special medical facilities, and 8 per cent reported the provision of female custodial staff.[10]

It is noteworthy that no country mentioned in its response special measures for the protection of detained women. Stories of what happens in women's prisons are rare, but the following is one example from Canada:

Suddenly, a scream. A hollow-sounding scream, filled with despair, that bounces off the walls and burns its way into the conscience. Everyone stops talking, glances furtively around, and then, as if

TABLE 7.1 CHRONOLOGY OF INTERNATIONAL STANDARDS FOR THE PROTECTION OF PRISONERS

1948 Universal Declaration of Human Rights

1950 European Convention for the Protection of Human Rights and Fundamental Freedoms

1955 United Nations Standard Minimum Rules for the Treatment of Prisoners

1964 Declaration of Helsinki [Biomedical research involving human subjects]

1966 International Covenant on Civil and Political Rights

1975 Role of Nurse in the Care of Detainees and Prisoners

Declaration of Tokyo [Non-involvement in maltreatment of prisoners]

1979 Code of Conduct for Law Enforcement Officials

1982 Principles of Medical Ethics relevant to the Role of Health Personnel, Particularly Physicians, in the Protection of Prisoners and Detainees against Torture, and Other Cruel, Inhuman or Degrading Treatment or Punishment

1983 Legal protection of persons suffering from mental disorders placed as involuntary patients

1984 Convention against Torture and Other Cruel, Inhuman or Degrading Treatment or Punishment

1987 European Convention for the Prevention of Torture and Inhuman or Degrading Treatment or Punishment

European Prison Rules

Statement from the WHO Consultation on prevention and control of AIDS in prisons

1988 Recommendation 1080 (1988) on a co-ordinated European health policy to prevent the spread of AIDS in prisons

Body of Principles for the Protection of All Persons under Any Form of Detention or Imprisonment

1989 Principles on the effective prevention and investigation of extra-legal, arbitrary and summary executions

Convention on the Rights of the Child

1990 Principles on infection with human immunodeficiency virus (HIV) and acquired immunodeficiency syndrome (AIDS) in prison

Basic Principles for the Treatment of Prisoners

United Nations Rules for the Protection of Juveniles Deprived of their Liberty

1991 World Medical Association Declaration on Hunger Strikers

Principles for the Protection of Persons with Mental Illness and for the Improvement of Mental Health Care.

order and action can somehow erase the haunting sound, they return to whatever they are doing. Minutes later, the prison grapevine begins circulating the story. One woman, held in segregation – known as 'the hole' – tried to hang herself. The guards cut her down in time and she's on her way to the hospital.

The pressure, palpable in this place, is winched up another notch. The Prison for Women at Kingston, Ontario, better known as P4W, is at flashpoint.

There is something very wrong at P4W. Although prison reform through the '70s and '80s has improved human rights in prison, and a federal task force has announced that this place must be closed and replaced with more suitable facilities, an insidious air of failure is thriving inside its walls. Five women hanged themselves in the last two years.[11]

WHY ARE WOMEN IN PRISON? Societal attitudes towards the protection of human rights of prisoners are influenced by the fact that prisoners are sent to prison as punishment. Public opinion often deems such punishment justified. Nevertheless, too little is known about 'crimes' which lead to women being imprisoned and, were more known, the pressure against the imprisonment of women for such 'crimes' would undoubtedly strengthen.

An illustrative example is Pakistan, where thousands of women found themselves in prison for the 'crime' of filing for divorce or even reporting rape:

According to an estimate by the Committee for the Repeal of the Hudood Ordinances, there are at least 3,000 women in jails in Pakistan awaiting trial under this law. Another estimate puts the figure of undertrial women at almost 6,000.

Women who have filed for divorce have found that an FIR (First Information Report) alleging Zina (adultery) had been lodged against them. Women who have been divorced by their husbands and have married a second time have been persecuted by their first husbands alleging Zina.

Ironically, the law couples Zina (adultery) with Zina-bil-Jabr (rape), and a rape victim who cannot provide proof of rape by the alleged rapist finds herself convicted of adultery. As a result of the Adultery Ordinance not only has there been miscarriage of justice in numerous cases, but also this law has increased the female population in prison drastically. The figures quoted above should be compared with the figure given by the Women's division: in 1980 there were only 70 women in jails all over Pakistan, either convicted or awaiting trial.[12]

Much attention has been focused on the ill-treatment of women political prisoners, particularly following the Amnesty International report *Women in the Frontline*, but this should not divert attention from the fact that most imprisoned women fall into the category of the poor, defenceless, increasingly migrant women, whose fate is seldom publicized. In its investigation of custodial rape the Indian People's Union for Democratic Rights found that most victims were migrant women:

In a large metropolis like Delhi the most common victims seem to be migrant women. Delhi has over 1.6 million migrant labourers, of whom at least 400,000 are women. Although they do usually have relatives or fellow villagers, they are practically devoid of any support mechanisms. Friends and neighbours, fellow workers at place of work, local leaders, and the usual informal social network are virtually absent. More than one fourth of custodial deaths that took place in the eighties in Delhi, for instance, were those of migrants. All the four women whose cases [of custodial rape] we have investigated and included in this report are migrants.[13]

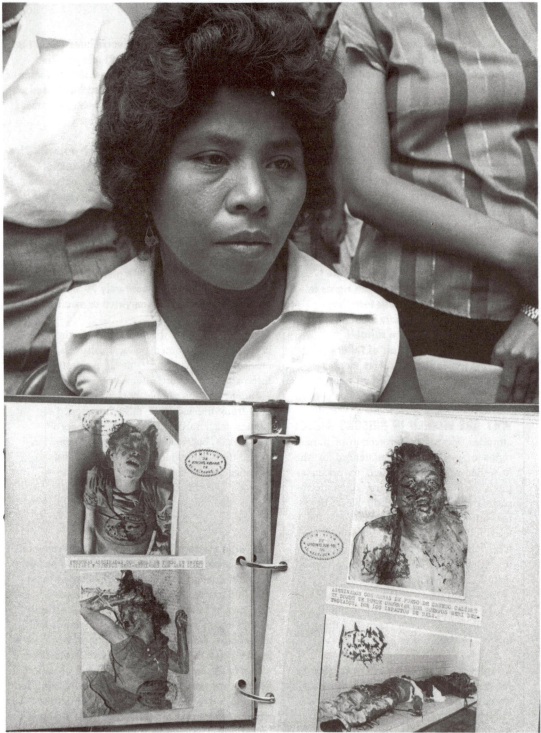

Women remain in the frontline: in El Salvador, the end of the armed conflict left the problem of human rights unresolved

WOMEN REFUGEES ☐ Much has been written thus far about the numbers and needs of refugee women. *Refugee Women*, one of the previous books in this series,[14] extensively illustrated their plight. Little has been written, however, about their human rights. The most important human rights aspect of the refugee problem is that refuge is often sought because of human rights violations. Refugees are thus in double jeopardy: in escaping from violations, refugees find themselves without human rights protection which should have been provided by their country of origin.

As elsewhere, women may face triple jeopardy. It is important to stress that women cannot obtain asylum if they are persecuted because of challenging gender discrimination in their country.

This may seem unfair, because asylum is intended for people who flee from repression and oppression and many women would qualify for refugee status if allowed to seek it. Women who seek refuge from an armed conflict or institutionalized violations of human rights have to prove – as do men – fear of persecution were they to return to their country of origin. However, various other grounds for persecution have been accepted for the admission of refugees, such as political opinion, ethnic origin, even sexual orientation, but not gender. A recent overview of the implementation of the Nairobi Forward-looking Strategies summarized the problem as follows:

[The refugee] instruments are gender-neutral, but in their application women may find it difficult to obtain the same refugee status as men, usually only on the basis of the principle of family unity under which granting of the refugee status to the men in the family leads to the spouse and children being given that status. Discrimination based on sex has not usually been considered as accepted reason for obtaining refugee status.[15]

A move towards change was made by the European Parliament which, on 13 April 1984, adopted a resolution suggesting that gender discrimination be included among the grounds for granting refugee status, so that women who face persecution because of transgressing discriminatory rules of conduct could seek and obtain refuge. The existing legal definitions of refugees remain, however, gender-neutral,[16] and pleas for change, in order to remedy the lack of recognition of gender-specific persecution as a ground for asylum, still remain unheeded. The decision whether or not to admit a refugee is within the competence of each state, hence national authorities could effect this change if they wanted to:

As a UNHCR legal adviser has noted, transgressing social mores is not reflected in the universal refugee definition. Yet, examples can be found of violence against women who are accused of violating social mores in a number of countries. The offence can range from adultery to wearing of lipstick. The penalty can be death. The Executive Committee of UNHCR has encouraged States to consider women so persecuted as a social group to ensure their coverage, but it is left to the discretion of countries to follow this recommendation.[17]

The case of Aminata, who fled from Mali to escape genital mutilation and sought asylum in France, illustrates the need for change. Her request for refugee status was first rejected, but following her appeal, in a historic decision on 17 September 1991, the French authorities found that female genital mutilation constituted valid grounds for granting refuge,[18] and thereby opened the way towards gender-specific grounds for refugee status.

The fate of women who seek refuge is more often than not characterized by

Triple jeopardy: a refugee, disabled, and a woman

double jeopardy: asylum-seekers do not enjoy much protection of their rights, while the fact of being female often exacerbates their ill-treatment. In the mid-1980s the United Nations High Commission for Refugees (UNHCR) reported that 2,400 'boat women' had been physically attacked by pirates in the South China Sea and 1,000 abducted.[19] Similar stories brought to public attention the plight of women refugees. Those involved in assisting refugee women acknowledge that violence against these women – as elsewhere – is seldom reported. However, this prompted increased attention to physical safety of refugee women. In 1980, the United Nations General Assembly already recognized 'the particular vulnerability of refugee and displaced women to intimidation, exploitation, and physical and sexual abuse' and urged states and donor agencies 'to ensure women's right to physical safety.'[20] The fact that the General Assembly

affirmed that refugee women have the right to physical safety moved the debate into the domain of human rights.

Not much has been accomplished in affirming specific rights of refugees, but special needs of refugee women have led to the elaboration of guidelines for equitable protection. UNHCR adopted detailed guidance on equitable protection of and assistance to women to prevent their marginalization:

Refugee women who are unable to feed, clothe and shelter themselves and their children will be more vulnerable to manipulation and to physical and sexual abuse in order to obtain such necessities ... Refugee women who must bribe guards to obtain firewood, water or other essential goods will be more susceptible to sexual harassment. Moreover, refugee women who formerly had a means of expressing their views in the community

may find themselves unable to do so in the camp management committees established by assistance organizations.[21]

This approach led to the addressing of systemic problems faced by women refugees, including violations of their rights:

Where there appears to be a recurrent pattern of violations of the security or legal rights of refugee women, UNHCR actions should focus not only on individual cases but should also seek to identify and ameliorate systemic reasons for the continuing protection problems. This will involve:

- **undertaking a systematic assessment of policies and practices implemented in the camp to determine if these policies are contributing to the protection problems and instituting changes as needed to prevent further abuses;**
- **establishing training programmes for responsible officials of UNHCR, NGOs, the host-country government and the refugee community to make them more aware of the rights of refugee women and their responsibilities to provide protection to refugee women;**
- **establishing education programmes for refugee women to appraise them of their rights and the recourse open to them if their rights are violated;**
- **making representations to those responsible for setting policies and implementing programmes, including strong requests to host governments to take action for the further protection of refugee women; and**
- **consulting with NGOs to inform them of the identified problems and seek their cooperation and assistance in finding solutions.[22]**

It is obvious from the preceding pages that protecting the human rights of refugee women has become an important area for refugee, rather than human rights bodies. The following excerpt from the dialogue between CEDAW and Thailand illustrates obstacles to the consideration of refugee problems by human rights bodies. Thailand's representative described the problem, during the CEDAW's consideration of its initial report under the Women's Convention, as follows:

In general, on refugee women, it was explained that Thailand had not acceded to the International Refugee Convention and the issue concerned asylum-seekers, about 60 per cent of whom were women and children, largely Indochinese. Under the law, asylum-seekers were considered to be illegal immigrants with duties rather than rights. Policy, however, was to bend the law for humanitarian considerations, with emphasis on screening, under the rule of first asylum. Those found to be legitimate refugees were allowed to stay temporarily while awaiting third-country placement and were not repatriated. The issue was both sensitive and complex.[23]

DISABLED WOMEN ☐ When discussing problems of disabled women in the human rights context the typical accumulation of grounds for discrimination emerges forcefully: women are often victims of discrimination because they are disabled and may be additionally discriminated against as women. This challenge remains: 'It must be admitted that whereas we have made some progress in the rehabilitation of disabled men, barely the fringe of the problem has been touched so far as disabled women are concerned.'[24] Indeed, most literature on the equalization of opportunities for disabled persons focuses on their disability, not on the additional factors that may jeopardize the exercise of their human rights further, such as sex, race, colour, ethnic origin. *Women and Disability*, a previous book in this series,[25] documented multiple problems

PHOTO: A. HOLLMANN/UNHCR

What fate for women seeking asylum in Germany?

encountered by disabled women.

Within a discriminatory act that targets a disabled woman it is sometimes difficult to discern whether she is victimized because of her sex in addition to her disability, or whether sex is irrelevant. For example, in a well-known court case in the USA, *School Board of Nassau County v. Arline,* a school-teacher was dismissed because she had active tuberculosis. The school board specified that the dismissal took place not 'because she had done anything wrong,' but because of the 'continued recurrence of tuberculosis'. After protracted legal proceedings, the US Supreme Court granted Ms Gene Arline reinstatement to her job and found generally that persons with contagious diseases enjoy protection against discrimination under the national law concerning the handicapped.[26]

This case set an important precedent in the protection of disabled persons; but that Ms Arline is a woman did not constitute a factor that led either to discrimination or to the judicial remedy. This difficulty of identifying whether the sex of the victim of discrimination is relevant in a specific case has largely hidden gender issues in the existing jurisprudence concerning the elimination of discrimination against the disabled. Nevertheless, it may well be that many disabled women are victims of discrimination because they are women in addition to being disabled. This is not known because there is insufficient information about the exercise of human rights by disabled women, and accordingly denials of their rights and their violations remain undocumented. The United Nations Special Rapporteur on human rights and disability strongly criticized this neglect:

We would would now like to focus our attention on the negative consequences for women of the persistence of certain

cultural barriers that make them the victims of a twofold discrimination: as women and as disabled persons. Much has been written on discrimination against women, but very little has so far been done to deal adequately with the problem of disabled women. The few attempts made have been based on a mistaken approach, since they treat the acute problem of disability as part of the general topic of discrimination against women. However, sex and disability are two separate factors which, when combined in the same person, usually reinforce each other and compound prejudices.

It has been proved that women in many countries are disadvantaged with respect to men from the social, cultural and economic points of view, which makes it very difficult for them to have access to health services, education, vocational training, employment, etc. This statement, which is valid for women in general, also applies to disabled women. For the latter, however, the lack of access to health services will certainly aggravate their disability or make it difficult for them to be rehabilitated quickly by making their participation in community life even more problematic.

All the arguments adduced in favour of women's full participation in the various spheres of cultural, political, economic life, etc., are doubly applicable to disabled women, not only regarding equal rights, but also with respect to the negative consequences for society in general of neglecting any human resource, for the community's failure to use it turns it into a burden for that community. It is sufficient to realize that over 250 million disabled persons throughout the world are women to understand the importance of the issue and its close links to all

development questions. Women make up three quarters of disabled persons in developing countries, with the highest proportion in Asia. From 65 per cent to 70 per cent, i.e. the great majority, live in rural areas.

Finally, the Special Rapporteur would like to express his disappointment at the virtually total lack of bibliographic material on the specific problem of women with disabilities. It is all the more surprising to find such a lack in women's literature, which is obviously very familiar with discrimination.[27]

Lack of information about a specific facet of discrimination may indicate that such discrimination does not exist, but it may also point to the permissive societal attitudes which allow such discrimination to continue. Occasional calls for increased attention to the problems that disabled women experience – because they are both disabled and women – testify to the fact that the dearth of information does not reflect the lack of a problem (see *Women and Disability*, an earlier book in the Women and Development series). The Nairobi Forward–looking Strategies stressed in regard to disabled persons that 'the recognition of their human dignity and human rights and the full participation by disabled persons in society is still limited' and added that 'this presents additional problems for women who may have domestic and other responsibilites'.[28]

The World Programme of Action Concerning Disabled Persons called upon international human rights bodies to ensure that international human rights instruments 'fully take into account the situation of persons who are disabled', and to pay increased attention to obstacles 'which inhibit the ability of disabled persons to exercise the human rights and freedoms recognized as universal to all mankind'.[29] This appeal remains a challenge for the future.

Overcoming obstacles: disabled women are rarely helped

1. T. van Boven (1982) *People Matter. Views on International Human Rights Policy*, Meulenhoff, Amsterdam, p. 122.

2. European Commission of Human Rights, *Survey of Activities and Statistics*, Strasbourg, 1989. p. 15.

3. E. Gimenez-Salinas i Colomer, 'Spain', in D. van Zyl Smit and F. Dunkel (eds) (1991) *Imprisonment Today and Tomorrow. International Perspectives on Prisoners' Rights and Prison Conditions*, Kluwer, Denveter, p. 359.

4. *Justice in Prison*, Justice, London, 1983.

5. 'Statement of basic principles for the treatment of prisoners', Annex to General Assembly resolution 45/111 of 14 December 1990, para.5.

6. Human Rights Committee General Comment 7[16], Article 7, and 9[16], Article 10, UN Doc. CCPR/C/21/REV.1 of 19 May 1989.

7. Economic and Social Council, 'Physical violence against detained women that is specific to their sex', resolution, 1986/29 of 23 May 1986.

8. K. Pease, 'Going to prison next year?' *The World in 1990*, The Economist, London, 1990, p. 130.

9. 'Survey of prison systems in the Member States of the Council of Europe', *Prison Information Bulletin*, No. 15, June 1990, p. 14.

10. 'Criminal justice processes and perspectives in a changing world. The fair treatment of women by the criminal justice system', Report of the Secretary-General, UN Doc. A/CONF.121/17 of 1 July 1985, paras. 65 and 67.

11. S. Armstrong, *P4W Home Maker's*, Montreal, September 1991, pp. 13–14.

12. N. Ahmed, 'Inequality before the law', *SUBHA*, A Newsletter on Women and Development, Karachi, vol. 4, March 1990, p. 1.

13. *Custodial Rape*, People's Union for Democratic Rights, Delhi, March 1990, p. 4.

14. S. Forbes Martin (1992) *Refugee Women*, Zed Books, London.

15. 'Implementation of the Nairobi Forward-looking Strategies for the Advancement of Women', Report of the Secretary-General, UN Doc. A/45/489 of 18 October 1990, para. 42.

16. A.B. Johnsson, 'The international protection of women refugees: a summary of principal problems and issues', *International Journal of Refugee Law*, Vol. 1, 1989, No. 2, pp. 221–32.

17. *Guidelines on the Protection of Refugee Women* (1991) UNHCR, Geneva, para. 54.

18. 'Story of a courageous young girl', *Inter-African Committee on Traditional Practices Affecting the Health of Women and Children, Newsletter No. 12*, Geneva, June 1992, pp. 10–12.

19. M.C. Amar, 'Boat-women: piracy's other dimension', *Refugees*, 18 June 1985, pp. 30–31.

20. 'Refugee and displaced women', General Assembly resolution 35/135 of 11 December 1980, preamble and para. 4.

21. *Guidelines on the protection of Refugee Women* (1991) UNHCR, Geneva, p. 9.

22. Ibid., para. 125.

23. 'Report of the Committee on the Elimination of All Forms of Discrimination against Women, Ninth Session', UN Doc. A/45/38 (1990), para. 250.

24. H.K.M. Desai, *United Nations World Programme of Action concerning Disabled Persons and the International Labour Office's Convention and Recommendation Concerning Vocational Rehabilitation and Employment (Disabled Persons)*, 1983, National Association for the Blind, Bombay, India (no date) p. 78.

25. Esther Boylan (1991) *Women and Disability*, Zed Books, London.

26. *School Board of Nassau Country v. Arline*, 480 US 273 (1987).

27. 'Human rights and disability. Final report prepared by Mr Leandro Despouy, Special Rapporteur', UN Doc. E/CN.4/Sub.2/1991/31 of 12 July 1991, paras. 140–42 and 145.

28. 'Nairobi Forward–looking Strategies for the Advancement of Women', UN Doc. A/CONF. 116/28 of 15 September 1985, para. 296.

29. World Programme of Action Concerning Disabled Persons, paras. 163 and 166.

8 RIGHTING WRONGS

Of all the violations of human rights, the most systematic, widespread and entrenched is the denial of equality to women. Despite some progress in recent years, there is no country in the world where women have achieved full equality. Although making up half or more than half of the population, they are treated as a minority group, disadvantaged and powerless.[1]

MOVEMENTS TO DEFEND HUMAN RIGHTS always emerge in response to violations. This has occurred with women's rights as in any other human rights issue. Another truism is that silence enables the continuation of violations. The worst response to violations is to do nothing; violations have to be recognized as human rights issues in order to be reported, prosecuted, condemned and remedied. Many violations of women's basic rights and fundamental freedoms continue unreported and unremedied, but much has been accomplished in exposing and opposing them.

Two areas have been selected here – violence against women; and traditional practices – to describe how the international momentum against the denial of women's rights has developed, and how victories in effecting changes have been achieved. An important change is the mere placing of the problem on the human rights agenda: it becomes a matter of women's entitlements and governmental obligations; it enables women to demand and obtain equal rights; it obliges governments to guarantee these rights to women.

TRADITIONAL PRACTICES ☐ No other issue has attained as much pub-

licity on the human rights agenda as traditional practices that harm women, particularly female children. The reason can be seen in the box on page 86.

One could easily argue that there are some modern practices that may be as harmful to women as traditional practices – some even more harmful. The detrimental effects of modernization are increasingly addressed by human rights organizations, particularly those working on indigenous rights; thus modern practices that are harmful to women are likely to be placed on the human rights agenda in the near future.

Similarly to many other problems, traditional practices were first brought to the attention of the United Nations human rights bodies by NGOs. Getting the United Nations and its specialized agencies, notably WHO, to address the genital mutilation of women was neither easy nor quick:

In 1958 the Economic and Social Council of the United Nations invited the World Health Organization to 'undertake a study of the persistence of customs which subject girls to ritual operations, and of the measures adopted or planned for putting a stop to such practices, and to communicate the results of that study to the Commission on the Status of Women before the end of 1960.'

The twelfth WHO Assembly in 1959 rejected this request on the grounds that 'the ritual operations in question are based on social and cultural backgrounds, the study of which is outside the competence of the World Health Organization.'

WHO was again asked to undertake a study on the subject by the African participants in a United Nations seminar in Addis Ababa, 'On the Participation of

FEMALE GENITAL MUTILATION

The little girl, entirely nude, is immobilized in the sitting position on a low stool by at least three women. One of them has her arms tightly around the little girl's chest, two others hold the child's thighs apart by force, in order to open wide the vulva. The child's arms are tied behind her back, or immobilized by two other women guests. Then the old woman takes her razor and excises the clitoris. The infibulation follows: the operator cuts with her razor from top to bottom of the small lip and then scrapes the flesh from the inside of the large lip. The nymphotomy and scraping are repeated on the other side of the vulva. The little girl howls and writhes in pain, although strongly held down. The operator wipes the bollo from the wound and the mother, as well as the guests, 'verify' her work, sometimes putting their fingers in. The amount of scraping of the large lips depend upon the 'technical' ability of the practitioner. The opening left for urine and menstrual blood is minuscule. Then the practitioner applies a paste and ensure the adhesion of the large lips by means of acacia thorn, which pierces one lip and passes through into the other. She sticks in three or four in this manner down the vulva. These thorns are then held in place either by means of a sewing thread or horsehair. Paste is again put on the wound. Exhausted, the little girl is then dressed and put on a bed. The operation lasts from 15 to 20 minutes according to the ability of the old woman and the resistance put up by the child.[2]

Against female circumcision: a Sudanese cartoon

1991 GIFT FOR ALL FAMILIES

هديّة عـام ١٩٩١

Women in Public Life', and this request was repeated by ECOSOC.

However, nothing happened for nearly 20 years. The first opportunity for discussion provided by the WHO was the seminar on 'Traditional Practices

Affecting the Health of Women and Children', organized by the WHO Regional Office for the Eastern Mediterranean in Khartoum, in February 1979.[3]

This Seminar condemned female circumcision (genital mutilation) as a health hazard, and constituted the first international step towards formulating a policy against it.

Twenty NGOs, including the Arab Lawyers Union, International Alliance of Women, International Commission of Jurists, International Council of Women, International Federation of Women Lawyers, League of Red Cross and Red Crescent Societies, Radda Barnen International, and Soroptimist International, formed a Working Group to co-ordinate their action in 1977. The Inter-African Committee on Traditional Practices was formed in 1984, at the Dakar Seminar. Its two principal tasks were (1) to initiate and support the creation of national bodies capable of addressing female circumcision and other traditional practices; and (2) to encourage action-orientated research to identify those traditional practices that are harmful to women, with a view to elaborating strategies for their elimination.

In 1981, NGOs raised traditional practices as a human rights problem before the Working Group on Slavery, which decided to disseminate the information received and seek additional data. The next year the Working Group recommended that a study be undertaken to examine 'all aspects of the problem', at that time confined to female circumcision,[4] and its parent body, the Sub-Commission, requested that two experts carry out such a study.[5] In 1984 the two experts were nominated to assist the Working Group on Traditional Practices Affecting the Health of Women and Children, and the Working Group issued its first report in 1986. Following the dissemination of this report, the Commission on Human Rights requested the Sub-Commission to consider measures to be taken towards the elimination of such harmful traditional practices.[6] The Sub-Commission appointed Mrs Halima Embarek Warzazi to study traditional practices further, and she submitted her final report in 1991.[7]

The inclusion of traditional practices on the human rights agenda, and the subsequent broadening and deepening of the understanding of what traditional practices are, and what effects they have on women, were – as were many others – accomplished by NGOs. They have kept the issue on the agenda now for more than a decade. Many reports have been prepared to describe various forms of traditional practices detrimental to women, and numerous legislative prohibitions, action plans for their elimination, and educational campaigns have been adopted and implemented.

TABLE 8.1 WHY WOMEN SUBMIT TO CIRCUMCISION

This table summarizes results of a survey of 400 women in Sierra Leone, co-ordinated by Olayinka Koso-Thomas, in January 1985. Women were interviewed at family planning centres, hospitals and nursing homes. The majority of the interviewed women (369) had been circumcised.

REASON GIVEN	NUMBER
● Tradition	257
● Societal acceptance	105
● Religion	51
● Increasing chances to marry	12
● Preservation of virginity	11
● Female hygiene	10
● Prevention of promiscuity	6
● Enhancement of fertility	3
● To please husband	2
● To maintain good health	1

SOURCE: O. KOSO-THOMAS, (1987) THE CIRCUMCISION OF WOMEN. A STRATEGY FOR ERADICATION, ZED BOOKS, LONDON, PP. 45–9.

Not every practice which is harmful for women is, or can be, subsumed under the existing human rights norms. It is indicative that a survey conducted in January 1977 at hospitals in Alexandria by Dr Taha Baasher revealed that women opposed to traditional practices (83 per cent of the respondents) perceived them as a violation of fundamental human rights. They held that 'even if female circumcision is a traditional custom and may be acceptable, it should be a matter of personal choice.'[8] The Working Group on Traditional Practices placed the problem in the human rights framework. It stressed that 'some traditional practices were aimed, in traditional societies, at the closer incorporation of the individual within his social environment in order to enable him to benefit from all the rights of the individual which these societies recognized', and added that 'today there is incompatibility between human rights obligations of governments and the maintenance of harmful traditional practices.'[9] Progress does not come easily, as the following excerpt from the report concerning Djibouti by the United Nations Special Rapporteur on Traditional Practices bears witness:

The team was made to understand that the issue of human rights and traditional practices was not considered a priority since the Government deals with other basic human rights problems which need immediate attention. No law has been decreed against female circumcision since the experience of other countries regarding legislation on this issue resulted in failure.[10]

FROM SON PREFERENCE TO FEMICIDE

Descriptions of the celebration of the birth of a son abound in historical and contemporary literature. Son preference is a reflection of patriarchal society and is worldwide. This constitutes a fact that many would not associate with human rights. Parents who prefer a son to a daughter are not breaching any law, nor could law even attempt to outlaw people's wishes. Son preference, however, becomes an important human rights issue when it results in discrimination against female children: 'Scientific evidence of the delete-

rious effect of son preference on the health of female children is ... scarce, but abnormal sex ratios in infant and young child mortality rates, in nutritional status indicators and even population sex ratios show that discriminatory practices are widespread and have serious repercussions. Geographically there is often close correspondence between the areas of strong son preference and of health disadvantage for females.'[11] Because of the dearth of gender-specificity in statistics there can be no worldwide picture of the fate of female children. This reveals the perverse paradox of gender discrimination: much of it cannot be proved due to lack of data, thus it is easy to pretend that it does not exist.

The movement against gender discrimination in India has significantly redressed this dearth of information, and also brought it into the human rights context. Indian human rights organizations have addressed the use of amniocentesis (originally designed to detect genetic abnormalities of a foetus, but widely applied to determine its sex),[12] and prompted the adoption of legislation to outlaw this practice of 'femicide'.[13]

The Human Rights Committee included 'femicide' in its questions on non-discrimination and equality between sexes in examining governmental reports under the ICCPR. The Committee 'wished to know whether any measures had been taken to combat the tradition according to which abortion of female foetuses was promoted in order to encourage families to have male children'.[14] The representative of the Government of India responded: 'Reports of destruction of female foetuses were alarming and the Government was currently developing an information campaign against the practice of identifying the sex of foetuses and aborting them on the basis of their sex.'[15]

Data generation showing different facets

of gender discrimination has much improved in the 1980s. In India, statistical evidence of gender discrimination has not only improved, it has also become a publicly debated issue. The 1991 Indian census affirmed that research on the impact of gender discrimination was accurate: the sex ratio decreased for the country as a whole from 934 women per 1,000 men in 1981, to 929 in 1991.[16] This apparently small decrease in the sex ratio should be translated into absolute numbers. Estimates of the numbers of 'vanished women' have reached 100 million for Asia,[17] and are put at 30 million for China, where the sex ratio is similarly low (934 women per 1,000 men in 1991) and decreasing (the ratio was 941 in 1982).[18]

The ultimate cause of 'femicide' is much more difficult to document. At the beginning of the 1980s, the World Fertility Survey included questions relating to sex preference for their next child in order to study motivations of women in child-bearing. Results provided the first data to document the known, but previously undocumented, son preference. Table 8.2 shows results from this survey, most importantly the fact that daughter preference existed in only two (Venezuela and Jamaica) out of 39 countries encompassed by this survey. The strongest son preference was documented in Pakistan, Nepal and Bangladesh. The data show as many as five women wanted a son for every woman who preferred a daughter.

The obvious question is what to do now that both the consequences and causes of discrimination against female children are more or less known. Nobody would expect a magic recipe whereby individual preferences of (female) parents would instantly change in favour of female children. Such preferences are, however, largely shaped by economic and social factors, and these are amenable to change. A study into health implications of sex discrimination,

prepared by Sundari Ravindran for WHO and UNICEF, suggested that, in addition to measures against gender discrimination, causes of son preference be addressed:

Long-term measures to deal with the phenomenon of son preference would include enactment and implementation of legislation against discrimination on the grounds of sex; provision of adequate social security for older people so that a son is no longer a must for security in old age; abolition of practices such as dowry and bride price; and changing laws to enable women to maintain their maiden name and pass it on to their children so that continuation of the family name is not threatened by non-birth of a son.

Needless to say, concerted efforts to improve the overall status of women are the backdrop against which all of the

---

TABLE 8.2 INDEX OF SON PREFERENCE

The index of son preference shows the ratio of mothers who prefer their next child to be male to those who wish the next child to be female.

COUNTRY	INDEX	COUNTRY	INDEX
• Pakistan	4.9	• Kenya	1.1
• Nepal	4.0	• Indonesia	1.1
• Bangladesh	3.3	• Peru	1.1
• Korea	3.3	• Guyana	1.1
• Syria	2.3	• Trinidad and Tobago	1.1
• Jordan	1.9	• Colombia	1.0
• Lesotho	1.5	• Paraguay	1.0
• Sri Lanka	1.5	• Costa Rica	1.0
• Sudan	1.5	• Panama	1.0
• Thailand	1.4	• Philippines	0.9
• Fiji	1.3	• Haiti	0.9
• Malaysia	1.2	• Venezuela	0.9
• Dominican Republic	1.2	• Jamaica	0.7
• Mexico	1.2		

SOURCE: UNITED NATIONS, WORLD FERTILITY SURVEY, CROSS NATIONAL SUMMARIES, NO.27, NEW YORK, OCTOBER 1983.

above measures have to be implemented. Improving the access of girls and women to education and training and to productive resources such as land and credit, which will improve the perceived and economic value of women, are the starting point in this respect.[19]

VIOLENCE AGAINST WOMEN □

Violence against women has continued throughout history unreported and unchallenged. The recent worldwide mobilization to condemn violence against women as a violation of their rights has encountered centuries of silence as an obstacle. Many opponents of tackling violence against women claim that it has nothing to do with human rights. According to such views, only relations between the state and the individual pertain to human rights, what people do to each other is excluded; governments do not have to act to protect women from being beaten, raped, killed. However, both women's and human rights NGOs are today well-equipped to show how erroneous such views are, and how detrimental they are to women: 'In a way the entire community is responsible for the continued assaults on women and in some cases their deaths: the friends and neighbours who ignore or excuse the violence, the physician who does not go beyond the mending of bones and the stitching of wounds, the social worker who defines wife beating as a failure of communication and the police and court officials who refuse to intervene. The violence is meted out by one man but the responsibility goes far beyond him.'[20]

The international movement against violence is one of the most notable recent developments with regard to the human rights of women. The number of organizations involved, the persuasiveness of their evidence and arguments, and their successes in effecting local, national and international changes are proof that global

mobilization is effective. The lead was taken by women themselves. As with many other issues, inter-governmental bodies were moved by a genuine flood of NGO pressures to act:

The collective power of women's organizations was demonstrated when a United Nations treaty body declared that gender based violence is an abrogation of women's human rights. In January 1992 the Committee on the Elimination of All Forms of Discrimination against Women (CEDAW), which monitors implementation of the women's human rights treaty, adopted a general recommendation and comments stating exactly how the Women's Convention covers violence against women and what governments should do to stop the violence.

When this Women's Convention was adopted in 1979, violence against women was a subject rarely discussed in public forums. Today dowry deaths, domestic violence, sexual harassment and rape cases make headlines in newspapers and on TV because women's groups in nations around the world have brought the problem of violence against women to public attention. They published newsletters, held demonstrations, wrote letters and called on public officials, told their stories, got media attention, and changed public opinion. They illustrated how common, pervasive and insidious the problem of violence against women is, and created the political will for change.[21]

It took women's organizations decades of constant and concerted effort to attain international recognition of the fact that violence against women is a human rights issue. The United Nations bodies started addressing the problem of violence in the 1980s, but neither women nor human rights were mentioned at first. The first resolutions were adopted under the title of 'domestic violence' or 'violence in the family'. Women were identified as victims alongside children, the problem was described as global and pervasive, and

Violence against women is opposed and exposed worldwide

numerous measures were suggested to assist victims.

PROTECTION AGAINST VIOLENCE IS A RIGHT

The relevance of placing violence against women on the human rights agenda may not be self-evident. Indeed, one may ask what human rights offer to women in addition to other measures against violence. The affirmation that violence against women is a human rights problem entails governments' obligation to recognize that women are entitled to be protected against violence, that this is their human right, which the government should guarantee and to which it should provide remedies when this right is violated. This is what human rights are all about: once an issue is brought into the human rights context, it is no more a matter of wishes and suggestions, but becomes a matter of individual rights and governments' corollary obligations. Violence against women is thus not a 'private' but a 'public' issue, and necessitates governmental action to protect women against violence, no matter who the perpetrators are. Similarly, private employers as much as public ones are bound by the prohibition of discrimination, and the government should ensure that this prohibition is implemented and enforced. The acknowledgement that violence against women violates their rights means that governments ought to ensure that women are safeguarded against it, that is, that violence against women is effectively prevented. This necessitates governmental incursion into an area which has traditionally been deemed 'private', clouded in impenetrable silence and often protected against governmental interference by invoking family autonomy, societal rules of conduct, or the need to preserve traditional patterns of behaviour. This makes violence against women a very difficult issue to tackle.

In 1986, the United Nations Economic and Social Council recognized that violence in the family was 'a grave violation of the rights of women'.[22] A full elaboration of the implications of dealing with violence against women in the human rights context was accomplished by CEDAW in 1992. First, the Committee stated that the general prohibition of gender discrimination 'includes gender based violence – that is, violence which is directed against a woman because she is a woman or which affects women disproportionately. It includes acts which inflict physical, mental or sexual harm or suffering, threats of such acts, coercion or other deprivations of liberty.' Secondly, CEDAW affirmed that violence against women constitutes a violation of their rights irrespective of whether perpetrators are public officials or private persons. Because the Women's Convention requires states to eliminate gender discrimination by any person, organization or enterprise, 'States may also be responsible for private acts if they fail to act with due diligence to prevent violations of rights, or to investigate and punish acts of violence, and to provide compensation.'

In addition, CEDAW provided a detailed commentary on the implications of violence against women for the specific rights guaranteed to all women under the Women's Convention, such as life, protection against ill-treatment, liberty and security, health, just and favourable conditions of work, equality in the family, and equal protection of the law. CEDAW recommended that states take all measures which are necessary to provide effective protection of women against gender based violence, and it stressed in particular the following:

(a) effective legal measures, including penal sanctions, civil remedies and compensatory provisions to protect women against all kinds of violence, including *inter alia* violence and abuse in the family, sexual assault and sexual harassment in the workplace;
(b) preventive measures, including public information and education programmes to change attitudes concerning the roles and status of men and women;
(c) protective measures, including refuges, counselling, rehabilitation and support services for women who are the victims of violence or who are at risk of violence.[23]

Efforts to strengthen the human rights protection of women against violence led the Organization of American States (OAS) to initiate the drafting of a regional convention. In 1991, the OAS convened an expert meeting to consider the viability of an Inter-American Convention on Women and Violence. This process is intended to produce a legally binding instrument, because previously adopted resolutions contain measures against violence but lack legal force. The Draft Convention aims to provide the broadest possible protection to women through a comprehensive definition of the violence against which women should be protected:

[Violence against women includes] any act, omission or conduct by means of which physical, sexual or mental suffering is inflicted, directly or indirectly, through deceit, seduction, threat, [harassment], coercion, or any other means, on any woman with the purpose or effect of intimidating, punishing or humiliating her or of maintaining her in sex-stereotyped roles, or of denying her human dignity, sexual self-determination, physical, mental and moral integrity or of undermining the security of her person, her self-respect or her personality, or of diminishing her physical or mental capacities.[24]

Such a definition challenges the persistent – and widespread – tolerance of violence against women by trying to outlaw a broad range of practices to which many women are subjected, but which few are equipped to challenge. The Convention is being drafted to lay down safeguards against such practices. This proposed definition is in a relatively early stage. When the passage quoted above was written, agreement on the inclusion of harassment into the definition was still pending; this is marked by brackets. It is hoped that reaching agreement within the Inter-American Commission on Women will be a relatively easy task; much more opposition to outlawing violence against women through an international treaty can be expected once the Draft Convention moves from the 'women's' to the 'mainstream' bodies, composed predominantly of men.

No examples are necessary to illustrate the globally prevalent view that violence against women is 'normal', nothing to talk about and least of all to complain about. Human rights in this area, as in many others, are on the slippery slope of challenging societal norms and attitudes, shared by men and women. One can safely state that enacting legal prohibitions of violence against women, difficult as this is, constitutes the easiest task. Translating such norms into rules of conduct for everyone, everywhere, and all the time, will require a consistent struggle to be continued by future generations. The obvious difficulty with such rules of conduct is that they affect everybody. When dealing with issues that pertain to public officials only, such as outlawing torture, disappearances, or ill-treatment of prisoners, most people perceive them as something remote from their lives – few are personally involved. Human rights norms which deal with interpersonal and family relations affect everybody's lives. The interest in them, but also the resistance to adjusting behaviour to conform to them, is therefore significantly higher.

Legal norms are proverbially ineffective in changing private behaviour, particularly relations between couples, between parents and children, within families and neighbourhoods. They are, however, indispensable even if they are far from sufficient to accord women protection against violence. They demonstrate not only political will, but also public authorities' firm undertaking to take the lead in eradicating violence against women.

THE ROLE OF PUBLIC OFFICIALS The scope of the challenge can be illustrated by thousands of examples of victimization of women through violence. Only a few are provided here. Rather, the focus of this text is on the response to such victimization in the human rights context. How far we have already travelled on the way from refusing to respond to violence against women as a violation of their rights can be illustrated by a conversation with the Director-General of Police, which took place in 1988 in Orissa (India), following the abduction and rape of a schoolgirl:

**[Director General of Police]:
There is no nexus between rape and law and order. The number of rapes is not inter-linked with crime in the area.**

By crime we mean professional crime. Like theft, murder, communal riots. If we use that yardstick, rape is not a crime. The motive of gain is not present in rape. I am giving you a professional's view.[25]

The importance of public authorities taking the lead in treating violence against women as a violation of their rights is highlighted by such attitudes, which in many countries conform to the national law and policy. This is not easy either, as can be seen in the reported attitudes of ministers and members of parliament in Papua New Guinea:

THE KILLING OF A CHILD BRIDE: NIGERIA

The control over a woman's life by her husband and relatives can be so absolute that women who refuse their authority sometimes even have to pay with their lives for daring to say 'no'. In February 1987, newspapers carried the story of a young girl who was betrothed at the age of nine to a man chosen by her parents. At the age of twelve the girl, Hauwa Abubakar, was taken to her so-called marital home. She ran away from the man twice because she did not want the marriage. The third time she ran away, the 'husband' caught up with her and chopped off both her legs with a sword. She died. Since then, Women in Nigeria (WIN) has started a nationwide campaign on the different ramifications of child abuse and child marriage.

BEATEN BLACK AND BLUE BY HER HUSBAND: INDONESIA

'Physical torture inflicted upon the wife by the husband is one of the grounds for divorce. According to the Indonesian criminal law, proof of physical torture is the fresh traces left on the victim's body at the time of the report. Thus a wife who has been beaten black and blue by her husband has to report immediately to have any chance of success in achieving her divorce.'[29]

VIOLENCE AND WOMEN'S HEALTH IN THE USA

'Lori Heise outlined issues of violence and health in the United States, where battering is the greatest single cause of injury to women, more than car accidents, muggings and rapes combined. According to former Surgeon General, C. Everett Koop, 3 to 4 million women are beaten by their partners each year

and 20 to 25 percent of women who go to hospital emergency rooms are there for symptoms related to on-going abuse. Battery is also the primary context for many other problems: it is associated with 45 percent of female alcoholism and 26 percent of female suicides.'[30]

HOW CAN ABUSED WOMEN SEEK REDRESS? AN EXAMPLE FROM ZIMBABWE

'In traditional law, a woman or girl will not report a rape directly to the authorities. As in all matters, it is her guardian who is responsible for her welfare, and therefore responsible for reporting. The victim of a rape traditionally reports either to her mother or to her auntie, who will then report to the girl's father or guardian.

In some communal land areas we found an elaborate reporting procedure. The girl might report to her mother, who reports to her husband, who reports to the Kraalhead, who reports to the headman or chief, who reports to the Vilco (Village committee), which reports to the Wardco (Ward committee), which reports to the Councillor, before the matter finally gets to the police. On farms and mines, she reports to the foreman and then the mine or farm owner, before the police.

Apart from the obvious problem of the length of time that this all takes, and the fact that any evidence which the police might have been able to collect will have disappeared long before the reporting protocol is completed, it is also important to consider the psychological effect all this reporting may have on the girl. Before she knows it, everyone for miles around knows what has happened to her.'[31]

PHOTO: DIDIER RUET/WCC

Women are victimized by armed conflicts and are taking action against them: a march for peace in Jerusalem

Recent parliamentary debate in Papua New Guinea on whether wife-beating should be made illegal clearly reflects the widely perceived link between bridewealth and the right to discipline ... Most ministers 'were violently against the idea of parliament interfering in traditional family life'. Minister William Wi of North Waghi argued that wife-beating 'is an accepted custom ... we are wasting our time debating the issue'. Another parliamentarian added; 'I paid for my wife, so she should not overrule my decisions, because I am the head of the family.'[26]

This parliamentary debate was probably a response by [male] parliamentarians to the information campaign conducted by the Women and Law Committee of Papua New Guinea in 1990–91 on violence against women. This campaign included distributing 150,000 copies of the leaflet 'Wife-Beating is a Crime' in the three main languages.[27] The campaign continues.

THE ROLE OF GOVERNMENTS ☐ The path towards eliminating violence against women is long and strenuous. The first steps should be taken by governments 'to recognize that the elimination of violence against women is essential to the achievement of equality for women and is a requirement for the full respect of human rights'.[28] The emerging United Nations Draft Declaration on Violence against Women suggests that governments recognize that the following measures constitute their human rights obligations:

(a) To condemn all forms of violence against women and agree to pursue, by all appropriate means and without delay, measures to be adopted to prevent, punish and eliminate this violence;
(b) To include in domestic legislation penal and civil sanctions to punish and redress the wrongs caused to women

WOMEN'S RIGHTS INITIATIVES PREDATING THE UNITED NATIONS

It is generally unknown that the United Nations Commission on the Status of Women created in 1946 was the product of a struggle waged over twenty-five years by certain of the women's NGOs. In 1919 proposals for a Women's Bureau were presented to the Secretariat by British and American women's societies. One such proposal, drafted by British lawyer Chrystal Macmillan, Executive Secretary of the International Alliance of Women, was for a permanent international women's office modelled on the International Labour Office complete with an annual general conference of women ... It is interesting to note that it set forth fundamental principles which were eventually to guide the work of the United Nations Commission on the Status of Women: 'that the status of women, social, political and economic, is of supreme international importance' and 'that social progress is dependent on the status of women in the community' ... Macmillan's draft also outlined the procedure to be taken for non-observance of conventions ratified by member states following the model of international labour conventions, with the notable innovation that the commission of enquiry would be composed of women proposed by national women's organizations rather than governments.

The greatest achievement was to have the entire status of women, with particular attention to an equal rights treaty, placed on the Assembly [of the League of Nations] agenda in 1934 by a joint request of ten Latin American delegations. These delegations asserted that as 'the League of Nations is an international organization designed to defend human rights' it should 'take cognisance of the present widespread and alarming encroachment upon the rights and liberties of women'.

The women's NGOs were invited by the Secretary-General to present statements to the Assembly of 1935 on the status of women ... The women's organizations were unanimous in voicing concern over the growing tendency for governments to over-ride clauses of constitutions and laws establishing equality between the sexes and to restrict the employment of women ... The Assembly invited governments to send information regarding political and civil rights of women in their country. The women's organizations, even those which would have preferred more immediate action by way of an international convention on equal rights, were satisfied that the campaign for the advancement of the status of women was placed 'in the forefront of world politics'.

Few countries at this time were willing to consider the status of women a matter of international concern. The government of the United Kingdom prefaced its response to the Assembly's request for information with a statement that 'the extent to which effect should be given in any State to the principle of equality of the sexes is a matter for that State to determine ...' Yet there was a growing responsiveness to ideas about the League's role in protecting fundamental individual rights. At the 1937 Assembly, M. Cassin (France) stated that 'the League could not ignore the inequalities of so gross a character in some countries that it left women under such disabilities as to cause much suffering'. For the first time the possibility of an international convention to promote women's rights was discussed, albeit for the distant future ...[32]

C. Miller, Paper to British International Studies Association, December 1991.

who are subjected to violence and to provide them with just and effective legal remedies, compensation and rehabilitation;

(c) To take measures necessary to ensure gender-sensitive training of all officials who implement the policy of preventing, eradicating, investigating and punishing violence against women;

(d) To adopt all appropriate measures to modify the social and cultural patterns of conduct of men and women;

(e) To compile statistics relating to the prevalence of different forms of violence against women;

(f) To exercise due diligence to prevent, investigate and punish acts of violence against women.[33]

Everybody recognizes the necessity to undertake immediate measures to deal with consequences of violence and provide victimized women with redress and assistance, but the need to address underlying causes too cannot be postponed. This was summarized in the 1989 United Nations study on violence against women as follows:

Specific legal provisions which indicate that violence against women is excusable or tolerable must be repealed as must any provisions discriminating on the basis of sex. Access to courts must be simple and cheap. Any legal disability, such as considering women legally to be minors, that prevents a woman from bringing an action, must be removed and any evidentiary barrier, such as provisions that prevent a woman giving evidence against her spouse, must be clarified.

Ultimately, however, the inferior status of women ... must be addressed. Violence against women in the family and elsewhere is the product of this inferiority, and the eradication of violence will only occur if steps are taken to guarantee women equality in all spheres of life.[34]

1. *Many Voices, One World*, UNESCO, Paris, 1980, p. 189.
2. 'Report of the Working Group on Traditional Practices Affecting the Health of Women and Children', UN Doc. E/CN.4/1986/42 of 4 February 1986, para. 40.
3. S. McLean and S. Efua Graham (1980) *Female Circumcision, Excision and Infibulation: The Facts and Proposals for Change*, Minority Rights Group, London, p. 8.
4. 'Report of the Working Group on Slavery on its eighth session', UN Doc. E/CN.4/Sub.2/1982/21, chapter IV, recommendation 9.
5. Resolution 1982/15 of 7 September 1982.
6. Traditional practices affecting the health of women and children, resolution 1988/57 of the Commission on Human Rights.
7. 'Study on traditional practices affecting the health of women and children. Final report by the Special Rapporteur, Mrs Halima Embarek Warzazi', UN Doc. E/CN.4/Sub.2/1991/6 of 5 July 1991.
8. T. Baasher, 'Aspects psychologiques de la circoncision femenine, Rapport au 5eme Congres de la Societe d'obstetrique et de gynecologie du Soudan', WHO Regional Office Alexandria, 1977.
9. 'Report of the Working Group on Traditional Practices Affecting the Health of Women and Children', UN Doc. E/CN.4/1986/42 of 4 February 1986, paras. 116 and 118.
10. 'Study on traditional practices affecting the health of women and children. Final Report by the Special

11. 'Report of the Working Group on Traditional Practices Affecting the Health of Women and Children', op. cit., para. 150.
12. V. Patel, 'Science in the service of mass murder of female babies in India', *Women in Action*, No. 3, 1988, pp. 27–8.
13. N. Dutta, 'Law relating to pre-natal diagnosis', *The Lawyers*, Bombay, August 1988, pp. 35-7.
14. 'Consideration of reports submitted by States Parties under Article 40 of the Covenant, India', UN Doc. CCPR/C/42/CPR.1/Add.9 of 10 July 1991, para. 16.
15. Ibid., para. 18.
16. 'Unwelcome sex: Census highlights effect of bias against females', *Far Eastern Economic Review*, 26 December 1991, pp. 18–19.
17. N.D. Kristof, 'Asia, vanishing point for as many as 100 million women', *International Herald Tribune*, 6 November 1991, pp. 1 and 7.
18. N.D. Kristof, 'Where have all the little girls gone? In rural China, no one knows', *International Herald Tribune*, 18 June 1991, pp. 1 and 4.
19. S. Ravindran, 'Health implications of sex discrimination in childhood'. A 1986 review paper and an annotated bibliography, Doc. WHO/UNICEF/FHE 86.2, p. 15.
20. R.E. Dobash and R. Dobash (1980) *Violence against Women: A Case against the Patriarchy*, Open Books, London, p. 222.

21. A.S. Fraser and M. Kazantsis (1992) *CEDAW 11. The Committee on the Elimination of Discrimination against Women, the Convention on the Elimination of All Forms of Discrimination against Women and Violence against Women*, IWRAW, University of Minnesota, Minneapolis, July 1992, p. 1.

22. The Economic and Social Council, 'Violence in the family', resolution 1986/18 of 23 May 1986, para. 2.

23. CEDAW, 'Violence against women', General recommendation No. 19 (eleventh session, 1992), UN Doc. CEDAW/C/1992/L.1/Add.15.

24. 'Report on the results of the Meeting of Experts to Consider the Viability of an Inter-American Convention on Women and Violence, Caracas, 5–9 August 1991', Inter-American Commission on Women, CIM/Doc.1/91, Doc. OEA/Ser./II.7.4.

25. N. Kapur and J. Purewal (1990) 'State violence, law and gender justice', *Third World Legal Studies – 1990*, INTERWORLSA, Valparaiso University School of Law, p. 135.

26. L. Heise, 'Crimes of gender', *WorldWatch*, March–April 1989, pp. 15–16.

27. *FEMNET News*, Vol. 1, January-April 1992, No. 8, pp. 16–17.

28. Commission on the Status of Women, 'Violence against women in all its forms, draft resolution recommended for adoption by the Economic and Social Council', UN Doc. E/CN.6/1992/L.8 of 16 March 1992, para. 1.

29. *Women Living under Muslim Laws. Women's World*, ISIS, Rome, 21–22 December 1989, pp. 21 and 34.

30. *Women, Violence and Human Rights*, 1991 Women's Leadership Institute Report, Douglass College, Rutgers University, May 1992, p. 31.

31. A. Armstrong, *Women and Rape in Zimbabwe*, Institute of Southern African Studies, National University of Lesotho, Human & People's Rights Project, Monograph No. 10, 1990. p. 22.

32. C. Miller (1991) 'The interaction of national and transnational women's networks with the League of Nations Secretariat'. Paper presented to the British International Studies Association Conference, December 1991.

33. Commission on the Status of Women, 'Draft Declaration on Violence against Women, Appendix to Violence against women in all its forms. Report of the Secretary-General', UN Doc. E/CN.6/1992/4 of 6 December 1991, p. 13, Article 4.

34. United Nations (1989) *Violence against Women in the Family*, Sales No. E-89.IV.5, New York, pp. 101 and 105.

9 EQUAL RIGHTS FOR ALL

The United Nations is committed to the principle of equality of men and women, meaning the equality in their dignity and worth as human beings as well as equality in their rights, opportunities and responsibilities. In its work for the advancement of women, the entire United Nations system has dedicated itself to ensuring the universal recognition, in law, of equality of rights between men and women, and to exploring ways to give women, in fact, equal opportunities with men to realize their human rights and fundamental freedoms.[1]

THE UNITED NATIONS CHARTER was the first to affirm explicitly the equal rights of men and women in its preamble and to lay down a person's sex among the prohibited grounds of discrimination, alongside race, language and religion. Moreover, the Charter proclaimed human rights to constitute one of the main purposes of the United Nations. Specifically, these main purposes are to achieve international co-operation in solving international problems of an economic, social, cultural, or humanitarian character, and in promoting and encouraging respect for human rights and fundamental freedoms for all without distinction as to race, sex, language or religion. By the Charter all members of the United Nations are legally bound to strive towards full realization of all human rights and fundamental freedoms. Human rights have thereby been elevated from being merely a noble aim to an obligation of all governments and of the United Nations.

The explicitness of the Charter regarding equal rights for women was thereafter refined in a multitude of international human rights treaties. Some have further elaborated rights and freedom for all, others have focused on particular sets of rights (such as labour rights, or safeguards against torture), and yet others on those categories whose rights are denied or violated unless specifically and effectively protected. Women have been included among those categories. The need to pay particular attention to women became evident in the years of drafting these different documents. Unless women were represented, they tended to be forgotten; if the drafters were not alerted to the fact that the term 'men' does not necessarily include women, their drafts tended to refer only to the masculine part of humanity.

Indeed the Universal Declaration of Human Rights, which in its final text reaffirmed and reinforced the Charter's postulate of the equal rights of women, represented a battlefield. In an early draft of the Declaration, its first article began: 'All men are brothers.'[2] This was indicative of the relative lack of gender-sensitivity at that time within the Commission on Human Rights, which was drafting the Declaration, even though it was chaired by Eleanor Roosevelt, and despite the efforts of its female members. The exclusion of the female part of humanity in the drafting of the future Declaration was effectively opposed by the Commission on the Status of Women. As a result, the Universal Declaration was in its final text genuinely universal. Keeping in mind that it was drafted in the late 1940s, the careful use of terms 'everyone' and 'no one' appears even more impressive.

Nevertheless, the drafting had started with the term 'men' in the first article, and the Commission on the Status of Women formally submitted an alternative draft, suggesting that 'all people' be used instead of 'all men'. Another alternative was proposed during the debate at the Commission, 'all human beings', and this

ELEANOR ROOSEVELT

'On December 10, 1948 at 3 a.m. the United Nations General Assembly, meeting in Paris, adopted the Universal Declaration of Human Rights, which stands to this day as the most widely recognized statement of the rights to which every person on our planet is entitled.

Then something happened that never happened in the United Nations before or since. The delegates rose to give a standing ovation to a single delegate, a shy elderly lady with a rather formal demeanor but a very warm smile. Her name, of course, was Eleanor Roosevelt.

Determined to press the declaration to completion, Mrs. Roosevelt drove her colleagues mercilessly. There were 16-hour days, and some delegates may secretly have whispered the prayer ascribed to President Roosevelt: "Oh Lord, make Eleanor tired!" A delegate from Panama begged Mrs. Roosevelt to remember that UN delegates have human rights too.

Although Mrs. Roosevelt was proud of her role in shaping the Universal Declaration, she was a realist. She knew that words were not self-enforcing. The real challenge, she liked to tell the UN delegates in later years, was one of "actually living and working our countries for freedom and justice for each human being".'

Source: R.R.Gardner, 'Eleanor Roosevelt's legacy: The Rights Declaration', *International Herald Tribune*, 10–11 December 1988.

one remained in the final text.[3]

The Universal Declaration constitutes the core of universal human rights guarantees. It is, however, a Declaration, thus not legally binding, and virtually as soon as it was adopted work began on translating the principles and norms of the Declaration into an international treaty, to make the basic human rights norms formally binding upon states, and to specify them to the extent that governmental agreement can be obtained. It should not be forgotten that the international community has no hierarchical structure whereby it could enact and enforce rules; such rules have to be explicitly accepted by each individual state represented by its government.

The drafting of an international treaty to further strengthen the provisions of the Universal Declaration was a long and conflictual process. First, the aim to draft one treaty had to be abandoned. Mainly as the consequence of the Cold War controversies, the conceptual integrity of human rights was violated by the adoption of two treaties: the International Covenant on Civil and Political Rights (ICCPR), and the International Covenant on Economic, Social and Cultural Rights (ICESCR). Secondly, this protracted process lasted until 1966, when the two Covenants were adopted, and it took ten additional years for them to come into force.

The texts of these two Covenants further reinforce the prohibition of discrimination, but contribute little to the articulation of the specific issues affecting women. The approach followed in human rights was generic rather than gender-specific; hence gender discrimination did not have prominence, and women were not addressed as women, but only as child-bearers and child-rearers, namely through the special protection of motherhood. Indeed, much of the United Nations work at the time, not only in human rights, tended to deal with 'women and children',

thus reducing women's concerns to motherhood. It took 13 more years, from 1966 when the Covenants were adopted, to the adoption of the Women's Convention in 1979, before the human rights of women obtained international legal regulation.

Progress was achieved towards eliminating racial discrimination, and later this was useful as a precedent in the drafting of the Women's Convention. It was realized that the formal prohibition of discrimination is indispensable but insufficient: it does not provide sufficient grounds for redressing the inherited consequences of decades, even centuries, of discrimination. Thus a solution was found in laying down norms on 'reverse discrimination', 'affirmative action', or to use the CEDAW term 'temporary special measures', aimed to assist categories victimized by discrimination to attain a status comparable to that of the rest of the population, so that all would be able to exercise their rights on equal terms.

> The multitude of human rights standard-setting efforts that the United Nations have undertaken (the main instruments are listed in Table 5.1) has led to the realization that specific norms relating to women have to encompass three levels:
> 1. The formal affirmation of human rights and fundamental freedoms;
> 2. The prohibition of discrimination, entailing equal opportunities irrespective of sex;
> 3. The identification and elimination of the obstacles to the equal exercise of rights by women that are gender-specific.

It is obvious that the third requirement involves unequal rather than equal treatment: obstacles to equality cannot be eliminated unless they are recognized, and because they hinder women's (but not men's) exercise of human rights, special measures in favour of women are necessary. Because such measures may appear to be discriminating against men they remain controversial.

TABLE 9.1
NUMBER OF UNITED NATIONS RESOLUTIONS AND DECISIONS ON WOMEN 1946–91

	COMING FROM THE GENERAL ASSEMBLY	COMING FROM THE ECONOMIC AND SOCIAL COUNCIL	TOTAL
1945–1955	12	15	27
1956–1965	13	10	23
1966–1975	30	68	98
1976–1985	111	107	218
1986–1991	51	118	145
TOTAL	225	318	511

Source: List of resolutions and decisions on the status of women adopted by the General Assembly and the Economic and Social Council 1946-90, Prepared by the Division for the Advancement of Women, United Nations Office at Vienna, Commission on the Status of Women, Thirty-fifth session, Vienna, 27 February - 8 March 1991, Background Paper 1, 31 January 1991, revision 2 (mimeograph).

THE UNITED NATIONS: WHO DOES WHAT? ☐ Anybody who wants to find out what the United Nations is doing for the women of the world is faced with a complicated and vast structure of organs, bodies and programmes.

The main characteristics of the present United Nations arrangements for women's advancement are multiplicity of focal points, diffused mandate, limited financial resources and inadequate interaction with national governments.[4]

Obtaining an overview is difficult indeed. Even understanding what the multitude of the commonly used abbreviations stand for takes time and patience. However, it is a sign of progress that so many parts of the UN family have included 'women' on their agenda. A recent report on the implementation of the Nairobi Forward-looking Strategies found:

A system of focal points [concerning the advancement of women] exists that consists of a network of responsible officials in 32 units of the United Nations Secretariat, seven United Nations programmes, 17 specialized agencies and 10 United Nations research institutes or inter-agency bodies.[5]

Not all of these parts of the UN are concerned primarily with the human rights of women, nor do they necessarily include human rights in their work, whatever their work is; indeed, few do. As wide-ranging and diffuse as women's issues are within the UN, women's rights additionally broaden them further by adding a different part of the United Nations structure, namely the human rights bodies. In theory, all women's issues should be co-ordinated by the Division for the Advancement of Women (DAW) while all human rights questions should be co-ordinated by the Centre for Human Rights. In practice, however, women's human rights fall through the cracks created by the lack of co-ordination – they are dispersed among different agenda items at the Commission and scattered among various human rights bodies. Nowhere is there a focal point for the human rights of women.

The United Nations represents an easy target for criticism – the UN can never do enough to solve the world's problems.

TABLE 9.2

SELECTED GENERAL ASSEMBLY RESOLUTIONS ON THE HUMAN RIGHTS OF WOMEN

11 Dec 1946	Political rights of women
23 Oct 1953	Technical assistance for the rights of women
23 Oct 1953	Political rights for women in territories where these rights are not fully enjoyed
17 Dec 1954	Status of women in private law: customs, ancient laws and practices affecting the human dignity of women
5 Dec 1963	Draft declaration on the elimination of discrimination against women
15 Dec 1975	Equality between men and women and elimination of discrimination against women
16 Dec 1976	Improvement of the status and role of women in education
29 Jan 1979	Improvement of the status and role of women in education and in the economic and social fields for the achievement of the equality of women with men
17 Dec 1979	Women refugees
14 Dec 1981	United Nations Decade for Women: equal right to work
16 Dec 1983	Prevention of prostitution
29 Nov 1985	Domestic violence
3 Nov 1989	Elderly women
14 Dec 1990	Women and literacy

TABLE 9.3 SELECTED GENERAL ASSEMBLY RESOLUTIONS ON WOMEN IN DEVELOPMENT

12 Dec 1960	United Nations assistance for the advancement of women in developing countries
5 Dec 1963	Participation of women in national, social and economic development
15 Dec 1970	Programme of international action for the advancement of women
18 Dec 1972	International Women's Year
17 Dec 1974	Women and development
15 Dec 1975	Integration of women in the development process
15 Dec 1975	Women in rural areas
16 Dec 1976	United Nations Decade for Women
21 Dec 1976	Effective mobilization of women in development
29 Jan 1979	Effective mobilization and integration of women in development
4 Dec 1981	Comprehensive outline of a world survey on the role of women in development
14 Dec 1981	Consideration within the United Nations of the role of women in development
14 Dec 1981	United Nations Decade for Women: Equality, Development and Peace
14 Dec 1984	Integration of women in all aspects of development
13 Dec 1985	Implementation of the Nairobi Forward-looking Strategies for the Advancement of Women

Note: These tables include resolutions selected by the criterion of their precedent-setting whereby new concepts or issues were placed on the agenda. Therefore they mention specific items only when they were first placed on the agenda. They do not include resolutions relating to the work of specific UN bodies and institutions nor resolutions dealing with UN programmes and meetings.

Some mention of its success is therefore appropriate. On the credit side the most notable success is in giving women's issues visibility worldwide and in laying down global norms for the eradication of gender discrimination. The series of UN awareness-raising activities, particularly in the 1980s, was a catalyst for introducing the gender component into the work of international organizations. There are few governments or inter-governmental organizations that do not have a women's department, section, or – to use the vogue term – a focal point. Promoting the application of norms against gender discrimination by these various bodies remains a task for the future. The mushrooming of such bodies followed the adoption of the major UN policy initiatives whereby gender aspects have been introduced into the key areas of international co-operation: development and peace. It is no coincidence that the motto of the International Decade for Women was Equality, Development and Peace. It is this first term, equality, which constitutes the bridge between the 'women's' and the 'human rights' agendas.

The UN human rights bodies have succeeded in overcoming the division of human rights into 'generations', which hinders progress in other areas, with regard to women. It is firmly established that the human rights of women include all rights: civil, political, economic, social and cultural. Moreover, elimination of discrimination includes both formally recognized rights and unequal opportunities for the enjoyment of these rights, thus de jure and de facto discrimination. And yet in addition to all this, the United Nations has recognized that the key to the progress of human rights in developing countries is to apply them in mainstream development. In fact, the gender perspective was included in international development co-operation before 'human rights' in 'development' became a global battleground.

HUMAN **RIGHTS ON WOMEN'S AGENDA** ☐ The progress in tackling human rights of women during the past four decades is noticeable. The United Nations started by arguing the need to recognize political rights for women, which – in the late 1940s – were recognized in few countries. Political rights were followed by a focus on gender discrimination in the private sphere, within family, neighbourhood and community. This was accomplished by the Commission on the Status of Women rather than by the UN human rights bodies. The focus in human rights has been and remains the public sphere, the relations between the government and the individual. This does not imply that women are not affected by these 'conventional' human rights problems. They are indeed, but women's human rights problems extend further and necessitate tackling the private alongside the public sphere.

The move beyond the formal recognition of equal rights to the identification of problems that specific categories of women face in trying to exercise their rights was apparent in changes of terminology. From demands that rights for women be equal to those enjoyed by men, international policies evolved towards the awareness that 'women' do not constitute a homogeneous group. Some categories are often deprived of their basic rights (rural, and refugee women, for example) and others are particularly susceptible to human rights violations (imprisoned women, prostitutes, for example). At the same time, women's concerns became articulated in international development policy and practice, in which the postulate of equality also moved far beyond the formal recognition of equal rights. It now entails the identification and elimination of multilayered gender discrimination: legal and factual, public and private, direct and indirect, visible and invisible, intentional and unintended. It also necessitates an understanding of the multiplicity of the grounds of discrimination affecting women: a woman may be subjected to discrimination because she is an asylum-seeker, disabled and a woman; because she is imprisoned, black, a foreigner, and a woman.

Whilst early efforts in standard-setting were aimed against the discriminatory heritage of humanity, the 1970s marked an orientation towards 'modernity'. It was realized that development might harm, rather than benefit women: when introduced into an unequal society, development tended to reinforce pre-existing inequalities.

The particular feature of human rights is that they are not spontaneously respected; improvements in human rights are not a necessary corollary of development. Therefore, human rights constitute governmental obligations. Non-discrimination is the key principle; hence promoting equal rights to and in development became the bridge between 'human rights' and 'development'.

The evolution of UN standard-setting is illustrated here by showing, first, how much attention has been paid to women, illustrated in Table 9.1 by the number of resolutions concerning women adopted in the past four decades. More than 500 resolutions have already been adopted by the UN's principal policy-making organ, the General Assembly. The Economic and Social Council (ECOSOC) is included alongside, as it co-ordinates the vast field of economic and social issues, which include both women and human rights.

The sheer number of adopted resolutions is subject to two interpretations: some see them as a tool for advocacy and an instrument for change, because they constitute the international community's recognition that a problem – such as the

THE FOURTH WORLD CONFERENCE ON WOMEN: ACTION FOR EQUALITY, DEVELOPMENT AND PEACE, BEIJING, 4–15 SEPTEMBER 1995

The Conference will focus on 'a limited number of issues that have been identified as representing a fundamental obstacle to the advancement of the majority of women'.* Among these, inequality figures prominently as do specific measures towards redressing it. The preparations for the Conference singled out the following nine priority areas:

- increasing awareness among men and women of women's rights under international conventions and national law;
- increasing the proportion of women in decision-making in the economic, social and political spheres;
- strengthening worldwide efforts to end illiteracy among women and girls by the year 2000;
- improving the conditions of women and girls living in poverty;
- improving women's and girls' health by ensuring them access to adequate maternal health care, family planning and nutrition;
- implementation of policies to prevent, control and reduce violence against women and girls in the family, the workplace and society;
- establishment or strengthening of national institutional mechanisms for the advancement of women;
- establishment of special programmes to meet the needs of refugee, displaced and migrant women and girls, and those living in conflict areas;
- elaboration of ways and means of using new and high technologies, as well as scientific research, to benefit women.*

The first area, namely increasing the awareness of women's rights, explicitly mentions women's human rights. Nevertheless, all the identified priority areas are relevant for articulating, promoting and defending human rights of women. The challenge of arguing them all in terms of women's human rights constitutes a challenge in the preparations for the Conference.

* SOURCE: *COMMISSION ON THE STATUS OF WOMEN – PREPARATIONS FOR THE WORLD CONFERENCE ON WOMEN IN 1995, RESOLUTION 35/4 OF 8 MARCH 1992*

TABLE 9.4 ILLUSTRATIVE HUMAN RIGHTS ISSUES ADDRESSED BY THE COMMISSION ON THE STATUS OF WOMEN

1947 Review of national legislation on the status of women
1952 Political rights of women
1954 Equal rights of spouses in matrimonial regimes
Rights of married women to work
1955 Equal rights of spouses regarding parental authority
Rights of a married women to independent domicile
1957 Citizenship of married women
1962 Equal rights relating to marriage
Equality of men and women in inheritance rights
1967 Elimination of discrimination against women
Equality in the exercise of parental authority
1968 Family planning and the status of women
1972 Equal rights for unmarried mothers
1974 Women and children in emergencies and armed conflicts
Full legal capacity of married women
Status of rural women
1975 Equal opportunities for women in development
1979 Women's Convention
1980 Persecution because of family affiliation
Prevention of exploitation of prostitution
Fundamental individual freedoms
1982 Women and children under apartheid
Elderly women
1984 Violence in the family
Physical violence against detained women
1986 Palestinian women
1987 National policies concerning the family
1989 Women and human rights in Central America
1990 Migrant women
Equality in political participation
1991 Violence against women
Disabled women

status of rural women, or domestic violence – merits its attention, and necessitates international co-operation towards its solution. Others see these resolutions as a substitute, rather than a basis for action, and point to the proliferation of resolutions adopted within the UN and the lack of evidence that these result in the changes that were advocated or requested by them.

These are really two sides of the same coin – resolutions can be an instrument for action only if used; tools which are not used serve no purpose.

The basic content of the major resolutions concerning the human rights of women is summarized in two tables: one (Table 9.2) identifies those that specifically address different human rights of

TABLE 9.5 DRAFTING THE WOMEN'S CONVENTION: CHRONOLOGY

1972 UN Secretary-General asked by the Commission on the Status of Women to solicit views of governments on the nature and content of a new international instrument on the human rights of women

1973 Following the positive views of many governments, ECOSOC accepts the proposal of the Commission on the Status of Women and appoints a 15-member Working Group to consider drafting a women's convention

1974 The Commission on the Status of Women decides to prepare a draft convention on the elimination of discrimination against women, originally intended as a contribution to International Women's Year (1975)

1975 The World Plan of Action, adopted by the Conference on International Women's Year, calls for 'convention on the elimination of discrimination against women with effective procedures for its implementation'

1976 The Commission on the Status of Women elaborates the draft convention; this draft is discussed by the Economic and Social Council and the Third (Legal) Committee of the General Assembly

1977 The General Assembly appoints the Working Group of the Whole to continue work on the Draft Convention

1978 The General Assembly recommends the Working Group to complete its task

1979 The General Assembly adopts the Convention and opens it for signature and ratification

1981 The Convention comes into force having received the required 20 ratifications

1982 CEDAW begins its work

women, and the other (Table 9.3) lists the main resolutions which relate to development, that is, aim to merge the first two parts of the Women's Decade motto, equality and development.

The terminology of the main United Nations policy documents relating to women in development illustrates changes in conceptualizing the gender dimensions of development. At the beginning the key-word had been to 'integrate' women into development, until it was realized that women are 'integrated' in development by carrying its burden, while absent from participation in the enjoyment of its benefits. The terminology recently changed to 'participation' to signify the need for participation in decision-making on both burdens and benefits, not only in the carrying of burdens.

COMMUNICATIONS CONCERNING GENDER DISCRIMINATION The Commission on the Status of Women deals with complaints concerning discrimination against women. This procedure is different from that for complaints of human rights violations. It aims to discern 'emerging trends and patterns of discrimination against women';[6] hence the focus is not on remedies for violations for the individual women, but on developing recommendations to the Economic and Social Council on policies that should be adopted to address specific and widespread types of discrimination affecting women which emerge from the communications as a whole. This procedure is orientated towards the identification of 'a consistent pattern of reliably attested injustice and discriminatory practices against women' and of 'the categories in which communications are most frequently submitted to the Commission';[7] information contained in such communications led in 1986 to the adoption of a resolution on the prevention of physical violence against women that is specific to their sex, and in 1991/92 to the elaboration of measures to prevent and remedy violence against women.

The purpose of this procedure, namely to identify emerging trends and patterns in gender discrimination, depends on whether the communications reflect the existing scope and severity of problems worldwide. While in theory every individual and organization can submit a communication, in practice the number of communications is small. One reason, which the Commission on the Status of Women often points to, is the lack of knowledge about this procedure. Another is the difference between this procedure and that for human rights violations, which diminishes the motivation to submit communications; this procedure does not provide redress to the affected women, it does not condemn – or even identify – those governments implicated in the communications. This special UN procedure specifically for women was designed not to give women an additional avenue for seeking redress but to examine global patterns and seek global solutions. A reason for the dearth of communications is, therefore, the fact that problems are experienced at the individual level whilst this procedure focuses on the global level. In 1990 this procedure was subjected to examination and governments were asked to comment on it. Only 24 responded; out of these the majority suggested that this communications procedure be modified. The debate continues.

HOW THE UN HUMAN RIGHTS SYSTEM WORKS ☐ International human rights law defines human rights, specifying the nature and scope of each right and freedom in turn. These rights constitute the corresponding obligations of governments. The acceptance of human rights as universal and inherent makes them subject to international scrutiny. Governments no longer have the ultimate say in judging how they treat their 'own' population. The international community, embodied in the United Nations, monitors the compliance of governments with their human rights obligations.

The human rights obligations form a part of international law and lay down the minimum, but universally applicable, standards. Because these are universal, human rights have been defined in such a way that any state, whatever its economic, political or legal system, is able to and must observe them. Nevertheless, challenges to the universality of human rights continue, and are particularly frequent with regard to equal rights of women, despite the fact that human rights obligations are fully binding on all governments and do not allow exceptions based on municipal law, cultural, religious or historical heritage.

Human rights entail two types of governmental obligations: (1) to prevent abuses of power (both political and economic); and (2) to create conditions for the realization of human rights and fundamental freedoms. Prohibitions have been defined quite well. Norms which require governments to undertake specific measures, rather than to refrain from a prohibited action, are more difficult to elaborate and monitor. Because they should be applicable universally, the existing differences in the capacity of countries to implement their obligations impede precise definitions.

Determining compliance is easier for prohibitive norms, which specify what a government should not do. It is also fairly easy with respect to human rights standards which require the government to achieve specified results. Compliance with norms requiring the government to undertake a specific type or method of action is more difficult to supervise.

The most important issue is, of course, the performance of the government. First and foremost, the government should incorporate universal human rights norms into its own rules of conduct. This means that the core obligation is to adopt human rights norms as part of the national law and apply them in policy and practice. The framework for monitoring compliance with human rights obligations therefore includes three levels of analysis: adherence to international human rights standards; their transformation into national law; and their implementation.

A government's adherence to international human rights instruments is indicative of its commitment to human rights. A mere ratification of a human rights treaty does not necessarily mean that human rights norms become operative in a country, but it demonstrates the willingness of the government to accept human rights obligations, adjust its laws and practice to international standards, and expose its record to international scrutiny. At least this is how it should be.

REPORTING Seven major human rights treaties envisage a system of international supervision, which obliges states parties to report on their implementation and enables supervisory bodies to evaluate their performance. This provides an insight into the governmental views on human rights, their efforts to implement human rights obligations or the lack thereof, and their reactions to criticism by international supervisory bodies.

These reporting procedures enable human rights bodies to determine whether national laws and practices conform to the international standards and to suggest necessary changes. Governments thereby submit their human rights records to international supervision. Reports are assess-

---

TABLE 9.6 HUMAN RIGHTS TREATIES – NUMBER OF COUNTRIES BOUND BY THEM

International Convention on the Elimination of All Forms of Racial Discrimination	132
Convention on the Rights of the Child	122
Convention on the Elimination of All Forms of Discrimination against Women	117
International Covenant on Economic, Social and Cultural Rights	116
International Covenant on Civil and Political Rights	113
International Convention on the Suppression and Punishment of the Crime of Apartheid	94
Convention against Torture and Other Cruel, Inhuman or Degrading Treatment or Punishment	68

Source: *Status of International human rights instruments. Report of the Secretary-General,* UN Doc. HRI/MC/1992/3 of 25 September 1992.

ments of the state of human rights by the government itself, a form of self-evaluation. Information is hence authoritative but not necessarily accurate. The reporting system is often criticized for the one-sided view of the state of human rights. The supervisory bodies rely primarily on information from governments and they, of course, do not advertise violations for which they may be condemned. The supervisory bodies, however, consist of experts acting in their personal capacity; they may and do rely on their knowledge of the countries under study, which broadens the sources of information used. The informal submission of information by human rights NGOs has become an accepted practice.

The multiple reporting procedures have created quite a burden for governments and changes are being introduced to ease it. Periodic meetings of chairpersons of all supervisory bodies have resulted in innovations. Thus governments can now prepare a core document in which generally the national situation and the human rights system are generally described for all different bodies. The number of overdue reports is also a serious problem. There is a paucity of reports from the developing countries, particularly from Africa. Already in 1985, the 'alarming number of overdue reports' was noted by the General Assembly.[8] If governments do not submit reports, the supervisory bodies cannot perform their functions. Solutions are sought in offering governments expert and technical assistance to facilitate the preparation of reports and of reporting manuals, and the organization of seminars for government officials.

The biggest success of the UN human rights system is the acceptance by all governments of the international community's power to scrutinize the observance of human rights. Virtually every country is party to some international human rights treaty which entails the obligation of reporting, hence its human rights performance is subject to international supervision.

Although the Women's Convention, monitored by CEDAW, deals specifically with the human rights of women, this also pertains to all human rights treaty bodies. Women constitute half of humanity, and protection from discrimination is the key human rights principle. It is worth repeating that there are no special or separate women's rights. If any 'special' right ought to be formulated it would be the right of women to be protected from gender discrimination. Human rights bodies are often criticized for addressing women's human rights in a fragmentary and superficial way. For example:

It has been only in more recent times that initiatives have been taken to address the violation of women's human rights and to give substance to women's equality with men. Indeed, it appears that the legal prohibition of gender discrimination was an incidental rather than a central concern of the institutions that the UN established to promote respect for human rights. The existing pattern of UN instruments and institutions for the protection and promotion of human rights may be regarded as offering women not so much the security that their rights are safeguarded as the opportunity for recognition that the wrongs done to them are violations of their rights.[9]

The examination of the state of women's rights can be illustrated by the work of the Human Rights Committee, which includes sex equality as an item in discussing every governmental report. This provides an opportunity to seek information about the description of the state of women's rights in these reports, but as such descriptions are rare, questions are more often asked about what should have been encompassed by the report but was absent. Two examples are provided below, representative of the dominant pattern of dialogues between the Human Rights Committee and representatives of governments: questions are numerous and wide-ranging, responses evasive.

Morocco: Members of the Committee asked whether an alien husband of a Moroccan woman was eligible for Moroccan citizenship on the same basis as a foreign woman married to a Moroccan husband; what was the basis for the different treatment under Moroccan law of men and women in respect of their capacity to transmit Moroccan nationality automatically to children born outside the country; what distinctions existed between men and women under the inheritance laws.
In addition, members of the Committee wished to know under what conditions women could join trade unions; whether a woman could obtain a passport without the authorization of her husband or, if she was not married, of her father; how many women held seats in Parliament and had access to the civil service, higher education and the liberal professions; whether the principle of 'equal pay for equal work' was applied in both the public and private sectors; why Morocco had not ratified the Convention on the Elimination of All Forms of Discrimination against Women.
In his reply, the representative [of Morocco] stated that a foreign woman marrying a Moroccan could, after two years of marriage, acquire Moroccan nationality simply by an order of the Minister of Justice; foreign husbands must have been married five years and obtain Moroccan nationality by decree ... Inheritance laws in Morocco were based directly on the principles of the Koran, and women were in a somewhat less favourable position in that respect. However, women had never requested the abolition of the Koranic rules applicable to them with regard to personal and inheritance status ... A husband's consent to the passport application and travel of his wife was required. Equality between men and women applied to the right to participate in elections either as a voter or as a candidate. Women were currently members of communal and provincial assemblies but although a number of them had stood for Parliament none had been elected.

Jordan: Members of the Committee asked for examples of any laws or regulations specifically prohibiting discrimination and providing appropriate penalties; for comments whether special difficulties were being encountered in ensuring respect for equality between men and women; for information on whether any specific remedies were available to a woman who claimed to have been a victim of discrimination and, in that connection, on whether there had been any cases where relief had been sought and, if so, with what results; and for clarification concerning the basis for the different treatment under Jordanian law of men and women. They also requested current data on the number of women in public office, the liberal professions, senior ranks of the civil service and private business; recent data on the proportion of women receiving primary, secondary and higher education ...
Members of the Committee also pointed out that sex was not included as one of the possible grounds for discrimination in the Jordanian Constitution ... They asked about the nature of dangerous activities women were prohibited from under the Jordanian Labour Act; whether men and women were equal in respect of the division of common property and the custody of children; and whether boys and girls had the same rights in relation to succession.
The representative of the State Party said that article 6 (a) of the Constitution prohibited any discrimination between Jordanians, who were equal before the law in respect of rights and duties ... The Jordanian government did not have any difficulty in ensuring equality between men and women ... women had always taken part and continued to take part in economic, social and cultural life. There were women in the upper house of the Parliament, and they played a

The Legal Resource Foundation (LRF) in Zimbabwe was established in 1984 to improve popular knowledge of law and thereby to make law more useful to people. This booklet guides the reader through different types of marriage and explains the consequences of each for the spouses and their children

particularly important role in education. There were nearly as many women as men in the civil service posts and in the private sector. In schools and universities, there were equal numbers of students of both sexes ... Matters of civil status relating to such matters as succession and inheritance, marriage and divorce were subject to the jurisdiction of religious tribunals in accordance with the belief of the individual.[10]

COMPLAINTS PROCEDURES The United Nations human rights work evolved from defining what human rights violations are, to condemning governments violating human rights, to developing procedures to prevent violations. The first steps, in the 1940s and 1960s, laid down the main substantive human rights standards in order to develop a globally applicable yardstick. It is worth recalling that the UN Commission on Human Rights started in 1947 by explicitly denying itself powers to consider complaints for human rights violations.[11] Only in the 1970s did it become possible to institute international complaints procedures; individuals experiencing human rights violations by their own state could now seek international investigation and condemnation. Critics of the international human rights system regularly emphasize that not all governments violating human rights are condemned, but they seldom stress the importance of this profound change: a government is no longer the judge in its own case; it can be held accountable internationally for what it does to its 'own' people.

Human rights work is perceived as denunciatory: governments are singled out for condemnation. However, condemning governments for human rights violations is neither the end nor the necessary means of human rights work. However (in)effectively it is done in an inter-governmental

111

system, it always comes too late. Hence procedures aimed at preventing the occurrence of violations were developed for those types of human rights violations that are universally considered to constitute violations – torture, summary and arbitrary executions, disappearances. Assistance to facilitate 'recovery from adverse consequences of a repressive regime'[12] constitutes a minuscule component of the United Nations human rights activities, and its orientation to meetings and publications rather than projects is often criticized.[13]

Complaints, addressed to the Secretary-General of the United Nations, have been estimated at 300,000 per year. In addition, there are several hundred human rights organizations contributing information on violations in their submissions to the UN's human rights organs. Individual complaints are submitted under the human rights treaties from those countries whose governments have accepted these treaty provisions. The larger part of complaints are not linked to treaties, but submitted to the 'political' bodies. In practice, there is not much difference between the 'political' and the 'legal' procedure, due to the inter-governmental nature of both. The main distinction between the two methods, the 'legal' and the 'political', is their ultimate purpose. A 'legal' complaint demands an investigation of the alleged violation and an authoritative pronouncement by the competent human rights body. The purpose is to seek the application of human rights law, to obtain an official determination of the violation and compensation for the victim.

An increasing number of human rights NGOs bring up particular cases of alleged human rights violations to the agenda of the UN human rights bodies, primarily the Commission on Human Rights and its Sub-Commission. NGO submissions and oral interventions today represent an influential source of information on human rights, although mainly on violations. The NGOs use their main weapon – information – to its utmost. A simple proposal to place a specific country on the human rights agenda for violations triggers off fierce diplomatic and political activity. Resolutions of the Sub-Commission and Commission consequently provide a list of governments whose blacklisting a sufficient number of other governments support, rather than include all countries where there are serious and widespread human rights violations.

VIOLATIONS OF WOMEN'S RIGHTS ON THE HUMAN RIGHTS AGENDA

☐ An overview of violations of the human rights of women necessitates sifting through mountains of documents produced by various human rights bodies. There is no separate agenda item specifically on women which would make such an overview easy and comprehensive. Reasons for this are many. One, often voiced by women's organizations, is the traditional disregard for women in human rights much as in other areas. Another reason is that it is often difficult to determine whether a specific human rights violation is gender-specific, or whether women are victimized for reasons unrelated to their sex. However, because such analysis is rare, even those violations which are gender-specific are often not dealt with as human rights issues.

Women's human rights are scattered amongst many items on the UN human rights agenda. For example, at the 1991 session of the Sub-Commission for Prevention of Discrimination and Protection of Minorities, specific problems of the human rights of women were discussed in the context of reports on the human rights situation in Iran and Kuwait, traditional practices affecting the health of women and children, the report of the Working Group on Contemporary Forms of

TABLE 9.7
COMPLAINTS OF HUMAN RIGHTS VIOLATIONS: 1503 PROCEDURE

Step 1	Complaints from individuals and organizations received and registered by the UN Centre for Human Rights.
Step 2	The Centre for Human Rights acknowledges receipt, and sends a copy to the government of the country where the alleged violation took place for its reply. The Centre analyses and summarizes the received complaints in a monthly confidential document.
Step 3	The Working Group on Communications meets annually before each session of the Sub-Commission on Prevention of Discrimination and Protection of Minorities and considers all communications, including replies from governments. It decides which communications appear to reveal a consistent pattern of gross and reliably attested violations and thus which should be brought to the attention of the Sub-Commission. The Sub-Commission, on the basis of the confidential report of its Working Group, decides at a closed meeting which country situations to refer to the Commission on Human Rights, and which to defer action or take no action on.
Step 4	The Working Group on Situations meets annually before each session of the Commission and examines cases referred to in the confidential report of the Sub-Commission. It elaborates recommendations to the Commission on what type of action to take regarding specific country situations.
Step 5	The Commission on Human Rights examines at closed sessions country situations which appear to reveal a consistent pattern of gross and systematic violations. This includes a dialogue with the respective governments about possible measures to remedy the situation. The Commission may ultimately condemn individual governments for violations of human rights.

Slavery, and the initative to seek an advisory opinion from the International Court of Justice (ICJ) on the validity of reservations to the Women's Convention.

It is a positive development that special rapporteurs on country situations have begun to include in their documents specific human rights problems affecting women, although this practice is recent and the absence of any mention of women prevalent. This development reflects, for the most part, not the fact that women's rights are fully protected, because special rapporteurs are appointed precisely to report on those countries where human rights violations are prevalent, but on the neglect of women. During the 1991 session, the Sub-Commission adopted a resolution on human rights in Iran, explicitly referring to the finding of the Special Rapporteur of 'gross violations of women's and children's rights', and deplored 'the widespread public flogging of women'.[14] The Special Rapporteur included in his subsequent report the following description:

On 26 July 1991, in downtown Isfahan, a group of women were allegedly harassed, beaten and arrested by Revolutionary Guards on the charge of being improperly veiled. Various groups of people attempted to free the arrested women from the Guards, and were allegedly shot and wounded by the Guards who opened fire in an attempt to disperse them; 355 persons were allegedly arrested. According to *Salaam* of 29 July 1991, the clash began after police and members of the 'Headquarters to combat social vices' organization stopped women in a central Isfahan square. *Salaam* referred to notorious elements who came to the support of women breaking the dress code, shouting 'deviationist slogans' before smashing windows in the city centre. According to a Reuters cable of 29 July 1991, the clash was the biggest reported in recent years over enforcement of the dress code.[15]

Much criticism has been focused on the UN human rights bodies by NGOs and scholars because of their insufficient attention to the violations of women's rights. This has been joined by self-criticism. The Vice-Chairman of the Commission on Human Rights, summarizing its work at its 1991 session, singled out this notable gap in the work of the Commission:

Another lacuna concerned the question of women's rights, the position of which within the Commission was distinctly marginal. Admittedly, the Vienna-based Commission on the Status of Women had done a great deal of work in that field, but this work should, perhaps, be consolidated by the Commission on Human Rights, with a specific agenda item allocated to the question.[16]

THE HUMAN RIGHTS COMMITTEE Of the complaints procedures established by the human rights treaties, the practice of the Human Rights Committee is the most advanced. The Committee receives individual complaints (called 'communications') from those countries whose governments ratified the Optional Protocol to the ICCPR, which allows individuals to pursue their complaints internationally after having exhausted domestic remedies. The list of these countries is found in Table 9.8. One reason for the paucity of complaints is that too few countries allow their citizens to utilize international human rights complaint procedures. Indeed, the list of parties to the Optional Protocol illustrates this well. However, even in countries which are party to this Protocol information about its provisions and available remedies is not widely known, particularly among women's organizations; hence the dearth of cases.

The few international cases brought before the Human Rights Committee show that African women are determined to seek redress – when they are allowed to and when they know about this procedure. It may have come as a surprise that the denial of equal rights concerning citizenship figured as the first prominent case. Many would expect, wrongly, that the priority issues for which women would resort to international human rights procedures would be land ownership or access to paid employment. Others would assume, wrongly again, that such basic issues as citizenship have been solved for all a long time ago. Such assumptions have to be dispelled to open the way for increased use of international complaints procedures by women.

The problems faced by African women regarding citizenship have been summarized as follows:

Is the African woman a national of her own country? In how many countries does she have legal citizenship? Research shows that some countries have still not rewritten their inherited or settler Constitutions whereby women were legal minors.[17]

Citizenship is not a negligible issue, because it determines the whole range of civic and political rights, including the right to vote. African women are discriminated against by the dominance of *jus sanguinis* in national laws, whereby the father's citizenship determines that of his children. A woman cannot transmit her citizenship to her husband or to her children and may indeed lose her own when marrying a foreigner. Similar provisions that adopt this approach are found in the laws of Botswana, Egypt, Mozambique, Swaziland, Tanzania, Zambia, and Zimbabwe.[18] The law of Botswana has recently been successfully challenged by Unity Dow, whose case has attained worldwide publicity.

THE WOMEN'S CONVENTION □

Evidence of the level of commitment to non-discrimination worldwide is apparent in the number of ratifications for each of the anti-discrimination conventions: the Convention against Racial Discrimination leads with more than two-thirds of countries being parties, and the Women's Convention comes second. The number of countries bound by each human rights treaty is given in Table 9.6. The Women's Convention had the fastest ratification record of all human rights treaties; the Convention on the Rights of the Child, adopted in 1989, has done even better.

Years of work towards a legally binding instrument against gender discrimination, illustrated by Table 9.4, resulted in 1979 in the adoption of the Women's Convention. The preamble of this Convention expresses the commitment 'to adopt measures required for the elimination of [gender] discrimination in all its forms and manifestations'. This is reflected in 'the unique character of the Women's Convention as an instrument among other human rights conventions [in] that it requires states parties to tackle discrimination in the private lives and relationships of their citizens, and not simply in public sector activities'.[19]

TABLE 9.8
PARTIES TO THE OPTIONAL PROTOCOL TO THE ICCPR

● Algeria	● Luxembourg
● Angola	● Madagascar
● Argentina	● Malta
● Australia	● Mauritius
● Austria	● Mongolia
● Barbados	● Nepal
● Belarus	● Netherlands
● Benin	● New Zealand
● Bolivia	● Nicaragua
● Bulgaria	● Niger
● Cameroon	● Norway
● Canada	● Panama
● Central African Republic	● Peru
● Chile	● Philippines
● Colombia	● Poland
● Congo	● Portugal
● Costa Rica	● Republic of Korea
● Cyprus	● Russian Federation
● Czechoslovakia	● St Vincent and
● Denmark	Grenadines
● Dominican Republic	● San Marino
● Ecuador	● Senegal
● Equatorial Guinea	● Seychelles
● Estonia	● Somalia
● Finland	● Spain
● France	● Suriname
● Gambia	● Sweden
● Hungary	● Togo
● Iceland	● Trinidad and Tobago
● Ireland	● Ukraine
● Italy	● Uruguay
● Jamaica	● Venezuela
● Libya	● Zaire
● Lithuania	● Zambia

More than half of the international community is today not only morally and politically, but also legally committed to eliminate discrimination against women. The number of parties would have been a sign of real success were it not for the fact that many, too many, states which ratified the Convention submitted reservations to

115

TABLE 9.9 COUNTRIES WHICH HAVE NOT RATIFIED THE WOMEN'S CONVENTION

- Afghanistan
- Albania
- Algeria
- Bahamas
- Bahrain
- Botswana
- Brunei Darussalam
- Burma
- Cambodia
- Cameroon
- Chad
- Comores
- Côte d'Ivoire
- Djibouti
- Fiji
- Gambia
- India
- Iran
- Korean DPR
- Kuwait
- Lebanon
- Lesotho
- Liechtenstein
- Lithuania
- Malaysia
- Maldives
- Marshall Islands
- Mauritania
- Micronesia
- Morocco
- Mozambique
- Namibia
- Niger
- Oman
- Pakistan
- Papua New Guinea
- Qatar
- Samoa
- São Tome and Principe
- Saudi Arabia
- Singapore
- Solomon Islands
- Somalia
- South Africa
- Sudan
- Surinam
- Swaziland
- Switzerland
- Syria
- United Arab Emirates
- USA
- Vanuatu

it. Those countries which have not yet become party to the Women's Convention are listed in Table 9.9.

In order to facilitate the process of undertaking human rights obligations, governments are allowed to reserve the right not to apply a specific part of a treaty. They must declare that this is so when ratifying a treaty by submitting a reservation. This procedure is designed to help the achievements of human rights by providing for exceptions to those human rights guarantees that governments cannot immediately and fully undertake at the time of ratification. It is not intended to enable governments to behave in a self-contradictory manner: to ratify a human

rights treaty and thus express their commitment to abide by it, but to reserve their right not to apply the crucial human rights safeguards that such a treaty requires.

Much controversy has been created regarding the Women's Convention because reservations in many cases seem contrary to the very aim of the Convention. Thereby individual governments have limited the recognition of the full scope of women's rights, as laid down in the Convention, for women on their territory. Table 9.10 lists parties to the Women's Convention and those which submitted reservations are marked. The content of reservations is presented in Table 9.11. Some reservations which relate to the adjudication of disputes concerning the interpretation and application of the Convention, where governments refused to submit their possible disputes to the ICJ, are not dealt with here.

As can be seen from Table 9.11, many reservations refer to specific provisions of the Convention, including the general principle of non-discrimination. These are important because they indicate governments' unwillingness to undertake a commitment to eradicate discrimination against women in all its forms, which is the aim of the Convention. Table 9.11 lists the main provisions of the Convention to which reservations have been submitted by specific countries. Those which submitted reservations when signing the Convention, namely when expressing their consent to be bound by its spirit but not undertaking a legal commitment to implement it, are marked by square brackets. The purpose of this Table is to show that there is a high degree of universal consensus with respect to some of its provisions. It is particularly noteworthy that no reservations have been entered with respect to the provisions concerning the improvement of the status of rural women, which is crucial in many

TABLE 9.10 PARTIES TO THE WOMEN'S CONVENTION [THOSE WHICH SUBMITTED RESERVATIONS ARE MARKED BY ASTERISK]

- Angola
- Antigua and Barbuda
- Argentina*
- Australia*
- Austria*
- Bangladesh*
- Barbados
- Belarus
- Belgium*
- Belize
- Benin
- Bhutan
- Bolivia
- Brazil*
- Bulgaria*
- Burkina Faso
- Burundi
- Canada*
- Cape Verde
- Central African Republic
- Chile
- China*
- Colombia
- Congo
- Costa Rica
- Cuba*
- Cyprus*
- Czechoslovakia
- Denmark
- Dominica
- Dominican Republic
- Ecuador
- Egypt*
- El Salvador*
- Equatorial Guinea
- Estonia
- Ethiopia*
- Finland
- France*
- Gabon
- Germany*
- Ghana
- Greece
- Grenada
- Guatemala
- Guinea
- Guinea-Bissau
- Guyana
- Haiti
- Honduras
- Hungary
- Iceland
- Indonesia*
- Iraq*
- Ireland*
- Israel*
- Italy*
- Jamaica*
- Japan
- Jordan*
- Kenya
- Laos
- Latvia
- Liberia
- Libya*
- Luxembourg*
- Madagascar
- Malawi*
- Mali
- Malta*
- Mauritius*
- Mexico*
- Mongolia
- Nepal
- Netherlands
- New Zealand*
- Nicaragua
- Nigeria
- Norway
- Panama
- Paraguay
- Peru
- Philippines
- Poland*
- Portugal
- Republic of Korea*
- Romania*
- Russia
- Rwanda
- St Kitts and Nevis
- St Lucia
- St Vincent and Grenadines
- Senegal
- Seychelles
- Sierra Leone
- Spain*
- Sri Lanka
- Sweden
- Tanzania
- Thailand*
- Togo
- Trinidad and Tobago*
- Tunisia*
- Turkey*
- Uganda
- Ukraine
- United Kingdom*
- Uruguay
- Venezuela*
- Vietnam*
- Yemen
- [Yugoslavia]
- Zaire
- Zambia
- Zimbabwe

developing countries. It is no coincidence that both the Convention and women-in-development guidelines make rural women their principal concern.

Table 9.11 clearly shows that most reservations have been entered with respect to non-discrimination in family law and citizenship, and to women's legal capacity. More importantly, countries which apply Shari'a Law (Bangladesh, Egypt and Iraq) submitted reservations concerning the very obligation to eliminate gender discrimination. Two examples below illustrate how far-reaching some reservations are:

Libya: **[Accession] is subject to the general reservation that such accession cannot conflict with the laws on personal status derived from the Islamic Sharia.**

Malawi: **Owing to the deep-rooted nature of some traditional customs and practices of Malawians, the Government of the Republic of Malawi shall not, for the time being, consider itself bound by such of the provisions of the Convention as require immediate eradication of such traditional customs and practices.**

Some reservations reflect the exclusively male heritage in the exercise of royal powers (Belgium, Luxembourg, Spain), others exclude women from employment in the armed forces or from access to combat duties (Germany, New Zealand, Thailand), yet others restrict the employment of women in night work or work deemed hazardous to their health (Malta, United Kingdom). Most, however, retain restrictions on equal rights regarding personal status – as to marriage, family, citizenship, legal status of women.

BATTLE FOR EQUAL RIGHTS CONTINUES

While reservations made possible the ratification of the Women's Convention by virtually all countries because they can opt

TABLE 9.11 RESERVATIONS TO THE WOMEN'S CONVENTION

Substantive provisions	Reservations
Definition of discrimination (Art. 1)	United Kingdom
Commitment to eradicate discrimination (Art. 2)	Bangladesh, Cook Islands, Egypt, Iraq, [Libya], Malawi, Tunisia, United Kingdom
Measures to accelerate *de facto* equality (Art. 4)	[Malawi]
Measures to eliminate prejudices and stereotyping (Art. 5)	Cook Islands, France, [India]
Elimination of discrimination in political and public life (Art. 7)	Austria, Belgium, Germany, Luxembourg, Spain, Thailand
Equal citizenship rights (Art. 9)	Cyprus, Egypt, France, Iraq, Jamaica, Jordan, Korea, Thailand, Tunisia, [Turkey], United Kingdom
Elimination of discrimination in education (Art. 10)	Thailand, United Kingdom
Elimination of discrimination in employment (Art. 11)	Malta, Mauritius, New Zealand, Thailand, United Kingdom
Equal labour rights (Art. 11)	Australia, Austria, Ireland, New Zealand, Thailand, United Kingdom
Equal access to financial credits (Art. 13)	Bangladesh, Ireland, Malta, United Kingdom
Full legal capacity (Art. 15)	Austria, Brazil, Ireland, [Libya], Jordan, Malta, Thailand, Tunisia, Turkey, United Kingdom
Elimination of discrimination in marriage and the family (Art. 16)	Bangladesh, Brazil, Egypt, France, [India], Iraq, Ireland, Jordan, [Libya], Luxembourg, Malta, Mauritius, Korea, Thailand, Tunisia, Turkey, United Kingdom

out of some of its requirements, they also jeopardized the integral and effective application of the Convention as a whole. In other words, the problem is that the formal adherence to the Women's Convention is not accompanied by full commitment to the Convention. This problem led to repeated calls upon the United Nations to secure an authoritative determination of the permissibility of reservations that apparently undermine the commitment to the core human rights obligations towards women. This has not precluded efforts to persuade individual governments to withdraw their reservations, and quite a few have done so: Belarus, Czechoslovakia, Hungary, Mongolia, Russia, and Ukraine all withdrew their reservations to the submission of possible disputes to the ICJ. Some substantive reservations have been withdrawn by France, Ireland, Malawi, New Zealand, Republic of Korea, and Thailand.

Following the initiative of CEDAW members, Canada placed the issue of reservations on the agenda of the meeting of parties to the Convention which took place in 1986. This meeting asked the UN Secretary-General to solicit all parties' views on reservations.[20] Few governments submitted their views on reservations: only 17 out of more than 100 states parties, thus less than 20 per cent of the parties to the Convention.[21] Moreover, these reiterated the disagreement(s) among governments, evidenced before and continued thereafter. The next meeting of the parties to the Convention, held in 1988, did not resolve the problem.[22] Reservations to the Women's Convention have entered the political arena, and debates have been held at the ECOSOC and the General Assembly. Because most explicit and all-encompassing reservations were entered by those governments which invoked the Convention's incompatibility with Shari'a, objections have been raised that the movement against reservations was anti-Islamic.

The prevailing attitude of governments seems to be that it is preferable to have the maximum number of countries formally participating in the Women's Convention than to uphold a commitment to the main requirements of the Convention.

Most recently, this issue has been placed on the agenda of the Sub-Commission. In 1991 it started debating the 'validity of reservations to the Convention on the Elimination of All Forms of Discrimination against Women', and in August 1992 adopted a resolution. It is worthwhile to cite reasons for seeking an authoritative determination of the validity of reservations:

[The Sub-Commission on Prevention of Discrimination and Protection of Minorities]
- **Stressing that the Convention on the Elimination of All Forms of Discrimination against Women was adopted to eliminate discrimination against women in all its forms and manifestations;**
- **Concerned, however, that over 20 of the 107 States Parties have filed more than 80 substantive reservations with respect to their obligations to implement the Convention;**
- **Concerned also that certain reservations to the Convention, in particular, those in relation to the adoption of policies and institutional measures to implement the terms of the Convention (art. 2), political and public life (art. 7), discrimination in the field of employment (art. 11), equality of men and women before the law (art. 15), and marriage and family relations (art. 16), might diminish the international legal norm and legitimize its violation;**
- **Bearing in mind that the frustration of the objectives of the Convention, because of such reservations, is contributing to the phenomenon of the exploitation of women.[23]**

The practical implications of reservations can be described by taking Bangladesh as an example. At the time of ratification, on 6 November 1984, the government submitted its reservations on a number of articles of the Convention, including the key article on the policy of non-discrimination. The prohibition of gender discrimination, equal rights of spouses and equal rights and responsibilities of parents with regard to their children were declared not binding upon Bangladesh 'as they conflict with Shari'a law based on Holy Koran and Sunna.'[24] Numerous objections were raised to this reservation, both by other states parties to the Convention, and by CEDAW. Mexico and Germany objected to Bangladeshi reservations, stating their incompatibility with the object and purpose of the Convention. The government of Sweden explained its objections at greater length. It said that the reservations in question, if put into practice, would inevitably result in discrimination against women on the basis of their sex, which was against everything the Convention stood for. It concluded by saying that, if tolerated, such reservations would make human rights obligations meaningless.[25]

During consideration of the initial report of Bangladesh on the implementation of the Convention, CEDAW raised the issue of reservations as the crucial problem; CEDAW hoped that the government would soon withdraw its reservations.[26] The role of international assistance in putting equal rights of women into practice was raised by the representative of Bangladesh, who inquired about possibilities of obtaining financial assistance to help with reporting. The response was, at the time, disappointing: 'no funds were available at present for assisting States Parties in the preparation of reports. However, the Committee might wish to adopt a recommendation on the subject. Assistance might perhaps be provided under the UNDP to countries requesting it.'[27]

The example of Bangladesh is far from unique regarding the need for international assistance. To begin with, the reporting system does not function well, because of the increasing number of overdue reports from governments. More importantly, it is easy to imagine how much investment is necessary to translate women's equal rights into national practice. Many developing countries simply do not possess sufficient resources, infrastructure and expertise to carry out their obligations under the Convention. Assistance to governments to implement their obligations in the field of women's rights could constitute a useful, non-controversial and welcome contribution towards the promotion of women's human rights. This assistance could include the preparation of manuals on reporting, training seminars, and financial support to those countries which do not have sufficient resources to prepare comprehensive overviews of the state of women's rights. However, much more could be done to promote support for the realization of women's equal rights through international development assistance. Thereby, the Women's Convention could become a genuine tool for development.

CEDAW ☐ The Women's Convention, much as any other human rights treaty, lays down human rights norms which are necessarily worded in abstract terms. Moreover, these treaties are negotiated during protracted and sometimes conflictual inter-governmental meetings. In the case of the Women's Convention, the draftspersons 'had to face the difficult task of preparing a text applicable to societies of different cultural characteristics and traditions. The ways in which discrimination against women manifested itself varied from one culture to another. The Draft Convention therefore represented a constructive compromise.'[28] Specificity and clarity are thus attained through the interpretation and application of the Convention. It is through the reporting process that the Convention is translated

EQUAL RIGHTS FOR THE GIRL CHILD:

An emerging strategy combining the Women's and Children's Conventions

The importance of building and developing common strategies for women and children has already emerged. The Commission on the Status of Women has supported a proposal of UNICEF's Executive Board to focus on issues concerning girl children by reference to standards sets in both Conventions. The Commission has also called for closer links between the monitoring committees set up under these two Conventions. Women's movements in various countries have protested against child pornography and child trafficking, and have lobbied actively for law reform and social policies for child victims of exploitation. Particular problems such as cultural practices that adversely affect the health of women and children have been identified as important areas for common action.

In industrialized countries, where equal opportunities for girls and boys is no longer a controversial issue, the link between child rights and women's rights may be seen as a regression to an era when these two groups were linked by common disabilities in patriarchal societies ... In developing countries, however, the enormous breakthrough required for the recognition of gender equality in terms of access to opportunity will not come about unless there is a committed effort to address the issue of discrimination against girl children. This must be combined with action on women's issues. Constitutions provide for affirmative action on behalf of women and children, but very little has been done to initiate policy interventions that address the special needs of girl children. Yet, only when attitudes change, inequalities are removed and increased opportunities are made available to girl children – the women of tomorrow – will become unnecessary to perceive women as a 'disadvantaged' sector of an adult population.

S. Gooneseke – 'Women's rights and children's rights: The United Nations Conventions as compatible and complementary international treaties', *Innocenti Occasional Papers, Child Rights Series*, No.1, Florence, September 1992, pp.37–8.

from abstract requirements into the yardstick to monitor the realization of the human rights of women. At least, this should be so in theory.

CEDAW has been established on the basis of the Convention, with its main task to monitor progress made in the implementation of the Convention. It consists of experts – all women – who have been appointed in their individual capacity rather than as representatives of their countries. What this entails in practice has been explained as follows:

Although **CEDAW is not a body of governmental representatives**, it is nonetheless created by governments and its members are nominated and elected to the Committee by States Parties [to the Convention]. Governments are also in a position to influence the allocation of resources to the Committee. Thus, the scope of its activities and its effectiveness are ultimately constrained by the support which States Parties are willing to give it. By the same token, the nature of the Committee means that it has a level of access to governments which other groups may lack.[29]

The Women's Convention does not allow individual women to submit complaints about violations of their rights as recognized by the Convention. The only means of examining the application of the Convention is therefore through governmental reports. The initial report has to be submitted within the first year of the entry into force of the Convention, with periodic reports every four years thereafter. CEDAW is, much as other human rights treaty bodies, severely constrained in its work by the failure of governments to submit reports or by delays in submission. An overview of overdue reports is presented in Table 9.12. When submitted, reports are sometimes very short, sometimes they do not respond to the requirements of examining the state of women's human rights. Regarding the length of reports, for example, it is easy to imagine how little is known about the realization of the human rights of women when a government submits a report which is just two pages long. This was the case of Mali in 1987.[30]

CEDAW has elaborated guidelines for the preparation of reports.[31] Another example of the manner whereby the Convention's requirements can be translated into guidance for reporting is provided by the International Women's Rights Action Watch (IWRAW) in its set of questions relating to the first articles of the Convention which deal with discrimination in general:

- **Are there policy statements or laws that define discrimination against women? What do they say?**
- **Is the definition of discrimination sufficiently broad or interpreted broadly enough to cover practices which are discriminatory in their effect, even if they are not intended to discriminate?**
- **Does the Constitution, if there is one, include a guarantee of non-discrimination on the basis of sex or a guarantee of equality? If not, what work is being done to amend the Constitution and what are the obstacles to such an amendment?**
- **What laws or administrative provisions, if any, discriminate against women? Are they in the process of being repealed or changed?**
- **What legislative or administrative measures have been adopted to prohibit or to eliminate discrimination against women?**
- **Are there any penalties, such as fines or loss of government contracts, imposed for discrimination against women? If so, what are they? Have they been applied?**
- **Do courts or other tribunals affirm or protect the rights of women? How many cases of discrimination have been brought before the courts or government bodies in the last four years? How were they decided?**
- **Are there policies or practices of government or other public institutions that discriminate against women?**
- **What measures, if any, have been adopted to advance or improve the situation of women and to guarantee women fundamental freedoms and equal rights?**
- **What are the practical obstacles that prevent women from attaining their full development, fundamental freedoms, and equal rights?**

Governmental reports are, not surprisingly, rarely self-critical. In most cases they reproduce the existing constitutional and legal provisions relating to non-discrimination, and do not venture into analysing their application nor indeed obstacles to the enjoyment of equal rights by all women. Not only is there often a wide gap between formal legal status and reality, but also the Convention itself requires the eradication of *de facto* discrimination. Without data on the actual position of women regarding all their human rights and fundamental freedoms *de facto* discrimination remains invisible, and policies for its eradication are difficult to elaborate.

CEDAW, following the practice of other human rights treaty bodies, has adopted the practice of 'constructive dialogue' in the examination of reports by states parties. These reports are discussed at public sessions in the presence of representatives of the State Party who introduce the report and respond to questions and comments by the members of CEDAW. Quite often these questions relate to issues which have not been addressed in the report, but they frequently venture into examining whether a specific law, policy or practice is consistent with the requirements of the Convention. CEDAW has been criticized for failing to move one step further and declare when and where a national law, government's policy, or country's practice constitutes a breach of the Convention.

TABLE 9.12 OVERDUE REPORTS UNDER THE WOMEN'S CONVENTION

Countries which have not reported as yet and the year when the first report was due

- Angola (1987)
- Antigua and Barbuda (1990)
- Belize (1991)
- Bhutan (1982)
- Brazil (1985)
- Cape Verde (1982)
- Congo (1983)
- Costa Rica (1987)
- Cyprus (1986)
- Dominica (1982)
- Ethiopia (1982)
- Grenada (1991)
- Guinea (1983)
- Guinea-Bissau (1986)
- Haiti (1982)
- Iceland (1986)
- Laos (1982)
- Liberia (1985)
- Luxembourg (1990)
- Paraguay (1988)
- St Kitts and Nevis (1986)
- St Lucia (1983)
- Sierra Leone (1989)
- Togo (1984)
- Trinidad and Tobago (1990)
- Tunisia (1986)
- Uganda (1986)
- Zaire (1987)

A particular manifestation of this avoidance of collective pronouncements is the fact that CEDAW has never formally pronounced a State Party to be in violation of the Convention, even though the members have clearly felt that some States have failed to carry out their obligations.[32]

This feature of CEDAW's practice has resulted in the impossibility of discerning how the Women's Convention should be interpreted and applied. Along with the absence of international jurisprudence concerning gender discrimination, this hinders progress towards a body of knowledge about violations of the human rights of women.

CEDAW did not have an easy start in the dominantly male inter-governmental structure. An illustrative example was the consideration of the report of the Philippines in 1984, during which the (male) representative of the Philippines had made some remarks, for which his government later apologized. He stated the following:

In replying to some of the questions raised, the Permanent Representative of the Philippines to the United Nations, in his capacity as representative of the State Party, explained that in his perception there were cultural and traditional aspects in every country which could not be legislated. His culture regarded both sexes not as equal but as complementary to each other.

In responding to questions raised by the experts, the representative of the State Party expressed some personal views and perceptions on the role of women in the Philippines. He said that it was preferred that its women retain their femininity and gentleness because, in such a way, they had obtained many advantages and progress. It was for that reason that no women's liberation movement had existed in the Philippines.[33]

Like other UN human rights bodies, CEDAW was earlier affected by the ideological battles between East and West. East European countries tended to report that no gender discrimination existed. For example, Romania reported that 'all discrimination against women, who are equal in rights with men, has disappeared'.[34] Such assertions were not confined to East European countries, as can be seen from the responses to CEDAW's questions by the representative of Egypt:

With respect to the prescriptions of the Islamic religious law, Shari'a, and its effects on a reservation made on Article 16 of the Convention, [the representative of Egypt] explained that Islamic law had given a prominent position to all women and liberated them from any form of discrimination.

Except for certain rights and responsibilities during marriage and at its dissolution, Islamic law had given to women all the necessary rights even before the ratification of the Convention.[35]

The reporting procedures are necessarily constrained by the government being the sole source of information. It is understandable that governments are not eager to publicize their failure(s) to implement their human rights obligations, although this constitutes the major obstacle to identifying such failures and remedying them. In practice, this obstacle has been considerably diminished by NGOs, many of which provide members of human rights treaty bodies with information which supplements and often contradicts that provided by the government. Some treaty bodies, the Committee on Economic, Social and Cultural Rights, the Committee against Torture, and the Committee on the Rights of the Child, are formally entitled to receive information from NGOs. Others, including CEDAW, do not have any formally adopted rules and procedures relating to NGOs.

1. United Nations (1984) *The United Nations and Human Rights*, New York, Sales No. E.84.I.6, p. 148.
2. 'Roll call of human rights instruments', *United Nations Chronicle*, Vol. XXI, No. 2, February 1984, p. v.
3. J. Morsink, 'Women's rights in the Universal Declaration', *Human Rights Quarterly*, Vol. 13, May 1991, No. 2, pp. 229–56.
4. K. Haq, 'The role of the UN for advancement of women – a proposal', *Development. Journal of SID*, Rome, 1989, No. 4, p. 51.
5. 'Implementation of the Nairobi Forward–looking Strategies for the Advancement of Women. Report of the Secretary–General', UN Doc. A/45/489 of 18 October 1990, para. 56.
6. Commission on the Status of Women, 'Communications on the status of women', resolution of 16 March 1992, para. 1.
7. Economic and Social Council, Resolution 1983/27 of 26 May 1983, paras. 4(a) and 4(b).
8. In 1985 there were 384 overdue reports, in 1986, 460. Countries with the largest number of overdue reports were Guyana (13), Libya (13), Zaire (12), Tanzania (11), Gambia (10), and Liberia (10); cf. 'Reporting obligations of States parties to United Nations conventions on human rights, Report of the Secretary-General', UN Doc. A/41/510 of 11 August 1986.
9. R. Cook, 'Women' in Schachter, O. and Joyner, C. (eds) (1992) *The United Nations and the International Legal Order*, American Society of International Law, Washington DC, mimeograph, p. 1.
10. Report of the Human Rights Committee (1991) UN Doc. A/46/40, paras. 243–6 and 579–83.
11. United Nations, *Commission on Human Rights. Report of the First Session*, UN Doc. E/259, 1947, paras. 21–2.
12. T. van Boven, 'Human rights and development: The UN experience' in D.P. Forsythe (ed.) (1989) *Human Rights and Development. International Views*, MacMillan, 130.
13. Cf. *UN Assistance for Human Rights*, Räda Barnen and International Commission of Jurists, Stockholm, September 1988.
14. Sub-Commission on Prevention of Discrimination and Protection of Minorities, Resolution 1991/9 on the situation of human rights in the Islamic Republic of Iran of 29 August 1991, preamble.
15. R.G. Pohl, 'Special Representative of the Commission on Human Rights, Report on the human rights situation in the Islamic Republic of Iran', UN Doc. E/CN.4/1992/34 of 2 January 1992, para. 190.
16. Commission on Human Rights, 'Summary record of the 57th meeting (second part) 6 March 1992', UN Doc. E/CN.4/1992/SR.57/Add.1 of 17 March 1992, para. 64.
17. M. Ogundipe-Leslie, 'In search of citizenship', 21 *Index on Censorship*, 4, April 1992, p.17.
18. 'Comparative study of national laws on the rights and status of women in Africa', UN Doc. ECA/ATRCW/3.5(ii)(b)/89/3 (1989), pp. 6–7.
19. R.J. Cook, 'Reservations to the Convention on the Elimination of All Forms of Discrimination against Women', *Virginia Journal of International Law*, Vol. 30, Spring 1990, No. 3, p. 706.
20. 'Report of the Third Meeting of the States Parties to the Convention on the Elimination of All Forms of

Discrimination against Women', UN Doc. CEDAW/SP/10 (1986).

21. The States Parties which responded were Canada, China, Cuba, Czechoslovakia, Denmark, France, Gabon, Germany, Ireland, Japan, Mexico, Portugal, Spain, St. Lucia, Sweden, Turkey, USSR. UN Doc. A/41/608 and Add.1(1986).

22. 'Report of the Fourth Meeting of the States Parties to the Convention on the Elimination of All Forms of Discrimination against Women', UN Doc. CEDAW/SP/14 (1988).

23. 'Report of the Sub-Commission on Prevention of Discrimination and Protection of Minorities on its forty-third session, Geneva, 5–30 August 1991', UN Doc. E/CN.4/Sub.2/1991/65 of 24 October 1991, pp. 145–6.

24. UN Doc. A/40/623 of 6 November 1984.

25. Objection by Mexico to a reservation made by Bangladesh upon accession, UN Doc. A/40/623 of 11 January 1985; Objections by Sweden to reservations made by Bangladesh, Brazil, Egypt, Jamaica, Mauritius, New Zealand, Republic of Korea, Thailand and Tunisia, UN Doc. A/41/608 of 17 March 1986.

26. UN Doc. CEDAW/C/SR.96 of 8 April 1987, paras. 61–97.

27. UN Doc. CEDAW/C/SR.99 of 10 April 1987, para. 38.

28. Division for the Advancement of Women, 'The origins and institutional context of the Convention', UN Doc. RS/CEDAW/1992/WP.1 of 24 March 1992, p. 8.

29. A.C. Byrnes, 'The "other" human rights treaty body: The work of the Committee on the Elimination of Discrimination against Women', *Yale Journal of International Law*, Vol. 14, 1989, No. 1, p. 6.

30. UN Doc. CEDAW/C/5/Add. 43 (1987).

31. 'General guidelines regarding the form and content of reports received from States Parties under Article 19 of the Convention', UN Doc. CEDAW/C/7 (1983), and 'Guidelines for the preparation of second and subsequent periodic reports', UN Doc. CEDAW/C/... (1988).

32. A.C. Byrnes, op.cit., p. 21.

33. *Report of the Committee on the Elimination of Discrimination against Women, Volume II, Third Session,* UN Doc. A/39/45 (1984) paras. 100 and 105.

34. 'Initial report of Romania', UN Doc. CEDAW/C/5/Add.45 (1987), p. 2.

35. *Report of the Committee on the Elimination of Discrimination . . .* op. cit., paras. 215–16.

Human rights education takes many forms: breaking the chains in a theatrical performance in Zaire

10 GUIDANCE FOR ACTION

Women are discriminated against, and there is now a major global movement to overcome this problem. No one will be unaffected by women's movements. If we truly value human equality, all of us will have to change.[1]

THOUGH HUMAN RIGHTS are guaranteed to all, internationally and nationally, they are not granted to people but conquered by them. Knowing one's rights, demanding them and securing their observance is everybody's task. There is no country in the world where all human rights problems have been solved, none where women enjoy full equality with men in daily life.

Intergenerational transmission of discrimination is perpetuated or eradicated starting with the individual, with the way that the girl child is educated and socialized. For this reason, this final part of the book starts with the individual and relations within the family. True, relations within families – and the prospects of the future generations of women – are influenced, and sometimes determined, by a multitude of factors behind individual control. It is therefore the obligation of governments to create conditions for a eradication of gender discrimination by taking the lead against discrimination. This guide thus moves from the individual towards the society and state and finally the international community.

EQUALITY FOR GIRL CHILDREN □
Whatever measures we may design for the world of adults, the fact remains that gender discrimination begins much earlier and many female children will not reach adulthood or, if they do, to remedy the effects of discrimination will be impossible. UNICEF has developed a series of policy guidelines towards eliminating discrimination against girls which propose, *inter alia*, the following.

- **Adopt political, legislative and development policies that eliminate gender disparity and discrimination in childhood. At present, there is inadequate appreciation of the problems and the special needs of the girl child by all involved in the development process.**
- **Undertake specialized research and investigation into the status of the girl child. Create databases on her by collecting data disaggregated by gender and age and demonstrating the anthropological, religious, legislative and socio-economic evidence of her unequal status and living conditions. Disseminate widely the findings of such research for advocacy, policy formulation and programme interventions.**
- **Formulate specific legal and social provisions to counteract the unacceptable negative image of the girl in traditional and non-traditional media, education, religion and culture.**
- **Set up adequate mechanisms to enforce such provisions.**
- **Advocate equal rights for girls in all national and international fora. Multilateral, bilateral and non-governmental organizations must place the girl child and women's issues higher on their development agendas.[2]**

The importance of the contents of education for the future generations of women is highlighted as the key to change. In particular, the emphasis is placed on the fact that it is women who have decisive influence on the education of their daughters:

Ironically, women have often been instrumental in carrying out and perpetuating the discrimination. Women, as the traditional bearers of culture, have often preserved the unfair status of the girl child by inculcating her with feelings of inferiority. They are

the key determining force in the setting of the bridal dowry, and after the bride enters her new family, the mother-in-law is the one who makes demands on her for work, often relegating the newcomer to a role little better than a slave. So, if generations of discrimination are to end, much of the educational work will have to be done with adult women.[3]

Educational curricula have received immense attention because of their importance for the elimination of the stereotyping of women, and their review is regularly suggested – less often carried out – by institutions working to promote equal rights for women. Mass media have not escaped the attention of critics, but specific suggestions concerning the eradication of sexism and sterotyping, even incitements to discrimination, are less frequent. The problem lies in the need to reconcile freedom of information with a 'directed' anti-discrimination orientation. The Council of Europe has summarized this as follows:

The development of mass communications policies designed to promote equality between women and men – at least in a binding form – is limited by respect of the fundamental principle underlying relations between media enterprises and the authorities: the freedom of expression enjoyed by the former and the obligation on the latter to respect the independence of those engaged in the exercise of this freedom, in the context of both the printed media and the audovisual media. Pending a development in the concept of equality between women and men towards the stage when it will be possible for the authorities to criticise sexism and the depicting of women in an unfavourable or sterotyped light in different media, the mass media policy has been restricted for the moment to making media professionals aware of the need to adopt socially aware attitudes in this field and help dispel prejudices.[4]

GRASSROOTS ACTIVITIES ☐ Human rights and women's organizations real-ized long ago that human rights are too important to be left to governments. Moreover, the guiding principle of their action is that silence is the best friend of violations – as long as violations are not exposed and opposed they continue unchallenged. In order to be able to recognize violations for what they are, not incidents or accidents but a threat to equal rights for all, basic knowledge of human rights is indispensable. This does not necessitate university education or legal training: everybody can obtain sufficient knowledge of what human rights are and are not, and an orientation as to where to get help when more information or different skills become necessary. Obtaining a basic knowledge of human rights is easy because human rights represent universally shared values. True, not all are guaranteed to the extent that the equal rights of women need protection. It is thus important for everybody to know what the current human rights guarantees are.

ACCESS TO INFORMATION This book provides an initial orientation in international human rights standards and procedures as these relate specifically to women. This can easily be the first step towards action: organizations can review whether all rights that should be guaranteed are recognized in their countries, in the national constitution and relevant laws, and join forces with others to demand that the minimum international standards be observed.

This is an activity which women have to do for themselves in every country because nobody will do this for them. There is a much lamented dearth of knowledge of which rights are denied to women in specific countries. It is indeed deplorable that women are often left in ignorance about the rights which they should but do not have, thus struggle against gender discrimination is left to

At the Chorillos Women's Prison, Lima, facilities are available for children to remain with their mothers while they are serving a prison sentence

victims themselves. Changing this is not easy but neither is it impossible.

The starting point is obviously to obtain and share knowledge about human rights guarantees that would benefit women. Determining what these guarantees are is an educational experience in itself. Moreover, information is power. Having accurate and detailed information on the rights that women should enjoy enables women to demand them and is the first step towards their enjoyment.

Texts of international human rights instruments can be obtained from relevant governmental offices. If they are not available, the closest United Nations Information Centre will have them, or organizations can obtain them by writing to the Centre for Human Rights of the United Nations (Palais des Nations, CH-1211 Geneva 10, Switzerland).

If, however, international human rights instruments are not available at governmental offices, this is a good indication that officials who should be observing these guarantees in their own work may not know them. Human rights work is often confined to ministries of foreign affairs and absent from local authorities dealing with employment, housing, family planning, child maintenance or inheritance. It is here that human rights of women should be: related to their everyday lives. Again, it is important to keep in mind that women have equal rights, that they are not asking for special privileges when claiming these rights.

LINKING HUMAN RIGHTS TO EVERY-DAY PROBLEMS
Human rights are sometimes perceived as remote from daily lives, as issues which pertain only to relations between government and opposition, to national elections, and political parties. Unequal rights of women in marriage, inheritance, at the workplace or within political parties, are wrongly dissociated

from human rights and become 'women's issues'. This is an important target for education and action by women's and human rights organizations. Action can be organized around any of the important women's problems – and there will be many everywhere – to demonstrate how human rights can reinforce demands for, and actually obtain changes.

A few issues are suggested here to provide inspiration as to what to do and how to do it:

● Investigate what are the major women's problems relating to marriage, divorce, and maintenance of children. List the typical problems and find out what the applicable human rights standards are: write to the closest human rights or women's organization or invite their representatives to come and explain this to the women concerned. Discuss ways of sharing this information with other women.

● Discuss women's access to available public services (education, health) in order to determine what special problems they face. Find out whether, as a consequence, women are deprived of such services or unable to use them as men do. Raise your findings with the relevant governmental office and try to suggest what changes should be introduced to promote women's equal access to educational or health care institutions.

● Find out what problems women face at work. In rural areas, women's position might be jeopardized by the fact that they cannot own the land on which they work. Investigate what the law says about women's property rights. In urban areas, women may be discriminated against in access to employment. Get in touch with organizations, such as trade unions, which are working on labour protection.

- Find out who else is working on women's and human rights issues and obtain information about their activities, organize a visit or a joint meeting. Explore possibilities of working together.

- Inquire into possibilities of using the existing legal aid programmes to assist women who need such help. If none is available, investigate possibilities of organizing an education and training programme on women's human rights.

HUMAN RIGHTS LITERACY □ The truism that information is power is particularly applicable to human rights, where it can be the only power there is. Contrary to what the image created by well-publicized cases of detention of opposition leaders or torture of political prisoners would lead us to believe, the vast majority of victims of human rights violations are people who are disempowered. Their names – sometimes even the number of victims – remain unknown. The essence of human rights is the prevention of abuses of power.

Empowerment has thus become the key word in human rights. The knowledge of one's rights may not be sufficient to be able to exercise them but it is indispensable.

Most people identify human rights with law and perceive human rights work as its application. This perception, particularly in the case of women, is erroneous. Law can sometimes be an obstacle to women's equal rights when it legalizes discrimination. Challenging the law by invoking women's entitlement to equal rights thus often becomes the first priority in national action. The existence of international law, which guarantees these equal rights to all women, is the strongest pillar of support for demanding and implementing such changes.

The United Nations publication 'Women: Challenges to the year 2000' thus suggested the following priorities for action:

- Increase awareness among men and women of women's rights under international conventions and national laws;

- Ensure equal rights for women under national laws;

- Guarantee enforcement of laws safeguarding women's equality; introduce affirmative action incentives and penalties for non-adherence;

- Establish a legal minimum age for marriage and ensure the mutual consent of both parties, as well as the woman's right to retain her own nationality;

- Guarantee the right of all women independently to buy, sell, own, inherit and administer property and other resources;

- Provide legal protection for women's equal access to land ownership, credit, training, investment and income;

- Establish national machinery in all countries to implement and monitor progress towards women's equality and to provide a mechanism for redress of grievances.[5]

The need to provide women with information on their rights and assistance to secure their enjoyment of them was realized long ago. Information on women's rights is not easy to obtain in all countries, while specific legal aid programmes for women remain scarce. It is, however, an encouraging sign that their number and reach is increasing worldwide. Women's and human rights organizations have initiated such programmes in India and Sri Lanka, Ghana and Zimbabwe, Colombia and Chile, to mention just a few examples.

PHOTO: UN 149, 501/SAW IWIN

CEDAW was established in 1982 to monitor the Women's Convention

Much research has been done to document the fact that too many women are not familiar with the rights they have, particularly in areas which determine their lives, such as ownership of property, disposal of family income, and maintenance of children. A UN Expert Group Meeting on Legal Literacy concluded: 'The most urgent requirement of legal literacy should be to facilitate women's awareness of the laws that affect them most, to make available legal remedies, and access to those remedies.'[6]

LEGAL ACTION Problems faced by women in their enjoyment of equal rights may well seem endless. It is therefore important to prioritize and undertake action in selected areas. The multitude and magnitude of problems can be reduced to manageable priority issues.

It is crucial, from the human rights viewpoint, to differentiate between those problems which emanate from the lack of formal guarantees of women's human rights, and those where women cannot exercise their guaranteed rights. The former necessitates action to change national law. This may sound impossible but it has been done; the fact that international law guarantees women equal rights greatly facilitates such change. Two examples:

In Tanzania a woman recently challenged the customary law that prohibited her from selling clan land that she had inherited from her father. A High Court held that customary law may and should be modified to meet the equality and human rights standards of the country's own constitution and those of international law to which Tanzania has subscribed. The judge found that the new (1984) equality provisions of the

Tanzanian Constitution applied to modify the customary law so that women had exactly the same rights as men to sell land. He backed the argument by noting that the Women's Convention and other international human rights treaties containing gender equality should apply in interpreting customary law and the Constitution. The case is Ephraim v. Pastory, High Court (Mwanza), 22 February 1990.[7]

A practising woman lawyer is being heralded a hero for women's rights after the High Court of Botswana struck down two citizenship laws on the basis that they discriminate against women and are unconstitutional. The law Unity Dow challenged provided that her children could not be citizens of Botswana because their father – her husband – is not a citizen of that country. 'I do not think', wrote judge Martin Horwitz in the ruling, 'that I would be losing sight of my functions or exceeding them sitting as Judge in the High Court, if I say that the time when women were treated as chattels or were there to obey the whims and wishes of males is long past.[8]

Access to courts is generally perceived as expensive and slow; many women cannot afford the cost of a lawyer, while court cases can take years. Free and easily accessible legal aid has increasingly become a priority activity for many human rights and women's organizations. Moreover, legal education is not indispensable for all necessary work – much can be done by persons with para-legal training. These options make women's access to justice feasible. Numerous successful projects of legal literacy and para-legal training testify to the fact that this can be done.

Additional strategies for changing the legal system have been outlined in the following manner:

1. Use existing laws for legal activism. Seek legal reform through reinterpretation of accepted laws by applying them to women's situations, such as using international human rights conventions for addressing violence against women.

2. Question the constitutionality of biased laws and justice system practices. Make linkages between violations of human rights and laws that are oppressive to women in many areas including personal and family law, labour rights, violence against women, and reproductive rights.

3. Affirm and argue the universality of women's human rights regardless of religion or culture.

4. Use international law and standards to push for reform, either through cases brought in international fora or by using international principles to set standards for domestic law.[9]

NETWORKING Struggle against human rights violations, against discrimination in particular, was – throughout history – always started by victims. Today this is much easier because the major victory has been won globally: human rights violations are not only outlawed, but governments are held accountable for them internationally, and human rights organizations work worldwide, for and with victims, to sustain this accountability. The important first step for women's organizations is thus to link up with human rights organizations and include women's issues in human rights work.

Existing women's groups and organizations can benefit by invoking human rights law to strengthen their pressure for change. The advantages of the fact that human rights has become *law* are great: recognizing women's equal rights in all areas is no longer left to the discretion of

INTERNATIONAL NETWORKING FOR RIGHTS IN HEALTH

While coalition building is as old as politics, the emergence of national and international women's health networks is relatively recent, based on the new wave of the women's movement that has developed rapidly since the late sixties in almost every country. Institutionalized sexism is nearly universal. As patients, women tend to be treated differently from men, our complaints often seen as trivial or psychological in origin. Our bodies and our reproductive systems are targeted by industry and health professionals as objects of research and product development. Indeed the vast array of oral contraceptives, inert and active intra-uterine devices, injectables, implants, vaginal rings, abortifacients, hormonal drugs and new reproductive technologies is staggering. Yet we are excluded from decision-making in most medical institutions and have no significant voice in determining research priorities and government health policies.

Most women, even the highly educated, have at times felt patronized or demeaned by doctors, reduced to uncomfortable silence, and made to feel too ignorant to even know what to ask. Once women begin to move past the isolation of silence and speak with others, these experiences can become a catalyst to question why things are so and what can be done to change the situation. The need for all women to be provided with information and understanding about sexuality and reproductive health is a great leveller of class and ethnic barriers and may lead to concerted political action.

Women who are victims of dangerous reproductive drugs or devices have organized in order to obtain good medical care and accurate information about their conditions, to seek legal redress from manufacturers, and to raise public awareness about industry practices and gaps in government regulations.

Depo Provera has become something of a cause celebre among women's health groups precisely because it illustrates a good deal about the politics of contraception. As women throughout the world are discovering, national regulatory bodies treat contraception with even less scrutiny than other categories of pharmaceuticals. Often this reflects a government's desire to promote national population control progams or to control reproduction among specific categories of women, such as indigenous, disabled, and immigrant women, and those classified as 'non-complaint'. Increasingly, women are protesting our lack of control over decisions made about our reproductive health. Organizing an international campaign to ban a drug or holding transnational discussions on reproductive technologies are formidable projects, made possible in the 1980s largely because of other networks already in place. Hazel Brown from Trinidad and Tobago was active in the Nestlé boycott and brought lobbying skills, creative tactics, and knowledge of the UN system to bear on other women's health issues. As she puts it, 'we never thought we'd win. At home we built on our successes and on what we have learned – know your facts, mobilize professionals to help you when possible, support each other, go after the top man, be creative in your strategies for confronting people and asking for help. Our group called itself the Housewives' Association. What could be less threatening than that, eh?'

S. Tudiver, 1986, 'International
women's health networks
in the eighties'[10]

individual authorities, national or local; it is their *obligation*.

Many national and international organizations have been set up to strengthen action for women's equal rights. A selective list is included in Annex III. These can be approached for assistance, to obtain relevant publications or documents, to get information about their work and identify possible areas of collaboration, to get information about what is happening in other countries. Even though women face problems which are specific to their region or country, the pattern of gender discrimination is similar worldwide. Hence the sharing of information on problems, and more importantly on responses to them and solutions, strengthens action for equal rights for all women.

GLOBAL MOBILIZATION FOR WOMEN'S HUMAN RIGHTS □ An unprecedented action of worldwide mobilization, the Worldwide Petition Drive, was started on 3 February 1992 by the Center for Women's Global Leadership, calling upon the 1993 World Conference on Human Rights to bring violations of women's human rights to the centre of its agenda. The Petition Drive aimed to raise the awareness within the human rights community and in the general public that gender-based violations of human rights are perhaps the most universal and systematic form of human rights abuse, to increase denunciation of violations of the human rights of women and prompt the Conference to decide on a long overdue gender-based analysis of violations, and to strengthen the growing international women's and human rights networks. The text of the Petition says: 'We call upon the 1993 World Conference on Human Rights to comprehensively address women's human rights at every level of its proceedings.' During the first six months this Petition was signed by over 75,000

people in 78 countries.

The sheer number of NGO initiatives aimed at placing women's human rights on the agenda of the 1993 Conference has been impressive and the variety of their proposals indicates how much needs to be done. This has been joined by CEDAW, which requested that emphasis should be placed on the fact 'that women's equality is a significant human rights issue'.[11] Governments have thus far remained silent. The importance of not remaining silent has been described as follows: 'The international community can play a decisive role in protecting women's human rights through vigilant and concerted action. Important steps towards protecting women's human rights worldwide include documenting human rights violations, publicizing these as widely as possible and campaigning to press government authorities for an end to the abuses. Governments which fail to protect fundamental human rights should be confronted with the force of international public opinion.'[12]

Specific proposals to redress the neglect of women's rights on the global human rights agenda are coming from all corners of the world, thus testifying to the universality of the problems, but also to the globally shared views of how women's human rights should be respected and protected. Parts of two sets of recommendations, one from Asia and the other from Latin America, are cited on p. 136.

Even a cursory look at these proposals shows how wide ranging the human rights of women are: they involve all levels, from global to individual; all actors, governmental and non-governmental, public and private; all sectors, from education and health, to employment, international assistance, and to migration and environmental protection; all methods of action, from legislative reform to legal literacy; last but not least, they pertain to all areas of human activity.

EFFECTIVE REALIZATION OF THE RIGHTS OF WOMEN

Resolution 5 of the World Congress on Human Rights, Delhi, December 1990

[The World Congress on Human Rights]

Urges governments to ratify the Convention on Elimination of All Forms of Discrimination against Women (CEDAW) and to establish commissions to monitor compliance with CEDAW;

Further urges governments of countries which have entered reservations to CEDAW to withdraw these reservations and to change their laws to the extent necessary;

Calls upon governments and the media to disseminate freely information dealing with human rights, especially those of women, and to take action at every level of society with a view to changing attitudes which may result in discrimination against women and girls;

Condemns all forms of gender discrimination, including discrimination in respect of the right to be born;

Considers it imperative to eliminate gender discrimination in respect of education, and calls for steps to ensure that education should be universal, free and compulsory, at least up to the age of 16;

Recommends that national laws be examined and revised in order to remove gender discrimination in the areas of marriage, inheritance, matrimonial property, matrimonial relations, adoption and guardianship;

Further recommends the establishment of family courts based on the following principles: simplified laws and procedures; privacy of hearings; appointment of family court judges in equal gender proportions; the provision of counselling and mediation services as part of the court procedures.[13]

Recommendation of the CODEHUCA Meeting on the Promotion, Defence and Protection of the Rights of Women, San José, April 1992

Emphasis on the gender perspective in the work of human rights organizations.

Joint efforts of human rights and women's organizations in making women aware of the defence of their rights.

Education of women's organizations on the Convention on the Elimination of All Forms of Discrimination against Women.

Dissemination of the Preliminary Plan for an Inter-American Convention to Prevent, Sanction and Eradicate Violence against Women.

Legislation to protect women and their work in factories, their domestic work, which should be recognized as part of the national economy, and women's work in the informal sector.

Promotion of non-formal educational institutions that will facilitate the training of women.

Sex education beginning from childhood.

Integral attention to women's health care.

Sanctions for irresponsible fathers.

Campaigns against those media which use women and their image for commercial purposes.[14]

What makes women's human rights difficult to put into practice is the fact that conventional human rights work, namely ensuring that the government does not violate human rights, does not suffice. When dealing with safeguards against torture or the free press, people can separate such public issues from their private lives.

When dealing with the education of their daughters or professional responsibilities of their wives, equal rights for women often interfere with issues people would much prefer to keep away from public scrutiny. Respect for equal rights for women extends to everybody's life and – much more demanding – necessitates changes in most. Few people, women or men, could claim that they have completely freed themselves of the universal heritage of gender discrimination.

It is, however, the responsibility of governments to take the lead in ensuring equal rights for women. It is thus not surprising that so many requests and petitions have been addressed to the United Nations, which embodies the global intergovernmental community – this is where global leadership is sought and, according to the number of critical proposals for change, where the global leadership has not yet done justice to women. This justice is being demanded as a matter of women's right to have past gender discrimination redressed and to be protected from it in the future.

WOMEN'S ACCESS TO THE UN RIGHTS SYSTEM
The global spread of knowledge of the existing norms and institutions for the promotion and protection of human rights is reflected in the number and precision of proposals for change. Many suggestions have been directed to the international and national human rights institutions and they all have similar content: the request that equal rights for women, affecting half of humanity, be treated with the priority they deserve.

The marginalization of women's rights on the global human rights agenda necessitates numerous changes, which can build further on those already in place. True, the main UN human rights bodies deal with 'women' as a sub-item among numerous items on their long agendas. Women's rights have, however, emerged throughout the agenda: the number of NGO submissions concerning various aspects of the human rights of women, be it rape of women political prisoners, the position of indigenous women, or the human right to environmental protection, has prompted an increased awareness that women's rights are human rights. Special rapporteurs have started to include observations on women's rights when reporting on specific country situations. However, proposals that a specific mechanism be set up, most often a special rapporteur, aim to streamline all these scattered issues and documents. This would provide grounds for stocktaking in order to identify the global pattern of problems and determine priorities.

The human rights treaty bodies supervising the implementation of the seven main conventions, which entail reporting by governments, have addressed the equal rights of women in varying degrees. Some, like the Human Rights Committee, include equal rights and pay special attention to gender discrimination throughout the examination of states' reports. Others, like CERD which deals with racial discrimination, rarely address problems of compounded discrimination which victimizes women. A thorough stocktaking of the work of these bodies is impossible because no overview of their work on women's rights has been undertaken, either by the United Nations or by independent researchers. Redressing this gap in our knowledge of this wealth of material on human rights in general and women's rights in particular should be made a priority. The periodic meetings of chairpersons of all human rights treaty bodies have addressed this issue. The most recent meeting, in October 1992, adopted suggestions leading to effective incorporation of 'women's issues' into the mainstream human rights work. *Inter alia*, this meeting suggested that CEDAW be serviced by the Centre for

Women rallying for the human rights of women in Zimbabwe

Human Rights in order to 'achieve the full and effective integration of the Committee into the overall human rights treaty regime'.[15]

Knowledge of the existence of the Women's Convention and about the work of CEDAW is still restricted to the professional community, and there is a wealth of proposals to make the Convention and CEDAW more widely known. IWRAW has formulated proposals on how to begin:

● **Has the Convention been translated into the local language(s)? What steps have been taken to make people aware of its provisions?**

● **Has the CEDAW report been translated into the local language(s)? What measures have been taken to ensure that people are aware of the content of the report? Has the government made copies of the CEDAW report, or a summary of the report, available?**

● **What media coverage has been given to the Convention? To the report to CEDAW? To independent reports on the status of women?[16]**

An additional avenue is the mobilization of NGOs and of the research community on numerous issues relating to the realization of equal rights for women. The formal relations between different human rights bodies and NGOs vary, but in practice NGO input is used by them all. Human rights NGOs realized long ago that human rights are too important to be left to governments and intergovernmental organizations, and the growth and global spread of NGOs is probably one of the most notable developments of recent decades. The 1980s saw the emergence of NGOs dealing specifically with women's rights, and the early 1990s saw increased activism by human rights organizations in exposing and opposing violations of women's rights.

TRANSLATING HUMAN RIGHTS INTO ECONOMIC POLICIES

The fact that human rights law, and law in general, is considered the least effective in tackling global economic issues is evidenced by suggestions on how better to link the human rights guarantees for women with global economic policies and practices. Under the title 'Engendering global economic development', the Commonwealth Human Rights Initiative has addressed this area:

Adverse economic trends in the 1980s affecting all developing countries, and structural adjustment programmes, which have borne heavily on women, have meant that the 1980s have been a decade of stagnation for women. The informal economy, of most significance to women, has been hardest hit. The momentum of the UN Decade for Women, which ended in 1985, has been lost.

The Commonwealth as a whole, and individual member countries, have sought to mitigate these trends through legislation, economic and other policies. As part of its Women and Development Programme the Commonwealth Secretariat commissioned a report to look at the impact of structural adjustment on women. Called Engendering Adjustment for the 1990s ... the report called for a recognition of the burden which the current economic situation is placing on women. It urged that governments should give more attention to the impact on women in their future economic planning.

This report was followed up in the Ottawa meeting in October 1990 of Ministers responsible for women's affairs. They proposed a continuance and preferably an increase in spending on measures which would help women to participate in market economies in the fields of nutrition, health, education and time-saving technologies. They also recommended more participation by women in policy-making that will affect them....

Recommendation: The Commonwealth secretariat should make a follow-up report to Engendering Adjustment, to be made available to Ministers responsible for women's affairs no later than 1995. This should indicate how far international agencies, governments and other bodies have changed their practices following the first report, and how the changing economic situation affects the rights of women then.[17]

At the local level, working women are often exposed to triple discrimination. The diagnosis was provided by the Regional Forum on Women and Economic Rights, held in Colombo, Sri Lanka, in August 1991, and accompanied by proposals for action as shown on p. 140.

FORTHCOMING INTERNATIONAL EVENTS

Besides the World Conference on Human Rights, the UN has planned a whole series of major international conferences for the coming years. These events may appear remote from women's everyday lives but such conferences are important as they represent opportunities to advance global policies relating to women. The World Conference on Human Rights may well prove to be a turning point in giving equal

REGIONAL FORUM ON WOMEN AND ECONOMIC RIGHTS – PROPOSALS FOR ACTION

During the discussion held at the Forum, the following concerns were expressed with regard to recent developments in the industrial sector:

(a) the denial of the right to organize and unionize especially in the free trade zones and home-based production industries;

(b) the non-implementation of labour laws in the sphere of minimum wages, maternity benefits, equal pay, leave, etc.;

(c) the revoking of certain types of legislation which guarantee international standards of dignity and equality, e.g. night work;

(d) the abdication of the judicial process and the setting up of administrative tribunals directly under the executive to determine labour disputes, thus depriving women of independent and impartial adjudication.

It was pointed out that the major settlement and colonization schemes under large development projects discriminated against women since the man was regarded as the head of household and all services and credit facilities were in his name, as was the title to land. This discrimination was exposed in many fora but remedial action has not been taken.

In most Asian countries plantation labour is predominantly female, brought into the country from another cultural context. This often results in a situation of triple discrimination of race, class and gender.

It is important to reaffirm the tribal woman's right to property which existed earlier in tribal custom and practice. Laws and regulations must be enhanced to protect the rights of tribal women and the community, and all development programmes in tribal areas must be evaluated with regard to their impact on the livelihood of those tribal groups.

Women migrant workers include housemaids, entertainers, bartenders and workers in the sex industry. Their vulnerability is heightened by the fact that they are often drawn into and used for criminal activity such as drug trafficking, prostitution and smuggling of prohibited articles. There is the demand for women to become migrant workers due to the lack of economic opportunities in their respective countries, as well as State policies which actively encourage women to become migrant workers for their foreign exchange remittances.

Women dominate the informal sector. It is therefore not surprising that it is the least regulated and the most unprotected sector in the economy.[18]

rights of women the priority they deserve regarding all human rights issues.

The 1993 International Year for the World's Indigenous People is a good opportunity to advance awareness of the plight of indigenous peoples and to promote the protection of their human rights. The main purpose of this Year is to strengthen international co-operation for the solution of problems that are facing indigenous peoples worldwide, particularly human rights, environment, development, education and health. The central theme of this Year is empowerment through partnership.

Figures show that half of the 300 million indigenous people in the world are women. A specific focus on the human rights of indigenous women is justified by the multiple discrimination victimizing them: 'They have less access to education, are economically exploited, oppressed and marginalized. They are discriminated against, not only for being indigenous but also for being women. Because they work mainly in the informal sector they are not protected by any form of law.'[19] The Draft Declaration of Indigenous Rights thus emphasizes in its preamble 'the importance of giving special attention to the rights and needs of indigenous women.'

In 1989 the UN General Assembly proclaimed 1994 as the International Year of the Family. During the preparation of the programme, attention has been focused on the equal rights of all family members, and specifically promoting equal rights for women within the family is an important aim. The General Assembly has stressed the need 'to ensure that all plans, programmes and activities related to the family are in accordance with the concept of equality between women and men as expressed in the Convention on the Elimination of All Forms of Discrimination against Women, and to ensure the incorporation into the programme of the Year of the principles relating to policies aimed at fostering equality between women and men.'[20]

The Fourth World Conference on Women will be held in Beijing, China, from 4 to 15 September 1995. The agenda for this Conference includes the second review of the implementation of Nairobi Forward-looking Strategies for the Advancement of Women, and the adoption of a Platform for Action.

Numerous national and international activities are planned in preparation for this Conference. These include, for example, collaborative UN/NGO action on Mother's Day 1994 against discrimination against women under the title 'Poor, powerless and pregnant'. For Human Rights Day 1994 UNICEF has chosen the theme of the girl child and is planning to focus on discrimination against girls through its worldwide activities.

1. B. Reardon (1977) *Discrimination. The Cycle of Injustice*, World in Focus, Vol. 2, No. 2, Holt, Rinehart and Winston, Sydney, pp. 38–9.
2. UNICEF (1990) *Towards an Equal Opportunity Environment for the Girl Child*, New York, pp.31–32.
3. 'Sorry plight of female: How it started', *UNICEF INTERCOM*, No. 55, January 1990, Focus: SAARC Year of the Girl Child, p. 5.
4. Report by the Secretary General on equality between women and men in the Council of Europe, Parliamentary Assembly, Doc. 6606, 4 May 1992, p. 12.
5. United Nations (1991) *Women: Challenges to the Year 2000*, New York, p. 14.
6. Division for the Advancement of Women, 'Women's legal literacy: Obstacles and measures', Expert Group Meeting on Increased Awareness by Women of their Rights, including Legal Literacy, Bratislava, 18–20 May 1992, UN Doc. EGM/IAWR/1992/WP.1 of 12 May 1992, para. 68.
7. 'Law and tradition: Challenge and change', *FEMNET News*, Vol. 1, No. 5, September–December 1990.
8. 'A legal victory for women in Botswana', *Human Rights Tribune*, Vol. 1, No. 1, Winter 1992, p. 14; 'A big win for Unity Dow – and for women everywhere', *The Women's Watch*, Vol. 5, No. 1, July 1991, p. 1.
9. Women's Leadership Institute (1992) *Women, Violence and Human Rights. 1991 Report*, Center for Women's Global Leadership, New Brunswick, New Jersey, p. 55.
10. S. Tudiver, 'International women's health networks in the eighties', in: K. McDonnell, (ed.) (1986) *Adverse Effects. Women and the Pharmaceutical Industry*, International Organization of Consumer Unions, Penang, Malaysia, 1986, pp. 187–213.
11. 'Contribution of the Committee on the Elimination of Discrimination against Women to the World Conference on Human Rights 1993', UN Doc. A/CONF.157/PC/23 of 17 March 1992, p.6.
12. Amnesty International (1991) *Women in the Front Line. An Amnesty International Report*, London, March, pp. 52–3.
13. Final Act. World Congress on Human Rights, 10–15 December 1990, New Delhi, 1991, mimeograph, pp. 17–18.
14. X. Suareaz, 'Women report violations of their rights', *Brecha*, Commission for the Defense of Human Rights in Central America (CODEHUCA), San José, Costa Rica, Vol. 3, 1992 No. 2, pp. 15–16.
15. Report of the fourth meeting of persons chairing the human rights treaty bodies, para. 84.
16. International Working Group on Women's Rights (1989) *Assessing the Status of Women: A Guide to Reporting Using the Convention on the Elimination of All Forms of Discrimination against Women*, IWRAW, Minneapolis, p.23.
17. Commonwealth Human Rights Initiative (1991) *Put Our World to Rights. A Report by a Non-governmental Advisory Group Chaired by Hon. Flora MacDonald*,

London, pp.112 and 114.

18. Report on the Regional Forum on Women and Economic Rights, organized by the Asia Pacific Forum on Women, Law and Development and Law and Society Trust, Colombo, Sri Lanka, 2–4 August 1991, *Law & Society Trust Review*, Colombo, 1 October 1991, pp. 5–7.

19. Report of the Working Group on Indigenous Populations on its ninth session, UN Doc. E/CN.4/Sub.2/1991/40/Rev.1 of 3 October 1991, para. 84.

20. General Assembly, 'Preparation for and observance of the International Year of the Family', resolution 46/92 of 16 December 1991, para. 12.

ANNEX I
LIST OF ABBREVIATIONS

ACP African, Caribbean and Pacific countries parties to the Lomé Convention

ARTEP Asian Employment Programme of the International Labour Office

CEDAW Committee on the Elimination of All Forms of Discrimination against Women

CERD Committee on the Elimination of All Forms of Racial Discrimination

CIDA Canadian International Development Agency

CODEH Committee for the Defence of Human Rights in Honduras

CSCE Conference on Security and Co-operation in Europe

CSDHA Centre for Social Development and Humanitarian Affairs of the United Nations

DAC Development Assistance Committee of the OECD

DANIDA Danish International Development Agency

DAW United Nations Division for the Advancement of Women

DPI Department of Public Information of the United Nations

EC European Community

ECA United Nations Economic Commission for Africa

ECOSOC United Nations Economic and Social Council

EEC European Economic Community

FAO Food and Agriculture Organization

GDP Gross Domestic Product

GNP Gross National Product

HDI Human Development Index

ICCPR International Covenant on Civil and Political Rights

ICESCR International Covenant on Economic, Social and Cultural Rights

ICJ International Court of Justice

ICJ International Commission of Jurists, Geneva

ICRC International Committee of the Red Cross

ILO International Labour Office

IMF International Monetary Fund

INSTRAW United Nations International Research and Training Institute for the Advancement of Women

IOCU International Organization of Consumer Unions, Penang

IPPF International Planned Parenthood Federation

IWGIA International Working Group for Indigenous Affairs, Copenhagen

IWRAW International Women's Rights Action Watch

LDCs The Least Developed Countries

NGLS United Nations Non-Governmental Liaison Service

NGO Non-governmental organization

NORAD Norwegian Ministry of Development Co-operation

OAS Organization of American States

ODA Official Development Assistance

OECD Organization for Economic Co-operation and Development

OXFAM Oxford Committee for Famine Relief

PCIJ Permanent Court of International Justice of the League of Nations

PQLI Physical Quality of Life Index

SIDA Swedish International Development Agency

UN United Nations

UNCTAD United Nations Conference on Trade and Development

UNDP United Nations Development Programme

UNESCO United Nations Educational, Scientific and Cultural Organization

UNFPA United Nations Population Fund

UNHCR United Nations High Commissioner for Refugees

UNICEF United Nations Children's Fund

UNIFEM United Nations Development Fund for Women

UNITAR United Nations Institute for Training and Research

UNRISD United Nations Research Institute for Social Development

USA United States of America

USSR The former Union of Soviet Socialist Republics

WHA World Health Assembly

WHO World Health Organization

WID Women-in-development

WIDER World Institute for Development Economics Research of the United Nations

ANNEX II
DISCUSSION GUIDE

THIS BOOK IS MEANT TO BE A TOOL for organizations, institutions and individuals wherever they may live and work. It therefore provides an overview of the global pattern of problems related to the enjoyment of equal rights by women. Although these problems are similar worldwide their specific manifestations vary in time and place. It is thus important to recognize such manifestations as human rights problems. This discussion guide provides a series of questions, arranged chapter by chapter, to facilitate the process of identifying key human rights problems which women may face.

CHAPTER 1

1. Has the history of women's rights been written in your country? If not, which institution or individual is best placed to write it? How far back does it go? Who were prominent women who fought for equality in different stages of history? What have they accomplished? Are these women well known? Are there any women who were persecuted, condemned or killed because of their opposition to gender discrimination? What can be done to make women aware of the path trodden by previous generations?

2. When did women in your country acquire the right to vote? Are there women who may not be aware of this right? Are there any obstacles women may face in registering to vote that do not apply to men? If so, what can be done to challenge such obstacles? How many women are active in political parties, civic associations, trade unions, community organizations? Are there any rules or guidelines for such organizations regarding the participation of women? How many women are elected to parliament? Are there any quotas for women? Are there any other measures to increase participation of women in national politics?

3. What terminology does your national or local language use in referring to the human rights of women? Does this terminology reflect gender equality? If not, what can be done to change it? Are laws written so as to reflect women's equality or do they use masculine terms only?

4. Are there any forms of exploitation of women in your country which should be classified as slavery? Are there any organizations protecting exploited women?

CHAPTER 2

1. Is protection of motherhood granted in your country? Are all women entitled to this protection aware of their entitlements? What obstacles do women face in enjoying them? Are there organizations working towards overcoming these obstacles?

2. What do laws say about family planning? Are women entitled to have access to contraceptive information and services? If not, what is being done to change this? If they do have entitlements, what obstacles do women face in benefiting from them? Are there organizations helping women to overcome obstacles? If not, how can their establishment be facilitated?

3. What are women's legal rights in regard to child maintenance and custody? Is such information widely available? Is legal aid available to women? What are the best ways to initiate or to improve women's access to information and help in this area?

CHAPTER 3

1. Do children have the right to educa-

tion? Is primary education universally available free of charge? If not, what can be done to improve children's access to education? Is educational enrolment lower for girls than for boys? If so, how much lower? Does it vary in time and place? What are the main reasons for lower enrolment rates for girls? What is being done to improve access to education for girls? What more can be done?

2. Do boys and girls go to different schools? Do educational curricula vary for boys and for girls? Has anybody investigated these curricula for possible discriminatory contents? Is any governmental body or institution working towards eradicating gender discrimination in education? Are any information or educational programmes available concerning the value of the girl child?

3. What is the public perception of gender discrimination in your country and in your community? Are discriminatory attitudes common? Are there examples of women questioning and challenging gender discrimination? Are these women supported? By whom? Are there any special programmes of human rights education available? Are any programmes available specifically on the rights of women?

CHAPTER 4

1. What is the minimum legal age of marriage for girls? Is it widely known? Is it observed in practice? Is anything done to inhibit marriages of girls below minimum age? Is there anything these girls can do, anywhere they can go to for help?

2. Do women lose some of their rights when marrying? If so, have some women challenged this? Is information and legal aid available to them? Does national law recognize equality of spouses? If not, have

there been attempts to change this?

3. What rights do women have in the case of divorce? Are these widely known? What means do women have to enforce these rights? Is legal aid available? How can it be broadened and strengthened? What are the rights of widows?

4. Are women entitled to own property? Do they have any restrictions because they are women? Does marriage further affect their property rights? Do girls have equal inheritance rights with boys? Is this information widely available? If women have lesser rights, what can they do to challenge this?

CHAPTER 5

1. Does your constitution prohibit gender discrimination? If not, has this been brought to the attention of the government? If gender discrimination is prohibited, does this apply in all areas? What do women perceive as the main problems? In which areas is gender discrimination perceived to affect women most? Are there court cases where women have succeeded in changing discriminatory laws or practices? Is there information and literature available on gender discrimination?

2. Does the government have a policy or strategy for the elimination of gender discrimination? If not, is one necessary? If it does exist, is its application monitored? Are there women's or human rights organizations working against gender discrimination? If not, how can such organizations be best started?

3. Do women face special problems in obtaining employment? What are these? Is there any remedy available to a woman refused employment because she is a woman? Are trade unions active in providing assistance against gender discrimination? What other organizations can

provide assistance to women? Is any protection available to women who are working but not formally employed? Is any organization or institution available to assist them? Are their problems well known? What do they identify as their principal problems? What are the feasible remedies for these problems?

CHAPTER 6

1. What rights do women have regarding access to productive resources? What rights do they have with respect to income-generation? Are there special policies or measures to increase women's participation in development? If not, what can be done? Who should do it?

2. Is there a special governmental office or institution dealing with women-in-development? Are there national programmes to improve women's participation in development? Are there any local programmes? Are there projects specifically targeting women? Could other projects be initiated? Is information about such opportunities available to women?

3. Is data available on distinctions between men and women regarding health and nutritional status? If not, how can the gathering of such data be initiated? How can such data be effectively used?

CHAPTER 7

1. Are there any offences which only women can commit? Is this considered discriminatory? Should it be? How much information is available about women in criminal justice? How much information is available about imprisoned women? Is any organization giving them assistance?

2. How many refugees are there in your country? Where do they come from? What have they escaped from? What is

being done to assist them? Are there any special measures or programmes to assist refugee women? Should there be?

3. How much is known about disabled women in your country or community? Do they face any problems which disabled men do not have? Are they entitled to any special measures of assistance?

CHAPTER 8

1. Are there any traditional practices in your country or community perceived to be harmful to women? If so, what is being done to prevent harm to women? Are such practices illegal? Is there any publicity for this? Is there any protection for women?

2. What protection does the law provide for women in your country against family violence? Does legal protection for women differ from that guaranteed to men? What is the sanction for rape? What protection and assistance is provided to victims of rape? Is wife-beating an offence? Can a woman get legal protection? Is such information available? Is there a safe house an abused woman can go to? Is there any organization to assist her?

CHAPTER 9

1. How much information is available about the United Nations? How often is the UN's work described in the media? What are popular perceptions of the United Nations? How much is known about the UN protection of human rights?

2. Is your country party to the Women's Convention? To other human rights treaties? Is this information widely available? Have international human rights instruments been translated into the languages spoken in your country? Are such publications widely available? Is the text of

the Women's Convention available? Do interested women know where to get it from?

3. What are the differences between the text of the Women's Convention and laws in your country? Where in your country can precise information about the legal rights of women be obtained? Do laws differ from the provisions of the Women's Convention? Are there some rights which are guaranteed in the Convention that women in your country do not have? Are there any organizations working on the human rights of women? Are women's organizations familiar with the Convention? Are human rights organizations familiar with specific problems faced by women in their quest for equal rights?

ANNEX III
LIST OF
ORGANIZATIONS

INTER-GOVERNMENTAL

Centre for Human Rights, Palais des Nations, 1211 Geneva 10, Switzerland

Council of Europe, BP 431 R6, 67006 Strasbourg Cedex, France

Division for the Advancement of Women, United Nations Centre for Social Development and Humanitarian Affairs **(DAW)**, International Centre, P.O. Box 500, 1400 Vienna, Austria

European Economic Community, rue de la Loi, 1049 Brussels, Belgium

International Labour Office (ILO), 4 route des Morillons, 1211 Geneva 10, Switzerland

International Research and Training Institute for the Advancement of Women (INSTRAW), Santo Domingo, Dominican Republic

United Nations Development Fund for Women (UNIFEM), 304 East 45th Street, New York, NY 10017, USA

United Nations Development Programme (UNDP), 1 United Nations Plaza, New York, NY 10017, USA

UNESCO, 7 place de Fontenoy, 75700 Paris, France

United Nations High Commission for Refugees (UNHCR), Centre William Rappard, 154 rue de Lausanne, 1202 Geneva, Switzerland

UNICEF, 3 United Nations Plaza, New York, N.Y. 10017, USA; also Palais des Nations, 1211 Geneva 10, Switzerland

United Nations Non-Governmental Liaison Service (NGLS), Palais des Nations, 1211 Geneva 10, Switzerland; also Room 6015, 866 United Nations Plaza, New York, N.Y. 10017, USA

United Nations Population Fund (UNFPA), 220 E 42nd Street, New York, NY 10017; also Palais des Nations, 1211 Geneva 10, Switzerland

World Health Organization (WHO), 20 avenue Appia, 1202 Geneva, Switzerland

NON-GOVERNMENTAL

African Centre for Democracy and Human Rights Studies, Kairaba Avenue, K.S.M.D., Banjul, The Gambia

Arab Women's Solidarity Association (AWSA), 4 A Dareeh Saad Street, Kasr El Ainy, Cairo, Egypt

Amnesty International, 1 Easton Street, London WC1X 8DJ, United Kingdom

Article 19, 90 Borough High Street, London SE1 1LL, United Kingdom

Asia Pacific Forum on Women, Law and Development, Development Centre, Pesiaran Duta, P.O. Box 12224, 50770 Kuala Lumpur, Malaysia

Asian Women's Human Rights Council, P.O. Box 190, 1099 Manila, The Philippines

Baha'i International Community, 15 route des Morillons, 1218 Geneva, Switzerland

Center for Women's Global Leadership, Douglass College, 27 Clifton Avenue, New Brunswick, New Jersey 08903, USA

Commission for the Defence of Human Rights in Central America (CODEHUCA), 1002 Paseo de los Estudiantes, San José, Costa Rica

Fiji Women's Rights Movement, P.O. Box 14194, Suva, Fiji

Human Rights Internet, 57 Louis Pasteur, Ottawa K1N 6N5, Canada

Human Rights Watch, Women's Rights Project, 1922 K Street N.W., Washington DC 20005-1203, USA

Inter-African Committee on Traditional Practices Affecting the Health of Women and Children, 147 rue de Lausanne, 1202 Geneva, Switzerland

Inter-American Institute of Human Rights, Women and Human Rights Project, P.O. Box 10.081, San José, Costa Rica

International Alliance of Women, 1 Lycavittou Street, 106 73 Athens, Greece

International Centre for Human Rights and Democratic Development, 63 rue de Bresoles, Montreal H2Y 1V7, Canada

International Commission of Jurists, P.O. Box 160, 26 chemin de Joinville, 1216 Cointrin-Geneva, Switzerland

International Council of Jewish Women, 1110 Finch Avenue West, Suite 518, Downsview, M3J2T2 Canada

International Council on Social Welfare, Les Crosets, Koestlergasse 1/29, 1060 Vienna, Austria

International Council of Women, 13, rue Caumartin, 75009 Paris, France

International Federation of Red Cross and Red Crescent Societies, 17 chemin des Crets, 1209 Geneva, Switzerland

International Federation of University Women, 37 quai Wilson, 1201 Geneva, Switzerland

International Human Rights Law Group, 1601 Connecticut Avenue, NW, Suite 2000, Washington DC, USA

International Women's Rights Action Watch (IWRAW), c/o Women, Public Policy and Development Project, Humphrey Institute of Public Affairs, University of Minnesota, 301 19th Avenue South, Minneapolis, MN 55455, USA

International Women's Tribune Center (IWTC), 777 United Nations Plaza, New York NY 10017, USA

ISIS-WICCE 3A, chemin des Campanules, 1219 Aire-Geneva, Switzerland

Japanese Association of International Women's Rights, Bunkyo Women's College, 1196 Kamekubo, Oimachi, Iruma-gun Saitama Prefecture, 345 Japan

Latin American Committee for Defense of Women's Rights (CLADEM), P.O. Box 11-0470, Lima, Peru

Lawyers Collective, Jalaram Jyot 4th floor, Ghogha St, 63 Janmabhoomi Marg, Bombay 400 001, India

Lawyers for Human Rights and Legal Aid (LHRLA), 702 Mohammadi House, I.I. Chundrigar Road, Karachi, Pakistan

Legal Services for Women, Profamilia, Calle 34, No. 14-52, Bogota, Colombia

Medical Women's International Association, Herbert-Lewin Str. 1, D-5000 Cologne 41, Germany

Women and Law in Southern Africa Research Project, P.O. Box UA 171, Union Avenue, Harare, Zimbabwe

Women for Women, 15 Green Square, Dhaka 1205, Bangladesh

Women Living under Muslim Law, P.O. Box 23-34790 Grabels, Montpellier, France

Women's Action Group, P.O. Box 135, Harare, Zimbabwe

Women's Global Network on Reproductive Rights, Nieuwe Zijds Voorburgwal 32, 1012 RZ Amsterdam, The Netherlands

Women's International League for Peace and Freedom, 1 rue de Varembe, 1211 Geneva 20, Switzerland

Women's International Network (WIN), 187 Grant Street, Lexington, MA 02173, USA

World Council of Churches, 150 route de Ferney, CH-1211 Geneva 2, Switzerland

World Federation of Methodist Women, Inglenook, Royal Terrace Lane, Dun Laoghaire, Co. Dublin, Ireland

World Union of Catholic Women's Organizations, 7c avenue Alfred-Cortot, 1260 Nyon, Switzerland

World University Service, 5 chemin des Iris, 1216 Geneva, Switzerland

Zonta International, 557 West Randolph Street, Chicago, IL 60661-2206, USA

The generation of the future: schoolgirls in Sri Lanka

SELECTIVE BIBLIOGRAPHY

Publications containing full text of international human rights instruments:

Compilation of Human Rights Instruments, Centre for Human Rights, United Nations, New York, 1988.

Compendium of International Conventions Concerning the Status of Women, Centre for Social Development and Humanitarian Affairs, United Nations Office at Vienna, 1988.

International Labour Conventions and Recommendations 1919–1991, International Labour Office, Geneva, 1992

International organizations: Official publications

CEDAW – *Reports of the Committee on the Elimination of Discrimination against Women*, Vols. I and II, 1982-1987, United Nations Office at Vienna

Commission of the European Communities (1986) *Community Law and Women*, Women's Information Office, Brussels.

Commonwealth Secretariat (1985) *The Convention on the Elimination of All Forms of Discrimination against Women: A Commentary on the Convention*, Commonwealth Secretariat, London

Commonwealth Secretariat (1988) *The Convention on the Elimination of All Forms of Discrimination against Women: The Reporting Process. A Manual for Commonwealth Jurisdictions*, Commonwealth Secretariat, London.

International Labour Office (1980) *Selected Standards and Policy Statements of Special Interest to Women Workers adopted under the auspices of the ILO*, Geneva.

International Labour Office (1985) *Equal Opportunity and Equal Treatment for Men and Women in Employment*, International Labour Conference, 71st session, Report VII, ILO, Geneva.

International Labour Office (1988) *Women Workers. Selected ILO Documents*, ILO, Geneva.

International Labour Office (1988) *Equality in Employment and Occupation. General Survey by the Committee of Experts on the Application of Conventions and Recommendations*, International Labour Conference, 75th session, Report III, ILO, Geneva.

International Labour Office (1990) *Special Protective Measures for Women and Equality of Opportunity and Treatment*, Meeting of Experts on Special Protective Measures for Women and Equality of Opportunity and Treatment, Geneva, 10–17 October 1989, ILO, Geneva.

OECD (1979) *Equal Opportunities for Women*, Paris.

World Health Organization (1979) *Traditional Practices Affecting the Health of Women and Children*. Female Circumcision, Childhood Marriage, Nutritional Taboos, etc. Report of a Seminar, Khartoum, 10–15 February 1979, WHO/EMRO, Technical Publication No. 2, Alexandria.

Studies

Brocas, A-M et al. (1990) Women and social security. Progress towards equality of treatment, ILO, Geneva.

Economic Commission for Africa (1990) Comparative study of national laws on the rights and status of women in

Africa, UN Doc. E/ACA/ATRCW/
ARCC.XI/90/6, ECA, Addis Ababa.

Economic Commission for Asia and the
Pacific (1989) Guidelines on upgrading
the legal status of women, UN Doc.
ST/ESCAP/832, ESCAP, Bangkok.

Al-Bourqadi, H. (1986) Economic and
social rights of women from the Islamic
point of view, UN Doc. E/ESCWA/
SDP/87/WG1.1, ESCWA, Baghdad.

Ibrahim (1986) Women's right to work,
UN Doc. E/ESCWA/SDP/87/WG1.2,
ESCWA, Baghdad

Ridane, F. (1989) Convention on the
Elimination of All Forms of
Discrimination against Women. Case
study of Tunisia, UN Doc. IRS/
CEDAW/1989/CS.10

Rodriguez Blandon, M. (1989)
Convention on the Elimination of All
Forms of Discrimination against
Women. Case study of Guatemala, UN
Doc. UN/DAW.

Hoofar, H. (1990) Legal barriers to
empowerment of female-headed
households: women and customary law
in the Middle East, UN Doc.
EGM/VM/1990/WP.6.

Best, F. (1985) Women's right to
education, UN Doc. ED-87/
CONF.809/COL.1, UNESCO, Paris.

Einhorn, B. (1991) Democratization and
women's movements in East Central
Europe: concepts of women's rights,
UNU/WIDER, Helsinki.

Holt, S. and Ribe, H. (1991) Developing
financial institutions for the poor and
reducing barriers to access for women,
World Bank Discussion Papers, No. 117.

Books

Amnesty International (1991) *Women in
the Front Line. Human Rights Violations
against Women*, Amnesty International,
New York.

Armstrong, A. (ed.) (1987) *Women and
Law in Southern Africa*, Zimbabwe
Publishing House, Harare.

Arnaoud, A.-J. and E. Kingdom (eds.)
(1990) *Women's Rights and the Rights of
Man*, Aberdeen University Press,
Glasgow.

Ashworth, G. (1991) *Of Violence and
Violations: Women and Human Rights*,
Change, London.

Bonnerjea, L. (1985) *Shaming the World:
The Needs of Women Refugees*, Change,
London.

Buckley, M. and M. Anderson (eds.)
(1989) *Women, Equality and Europe*,
Macmillan Press, London.

Bunch, C. and R. Carillo (1991) *Gender
Violence. A Development and Human
Rights Issue*, Center for Women's Global
Leadership, New Brunswick, New
Jersey.

Buquicchio-de Boer, M. (1989) *Sexual
Equality in the European Convention on
Human Rights: A Survey of Case Law*,
Council of Europe, Strasbourg.

Chen, M. (1989) *Women and
Discrimination. New Zealand and the
UN Convention*, Institute of Policy
Studies, Wellington, New Zealand.

David, H. (1986) *Femmes et emploi. Le
defi de l'égalité* [*Women and Work: The
Challenge of Equality*], Presses de
l'Université du Quebec, Montreal.

Evatt, E. (1990) *Ten Years of the
Convention on the Elimination of All
Forms of Discrimination against Women*,
Human Rights and Equal Opportunity
Commission, Sydney, Australia.

Flanz, G. (1983) *Comparative Women's
Rights and Political Participation in
Europe*, Dobbs Ferry, New York.

Gajerski-Cauley, A. (ed.) (1989) *Women,
Development and Disability*, Coalition of
Provincial Organizations of the
Handicapped, Winnipeg.

Gallagher, M. (1985) *Becoming Aware:*

Human Rights and the Family, UNESCO, Paris.

Gonzalez de Pazos, M. (1989) *La Mujer y la Reivindicacion Internacional de sus Derechos [Woman and International Recognition of Her Rights]*, Universidad Autonoma Metropolitana, Azcapotzalco, Mexico.

Hevener, N. (1983) *International Law and the Status of Women*, Westview Press, Boulder, Colorado.

Hilmy, N. (1988) *Rights of Women in the Muslim Societies*, University of Zagazig, Zagazig, Egypt.

Ivan-Smith E., N. Tandon, and J. Connors, (1988) *Women in Sub-Saharan Africa*, Minority Rights Group, London.

Khushalani, Y. (1982) *Dignity and Honour of Women as Basic and Fundamental Rights*, Martinus Nijhoff Publishers, Dordrecht, Netherlands.

Landau, E. (1985) *The Rights of Women in the European Community*, Commission of the European Communities, Brussels.

Langley, W. (1991) *Women's Rights in International Documents: A Sourcebook*, McFarland, New York.

van Maarseveen H., D. Pessers and M. Gunning (eds.) (1987) *International Recht en Vrouwen [International Law and Women]*, Tjeenk Willink, Zwolle, Netherlands.

McLean, S. and N. Burrows, (eds.) (1988) *The Legal Relevance of Gender: Some Aspects of Sex-based Discrimination*, Macmillan Press, London.

Meza-Ingar, C. (1986) *Mas Alla de la Igualdad: Los Derechos de la Mujer al Año 2000 [Beyond Equality: Women's Rights towards the Year 2000]*, AMARU Editores, Lima, Peru.

Plata, I. and M. Yanusova (1988) *Los Derechos Humanos y la Convencion sobre la Eliminacion de Todas las Formas de Discriminacion contra la Mujer 1979 [Human Rights and the 1979 Convention on the Elimination of All Forms of Discrimination against Women]*, Printext Impresores, Bogota, Colombia.

Ruano Rodriguez, L. (1984) *Guia de los Derechos de la Mujer [Guide through Woman's Rights]*, Instituto de la Mujer, Madrid.

Russel, D. and N. van de Ven (eds.) (1984) *Crimes against Women: Proceedings of the International Tribunal*, Palo Alto, California.

Nation Newspapers (1987) *S.M. Otieno. Kenya's Unique Burial Saga*, A Nation Newspapers Publication, Nairobi.

Schuler, M. (ed.) (1991) *Empowerment and Law: Strategies of Third World Women*, OEF International, Washington, DC.

Stewart, J. and A. Armstrong (eds.) (1990) *The Legal Situation of Women in Southern Africa*, University of Zimbabwe Publications, Harare.

Ullah Shekab, R. (1991) *Rights of Women in Islamic Shariah*, Indus Publishing House, Lahore, Pakistan.

Women, Family and Civic Rights. International Women Lawyers Conference, Lahore, Pakistan, 4–6 November 1985.

The Women's Rights Project and Americas Watch (1991) *Criminal Injustice: Violence against Women in Brazil*, Human Rights Watch, New York.

Articles

An-Na'im, A. (1987) 'The rights of women and international law in the Muslim context', *Whittier Law Review*, Vol. 9, No. 2.

Bayefsky, A. (1982) 'The Human Rights Committee and the case of Sandra Lovelace', *Canadian Yearbook of*

International Law, Vol. 11.

Boulware-Miller, K. (1985) 'Female circumcision: challenges to the practice as a human rights violation', *Harvard Women's Law Journal,* Vol. 8, No. 1.

Buquicchio-de Boer, M. (1985) 'Sexual discrimination and the Convention on Human Rights', *Human Rights Law Journal,* Vol. 6, No. 1.

Burrows, N. (1984) 'Monitoring compliance of international standards relating to human rights: the experience of the United Nations Commission on the Status of Women', *Netherlands International Law Review,* Vol. 31, No. 2.

Busschere, B. (1990) 'The humane treatment of women in times of armed conflict: equality and the law of humanity', *Revue de Droit Penale Militaire,* Vol. 26, No. 4.

Byrnes, A. (1989) 'The "other" human rights treaty body: the work of the Committee on the Elimination of Discrimination against Women', *Yale Journal of International Law,* Vol. 14, No. 1.

Clark, Y. (1991) 'The Vienna Convention Reservations Regime and the Convention on Discrimination against Women', *American Journal of International Law,* Vol. 85, No. 2.

Coliver S. (1989) 'United Nations machineries on women's rights: how could they better help women whose rights are being violated?' in E. Lutz, H. Hannum and K. Burke, (eds.) *New Directions in Human Rights,* University of Pennsylvania Press, Philadelphia.

Cook, R.J. (1989) 'The international right to nondiscrimination on the basis of sex. A bibliography', *Yale Journal of International Law,* Vol. 14, No. 1.

Cook, R. (1990) 'Reservations to the Convention on the Elimination of All Forms of Discrimination against

Women', *Virginia Journal of International Law,* Vol. 30, No. 4.

Cortes, I. (1984) 'Monitoring progress in the implementation of the Convention on the Elimination of All Forms of Discrimination against Women', *Asian Newsletter on Human Rights Documents,* Manila.

Daw, R. (1970), 'Political rights of women: a study of the international protection of human rights', *Malaya Law Review,* Vol. 12, No. 3.

D'Sa, R. (1987) 'Women's rights in relation to human rights: a lawyer's perspective', *Commonwealth Law Bulletin,* Vol. 13, No. 6.

Easman-Taal, L. (1987) 'Constitutional rights of women under national and international law: present standards and further possibilities', *Santa Clara Law Review,* Vol. 18, No. 3.

Freeman, M. (1989–90) 'Measuring equality: an international perspective on women's capacity and constitutional rights', *Berkley Women's Law Journal,* Vol. 5, No. 1.

Galey, M. (1984) 'International enforcement of women's rights', *Human Rights Quarterly,* Vol. 6, No. 4.

Guggenheim, M. (1977) 'The implementing of human rights by the UN Commission on the Status of Women', *Texas International Law Journal,* Vol. 12, No. 2.

Howards, R. (1984) 'Women's rights in English-speaking Sub-Saharan Africa' in R. Meltzer, and C. Welch (eds.) *Human Rights and Development in Africa,* State University of New York Press, Albany, New York.

Johnsson, A. (1989) 'The international protection of women refugees: a summary of principal problems and issues', *International Journal of Refugee Law,* Vol. 1, No. 2.

Langley, W. (1987) 'The rights of

women, the African Charter, and the economic development in Africa', *Boston College Third World Law Journal*, Vol. 7, No. 1.

Loranger, J. (1982) 'Convention on the Elimination of All Forms of Discrimination against Women', *Canadian Yearbook of International Law*, Vol. 20.

McKenzie, D. (1991) 'China and the Women's Convention: prospects for the implementation of an international norm', *China Law Reporter*, Vol. 7, No. 1.

Medina, C. (1985) 'Women's rights as human rights: Latin American countries and the Organization of American States' in M. Diaz-Diocaretz and I. Zavala (eds.) *Women, Feminist Identity and Society in the 1980s. Selected Papers*, John Benjamin Publishing Company, Amsterdam.

Meron, T. (1990) 'Enhancing the effectiveness of the prohibition of discrimination against women', *American Journal of International Law*, Vol. 84, No. 2.

Neuwirth, J. (1987) 'Towards a gender-based approach to human rights violations', *Whittier Law Review*, Vol. 9, No. 2.

Parpart, J. (1986) 'Women's rights and the Lagos Plan of Action', *Human Rights Quarterly*, Vol. 8, No. 1.

Rahman, A. (1990) 'Religious rights versus women's rights in India: a test case for international human rights', *Columbia Journal of Transnational Law*, Vol. 28, No. 2.

Reanda, I. (1991) 'Prostitution as a human rights question: problems and prospects of United Nations action', *Human Rights Quarterly*, Vol. 13, No. 2.

Ricafrente, C. (1975) 'International labour standards for working women', *Philippine Law Journal*, Vol. 50, No. 1.

Schirmer, J. (1988) 'Those who die for life cannot be called dead: women and human rights protest in Latin America', *Harvard Human Rights Yearbook*, Vol. 1.

Shelton, D. (1975) 'Women and the right to education', *Revue des Droits de l'Homme*, Vol. 7, No. 1.

Strumpf, A. (1985) 'Re-examining the UN Convention on the Elimination of All Forms of Discrimination against Women: the UN Decade for Women Conference in Nairobi', *Yale Journal of International Law*, Vol. 10, No. 2.

Sweeney, J. (1984) 'Promoting human rights through regional organizations: women's rights in Western Europe', *Human Rights Quarterly*, Vol. 6, No. 4.

Tomaševski, K. (1988) 'Women-in-development: a human rights perspective', *Netherlands Quarterly of Human Rights*, Vol. 6, No. 4.

Wadstein, M. (1988) 'Implementation of the UN Convention on the Elimination of All Forms of Discrimination against Women', *Netherlands Quarterly of Human Rights*, Vol. 6, No. 4.

Wean, D. (1988) 'Real protection for African women? The African Charter on Human and People's Rights', *Journal of International Dispute Resolution*, Vol. 2, No. 3.

INDEX